D1571996

Alias

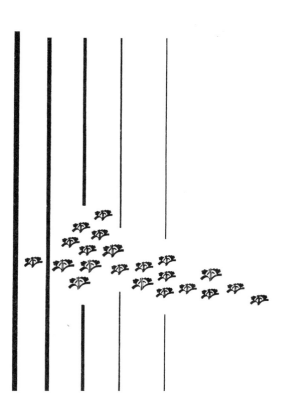

THE
BUFFALO
DOCTOR

by Jean Cummings

THE SWALLOW PRESS
OHIO UNIVERSITY PRESS
Athens, Ohio

Chicago

London

Dedicated to
Bruce, Beth and Brenda

Library of Congress Catalog Card Number 80-81714
ISBN 0-8040-0815-9

Harlo Press

First pre-publication printing June, 1980
Second pre-publication printing July, 1980

Ohio University Press

Third printing August, 1980
Fourth printing February, 1981

Printed in U.S.A.

Contents

Foreword

Dr. Bill Cummings, friend of Indians and bison, and a first-class surgeon, was introduced to a sizeable public by that amusing book *Why They Call Him the Buffalo Doctor.* This second Buffalo Doctor volume, in some ways even more lively than the first, ought to enjoy the success of Jean ("Pinky") Cummings' first study of her husband's doings.

For *Alias the Buffalo Doctor,* in large part, describes Bill Cummings' derring-do at Wounded Knee: the story of his airplane flight to carry supplies to the women and children of the Indians entrenched there. Of all those involved in that long fracas, Dr. Cummings was the most innocent; nevertheless, he was about the only one to suffer a penalty at law for his part.

There is more besides in this book, for Bill Cummings and Jean Cummings are humorous, energetic, generous, courageous people endowed with a diversity of talents. In these pages the reader learns all sorts of things about buffalo and about Indian ways that one doesn't encounter in standard works of reference. Also the reader picks up a good deal about varieties of human nature, including the behavior and notions of federal agents, lawyers, and backcountry people white and red.

His adventurous undertakings notwithstanding, Dr. Cummings possesses strong scientific interests: some chapters of this book touch on his endeavor to develop a "buffalo serum" for cancer. A champion of the humane scale, Bill Cummings strove to establish a model rural hospital; and in other ways, too, he has been an ornament of the medical profession, though far from ornamental merely. As a surgeon, he has worked wonders on occasion: he had this writer walking around two and a half days after a serious double operation. Jean Cummings does not exaggerate her husband's cheerful abilities.

In this bent time of ours, the unselfish vigor of Bill and Pinky Cummings reminds us that determination and imagination still may triumph over huge obstacles. The next best thing to a firm friendship with this couple and their children is to get to know them through the chapters of this honest, sprightly narrative by Mrs. Cummings. The two of them win, and deserve, the affections even of buffalo bulls.

—Russell Kirk

*"The white man does not obey
the Great Spirit;
that is why the Indians
never could agree with him."*
  —Flying Hawk

•

Wanted

1 When a telephone rings in the middle of the night it usually means bad news or tragedy to most people. But not in our household, where nighttime phone calls are commonplace. My husband, Bill, is a surgeon, and seldom does a night pass without the phone ringing at least once. I scarcely hear these calls, rousing only enough to hear Bill give instructions to a hospital nurse or question a patient about symptoms. If Bill gets out of bed, I know this means he must go to the hospital. I suffer a brief wave of pity for him, then roll over and drift back into sleep.

One March night the phone call seemed different. I heard Bill say, "When?" and then, "Okay, I'll be expecting you out here."

I heaved myself onto one elbow and squinted at the alarm clock. Four fifteen in the morning. No time for visitors.

"What is it?" I asked.

"The F.B.I. They want to come out and ask me some questions about my flight to Wounded Knee."

I laughed. "Oh, come on, you're kidding." But when I looked at Bill's face, I knew he wasn't kidding.

Hastily we pulled on the clothes we'd taken off when we

went to bed. I tidied up the living room, plumped pillows, stacked rumpled newspapers, and dumped ashtrays. Unexpected visitors are a real threat to casual homemakers, and a nighttime visit by the all-seeing, all-knowing agents of the F.B.I. was terrifying. As I slumped into my favorite red armchair, I glanced about the room for signs of dust, which might mean "bad character" to the F.B.I. My eyes fell upon a rectangular cardboard box beside the fireplace. This was one piece of evidence I didn't want our callers to see. The box contained a new, colorful Indian chief's headdress. It was Bill's dearest possession, but at the moment, a most incriminating one. I grabbed the box and headed out of the living room in panic. Where could I hide it? I knew I was no match for the F.B.I. if they intended to search our home. Stuffing it into the washing machine or under the bed seemed useless. I slid it under the kneehole of my desk in our bedroom where at least it was out of sight.

We turned on the porch light and sat in the living room, waiting. Bill rubbed the crown of his uncombed dark hair, shaggy and tousled from sleep. He gave me a weak smile. "So the F.B.I. wants to talk to me about my trip to Wounded Knee." He leaned back, propping his feet on the coffee table.

Numbly I stared at his bare ankles and patched, worn moccasins.

A loud crash came from our back door, but we weren't alarmed. We knew what it was. Our turning on the lights had awakened Little Joe. I went to the back door and switched on the yard light. I could make out the shapes of two shaggy buffalo cows, Sisseton Sioux and Good Cow, sleeping under my clothesline, not twenty feet from the house. Little Joe, our tame yearling buffalo, stood on the back porch, bunting at the aluminum storm door. He wanted his morning baby bottles of warm milk.

"No, Joe," I grumbled. "Not now. Go eat some hay, or go back to sleep."

Frowning, I returned to the living room and sat down beside Bill on the davenport. What a mess we were in!—

and buffalo had much to do with it. If Bill and I hadn't begun raising buffalo, we'd both be sleeping peacefully right now. Buffalo! I groaned. Buffalo and Indians. The buffalo brought on the Indians.

*"If we Indians
could be named an 'endangered species,'
we might survive."*
    —Modern Indian saying

•

The
Buffalo
Doctor

2 On a bleak and chilly April morning in 1964 our newly-purchased buffalo herd arrived from Iowa. The thirteen shaggy beasts jumped off the huge stock truck into the fifty-acre pasture we'd prepared for them and galloped down the fenceline, kicking up a fog of powder snow.

I shivered with excitement and a little apprehension. What did we know about buffalo? But then, who did know much about buffalo? For five years Bill and I had been reading everything available about this magnificent American animal. We'd learned about the buffalo's place in American history, but as to breeding, raising, and caring for buffalo, we found nothing.

Bill's dark eyes were shining as he watched his buffalo herd speed past on their second inspection lap of the pasture. "We did it, Pinkie!" he grinned. "We've got our buffalo!"

I nodded, shivering again. Maybe I had a premonition that the buffalo were going to change our lives, though my wildest imagination never could have suspected how much, and in what strange ways. How could I have guessed that the buffalo would be a major factor in Bill's being arrested by the F.B.I. and having to face a five-year

13

prison term and the loss of his license to practice medicine?

Bill's interest in buffalo was innocent enough, and understandable. He had been raised on the Sisseton Indian Reservation in South Dakota. As a little boy he'd listened to the oldtimers sunning themselves on the wooden bench in front of the feed store. Wistfully, they spoke of the good times long ago when buffalo, elk and antelope wandered the prairie. Bill felt cheated, wishing he could have lived when delicious wild game was plentiful.

The decade of the 1930's was a hungry time in South Dakota. Though the whole nation suffered during the Great Depression, South Dakota was hit an extra punch of devastating weather. Winter temperatures were exceptionally frigid, and there were fearsome blizzards. For several consecutive summers Dakota was punished by drought. The hot sun and constant wind turned the earth into a cracked, stone-hard floor. Crops failed. Grasshoppers swarmed in, eating any surviving vegetation. For awhile the fish in Lake Traverse nourished Bill's family, though they needed a good catch of pike, perch, and bullheads to feed the large brood of ten children. The drought persisted and Lake Traverse dried up. All the fish perished. The stench of rotting fish settled over the parched reservation. White fish skeletons gleamed from the cracked lake bottom. But the Cummings family survived, mainly on goat meat from their small herd of goats.

In 1942 Bill's parents received an astonishing letter from relatives in Illinois. The relatives claimed that the Great Depression was over, that a war boom was occurring. In Illinois, the letter said, jobs were plentiful.

To check out this wondrous news, Bill's mother and father went to Illinois. The news was true. Off the reservation and far from South Dakota, the nation was prospering. Both parents found jobs in a munitions factory. The meager family belongings were piled into a farm truck, and Bill waved good-bye to his boyhood friends.

He hated his new home in Savanna, Illinois, a town built on a steep bluff overlooking the Mississippi River.

Bill's new home, an ancient dilapidated house, clung to the hillside half-way up the slope. The houses above poised threateningly over them, and the view from their front windows consisted of the rooftops of the homes below. At best a raucous river town, Savanna was now a noisy boom town, peopled with newcomers working in the wartime factories. Accustomed to his gentle friends back on the reservation, Bill was bewildered by the indifferent and hostile environment. Neighborhood toughs beat him up, knocking out his front teeth. His mother and father worked different shifts at the factory so the togetherness of their Dakota existence disappeared. Bill wasn't home much either. Before school in the morning he swept out and cleaned a shoe store. After school he clerked in the store, and evenings he ran the projector at a movie theater.

After two years Bill's family moved to Waterloo, Iowa, where better jobs were available. Bill finished high school there and enlisted in the Navy, where he served in the South Pacific. When World War II ended, he returned home with the intention of loafing around a bit and "finding himself," but an energetic brother-in-law squelched those plans. The brother-in-law took Bill to a tavern, got him drunk, and drove him to college to register for classes which were to start the next day. Within a week from the time his ship steamed under the Golden Gate Bridge, Bill was a pre-med student, sitting in a college classroom.

The GI bill helped in financing college, but Bill had to have a job besides. He was working in the violent ward of a psychiatric hospital when I met him at the beginning of his senior year of college. After graduation Bill went off to Des Moines to begin his medical studies. After six months of separation and misery we decided to get married. I got a full time job to support us, and completed my college work through night school. Bill held a variety of part-time jobs—cab driver, drugstore clerk, restaurant cook. Several summers he worked at a meat packing slaughter house, and one summer he dug graves in a cemetery. Somehow we made it through the four years of medical school and then through another four years of residency in surgery.

By this time Bill was thirty-one years old, and all those years had been lived in poverty. He was offered several promising opportunities as a surgeon, and he investigated them all. I was expecting our third child momentarily, so Bill travelled alone to check out the offers. An opportunity in the Detroit area sounded appealing, so Bill flew to Michigan where he stayed overnight with a former college roommate, now also a doctor. The friend told him about a small forty-bed hospital in a village nestled in the woods of central Michigan.

"They really need a surgeon up there," he said. "Why don't you take my car and drive up there? Look it over."

Bill never got to the Detroit area interview.

He telephoned me that evening. "I've found where I want to practice! It's Mecosta Memorial Hospital, a nice little place in a tiny, quiet village. I believe a hospital should be a sanctuary where a patient can get away from the pressures of city life to recover from illness." He chuckled. "And Mecosta Memorial is a long way from city life."

"What's the name of the town?" I asked.

"Stanwood, Michigan."

I scribbled the name on a scrap of paper.

"Pinkie," Bill added softly, "they really need me there."

Ah, I thought. That was the hooker. They needed him.

When I found a Michigan road map I searched for the location of our new home. Stanwood, Michigan, wasn't on the map. Bill had said the town was fifty miles north of Grand Rapids. Though I studied the area thoroughly, no Stanwood could be found.

Two days later when Bill returned I found out why Stanwood wasn't on the map. Its population was 189.

The reason for there being a hospital in such a tiny hamlet was that the hospital building had once been the

16

county poorhouse, and the farm surrounding it had been the county poor farm, where the destitute inmates had grubbed out food and grain. When retirement plans and social security benefits made poorhouses obsolete, Mecosta County's poor farm was converted into a hospital. For ten years the little hospital had been struggling against threatened closure by new state requirements, edicts which called for expenditures of money. Money was a scarce item in this disadvantaged rural pocket. The hospital always had an adequate supply of patients. It was *paying* patients who were scarce.

Bill worked hard in establishing his surgical reputation in Stanwood. He fretted over how he could help the little hospital survive. The county decided to sell the rolling pastures surrounding the hospital, and Bill bought the farm.

Though our three children were very young, we found they could perform a fair amount of farm labor, and the five of us set about fencing fifty acres of pasture with what we hoped would be a buffalo-proof fence. It took us nearly a year, and the fence was completed by the time the buffalo arrived. As the herd churned about, investigating their new home, Bill and I sighed with relief that they seemed to respect our fence.

Our buffalo were young, far from full grown. Four were two-year-olds, and nine were but yearlings. Even so, they looked large and powerful to us. There was always that finger of uneasiness prodding us. Did we have a tiger by the tail?

Almost immediately, the buffalo herd began showing its value. The hospital patients loved watching the shaggy animals cavort and graze. Relatives and friends came to visit the elderly patients more often now that they also could see a herd of buffalo. Mecosta Memorial Hospital became "that hospital where the buffalo are," and we hoped that the state regulatory bureaucracy would not close a well-known hospital so quickly and so unthinkingly.

Our woolly animals began to dominate our thoughts, our time, and even our social relationships. People no longer asked, "How are you?" but "How are the buffalo?" And, of course, Bill became known as "The Buffalo Doctor."

"Beast knows beast;
birds of a feather
flock together."
     —Aristotle (384-322 B.C.)

●

Cross-breeding Buffalo and Cattle

3 Those first years as buffalo raisers we performed all the farm labor ourselves, usually with inadequate tools and equipment. We fenced more pasture to accommodate our multiplying herd. We kept learning new and fascinating things about the Great American Bison, or buffalo, as they are known to most of us.

The buffalo is a bovine, a relative to cattle. But it isn't a docile servant to mankind like Elsie the Borden Cow. The buffalo is a wild animal, a rugged creature capable of surviving extremes of temperature and weather conditions. You don't put buffalo in a barn. In fact, you don't *put* them anywhere. We buffalo raisers have the saying, "You can herd a buffalo anywhere *he* wants to go!"

One of the most important principles in buffalo-raising is to keep the proper male to female sex ratio in a buffalo herd. It's best to have one bull for every ten cows in the herd. If there are too many bulls, they spend all their time fighting each other, neglecting their romancing duties. Then you have no calf crop the following spring. Buffalo are like deer in that they have a mating season but once a year, in early autumn. The buffalo cow must become pregnant during this short mating season.

19

When we attended meetings of the National Buffalo Association, we became friends with several western ranchers who raised both cattle and buffalo. Talks with these cattlemen impressed us with the rugged superiority of buffalo over cattle.

Ranchers in the northern plains region of the United States lose many cattle during winter blizzards. Cattle tend to drift with the wind, piling up against the fences and freezing to death. During prolonged snowstorms, many cattle starve. Yet another hazard faces the livestock grower once the storm has ended, and he can get feed to his cattle. The hungry cattle may eat too much and die from bloating. These western ranchers were impressed with the fact that they never lost any buffalo during severe winter storms. Impervious to cold and snow, the buffalo weren't bothered by the blizzards, nor did they starve to death. Their survival instincts yet intact, the buffalo pawed through the snow to graze, or nibbled on brush and twigs. Once the blizzard ended, the buffalo again showed an instinct for self-preservation. They never overate, but nibbled sparingly for a few days on the feed provided.

"If my cattle just had a little buffalo-sense!" many a rancher wished.

The buffalo's tremendous resistance to cold makes it an ideal animal for our northern range lands, where the winters are long, and the cold is severe. Some European breeds of cattle, such as Scottish Highland and Galloway, are considered winter-hardy because of their coat of long winter hair. Though this long hair keeps them warm, it causes trouble when it cakes with sleet and snow. Huge chunks of ice form in the hair, weighing the animal down and making it difficult for him to move about. Buffalo fur is not long, but extremely dense, forming a soft body-covering which fends off cold, but will not hold large chunks of ice.

Hereford cattle, a popular breed on the northern plains, have only four thousand five hundred hair fibers per square inch, while buffalo have over nineteen thousand fibers per square inch. The hair-covering of the buffalo is said to be the warmest possessed by any four-legged animal except the Arctic musk-ox.

We became intrigued with the possibilities of crossing buffalo with domestic cattle to introduce the hardy traits of buffalo into the less rugged species. In the past there had been several attempts at this crossbreeding. The resulting hybrid was called a "cattalo." Bill and I were impressed with the fast-growing, rugged cattalo, but we learned that crossing buffalo and cattle was difficult.

A big drawback was that male cattalo were sterile unless they had less than one-sixteenth buffalo blood. Of course, crossbreeding still could be conducted through the female lines since cattalo heifers didn't seem to be sterile.

When using a buffalo bull for the father, and a domestic cow for the mother, a major difficulty could be encountered. The pregnant cow often developed a condition known as "polyhydramnios." In plain language this means that a huge amount of amniotic fluid, as much as fifty gallons, may build up around the unborn calf. The pregnant cow also may retain large quantities of fluid in her tissues and suffer huge swollen ankles. This sign indicates that the cow has developed congestive heart failure, brought on by the strain of carrying the extra four hundred pounds of excess amniotic fluid surrounding her unborn calf. If the cow doesn't die from the congestive heart failure, she faces another hazard when she goes into labor. At the onset of labor, when the cow expels the large amount of amniotic fluid, she may go into shock and die. The mortality rate of cows bearing half-buffalo calves is very high, we learned.

A South Dakota rancher friend told us about his sad experience with losing pregnant cows. When he crossed a buffalo bull with thirty domestic cows, twenty-eight cows died before the end of their pregnancies. Caesarean sections were performed on the remaining two cows. The calves survived, but the mothers died. Bill and I saw these two resulting cattalo when they were three years old. Now grown into thirty-five hundred pound monsters, they demonstrated beautiful beef configuration and were of

21

great size, towering over six feet at their slightly-humped backs. Cream-colored beasts, freckled with liver spots, they showed some buffalo characteristics and some cattle traits.

Though intrigued by these two magnificent cattalo, we were sobered by the one-hundred percent mortality rate of the mother cows.

According to the small amount of scientific literature available on the subject, it appeared that buffalo cows didn't suffer great dangers when pregnant with a half-domestic calf. But even with this method of crossbreeding, there was a major difficulty—one called "breeding indifference." Apparently, buffalo and cattle just aren't especially attracted to each other. Unless they're raised together as calves, it's difficult to get them to interbreed.

Nonetheless, we decided to try to cross buffalo and cattle. Our huge buffalo herd bull, whom we'd named "Kahtanka" (meaning 'Chief Bull' in the Sioux language) would be the father. Whenever we could afford it we'd buy domestic cows and put them in the buffalo pasture with Kahtanka.

First we purchased two black Angus heifers. Hornless, they remained on the outskirts of the herd, but there seemed to be no antagonism. Monthly, during their estrous cycle, they cavorted and danced flirtatiously before Kahtanka, trying to attract his amours. Kahtanka remained indifferent to the fat, hornless heifers. We were prepared to be patient. Once the two Angus heifers had dwelled there long enough to become accepted as part of the group, perhaps Kahtanka's roving eye would pause upon them.

The Angus heifer we'd named "Angie" was the more aggressive in her flirtations, and she tried hard to perform the mating game properly, according to buffalo standards. Her approach to Kahtanka was vigorous and enthusiastic. Angie lowered her hornless head and lunged at Kahtanka, hitting him in the chest with a tremendous whack. The wind knocked out of him momentarily, Kahtanka swung his massive head and walked slowly toward a nearby elm tree. With deliberate upward swings of his horns, he dug deep grooves in the tree trunk, stripping away large sections of bark. Next he stomped to the tag elder thicket and began tearing brush out by the roots. The uprooted elder bushes collected on his head and horns. Turning back toward the watching Angie, Kahtanka swung his great head back and forth, scattering brush in every direction. This was the buffalo bull's way of saying, "I'm a big, strong bull. Stronger and more powerful than you!"

Several times over the next year Angie appeared to be pregnant, but each time it proved to be a false pregnancy. The poor animal was so anxious to become a mother that she talked herself into exhibiting all the usual pregnancy signs. We suspected that the two young Angus heifers were too inexperienced and naive to appeal to the worldly Kahtanka.

We decided what we needed was a "sexy" cow, one who had "been around." A red Durham cow named "Mable," seemed to fill these qualifications, according to her owner. We bought Mable, put her into the buffalo pasture, and within a few months she began showing signs of pregnancy.

Bill kept a close watch on Mable as her pregnancy advanced. His concern nearly cost him his life. One day he found Mable off by herself, some distance from the buffalo herd, and he crawled under the fence. As he bent over her, pressing his stethoscope against Mable's belly to listen for fetal heart tones, Kahtanka slipped up on him from behind. The monstrous buffalo bull gave Bill's rear end an assertive nudge, driving Bill's head into the cow's flank. With a groan, Bill crumpled to the ground in great pain. Though only half-conscious, he instinctively rolled under the fence to get out of the pasture. As Bill's eyes began to focus once again, he looked up through the fence into the furious eyes of Kahtanka. The shaggy bull pawed the ground and roared.

Bill managed to get to the hospital, and x-rays showed a broken bone in his neck. An extension neck brace was applied and this relieved some of the pain, but not the persistent numbness and cramping of his right arm. For awhile, Bill feared that his surgical career might be ended by a paralyzed right arm. By combining rest and exercise he recuperated and eventually regained good health.

Though Bill continued his close supervision of Mable's pregnancy, her health deteriorated, and it became obvious that she was going to die. In hopes of saving the unborn calf, we shipped Mable to the slaughterhouse with instructions for them to take the calf by Caesarean section immediately. Too premature to survive, the little calf lived only forty-five minutes. The bull calf showed the superior traits of the rugged animal we hoped to breed. The rounded head was small, like a buffalo calf's head, an important trait for range animals, since they must give birth easily and unassisted. The yet hairless body had a short neck, deep chest, and short legs, characteristics of a good beef-producer.

The near miss we'd had in achieving a cattalo calf with Mable whetted our interest in crossbreeding.

The once serene Kahtanka had become mean and threatening. He seemed to think of Bill as a rival bull. A mean bull can't be tolerated. When aroused, bulls are too strong to restrain, and with those powerful shoulders and deadly horns, a bad-tempered buffalo bull was sure to kill. Kahtanka had to be destroyed. We donated him to the hospital's annual fund-raising Buffalo Barbecue.

With Kahtanka no longer around to endanger domestic bulls, Bill decided to attempt crossbreeding by using domestic bulls with our buffalo cows.

First we purchased a young bull calf, a Hereford, and turned him loose in the buffalo pasture. He was strictly pre-adolescent, incapable of performing the usual bull functions. We hoped that by growing up with buffalo, breeding indifference in the future might be lessened. The children thought the little white-faced calf adorable and named him Vindicator. We hoped that within a year Vindicator might begin to father cattalo calves.

In the meantime a neighboring farmer asked if we

would pasture his Hereford bull, Oscar, for a few months. Oscar was growing fierce and mean, he said. The farmer's children were responsible for feeding his livestock, and as Oscar's disposition deteriorated, the farmer worried for the safety of his children. Oscar appeared to be a fine specimen, and we agreed to pasture Oscar as a "guest bull."

Bill and the farmer hauled Oscar in a truck to the buffalo pasture and turned him loose near the small creek which runs the length of the pasture. At a distance the buffalo herd grazed contentedly. Oscar planted his huge hoofs and stared. Good Cow, one of the older cows, left the herd and walked slowly toward Oscar. She approached to within ten feet of the white-faced bull, then stopped and returned his stare. Oscar decided it was time to put on his bull act. Pawing deep furrows in the earth, Oscar bellowed and roared. He hunched his shoulders and swung his head, all of which meant, "I'm really tough, I am!"

For awhile Good Cow watched Oscar's exhibition. Then with an abrupt grunt, she jumped twelve inches toward Oscar and stopped short. Oscar sort of went "Eek!" and tore off into the creek bed where he hid in the elder bushes.

For several days Oscar continued to hide from those frightening buffalo cows. Curiosity-driven, the buffalo cows persisted in the game of hide-and-seek, hunting out the terrified Hereford bull. At last, Oscar's nerves could stand it no longer. As the buffalo cows crashed through the brush, seeking out his hiding place, Oscar, with a mighty lunge, went through the high buffalo fence. He galloped off, leaving the whole terrifying situation behind. Unfortunately, the route of his flight took him down the main highway, where he encountered an automobile. Oscar and the driver of the car were unhurt, but the automobile was hauled to the junkyard.

We returned the cowardly Oscar to his owner, explaining that we must find a braver bull.

Shortly after Oscar's failure to cope, we attended a rodeo. There we saw what we thought was the bravest, fiercest bull one could imagine. A hump-backed Brahma, this bull was called Big John. His duty in the rodeo was to be ridden by the cowboy contestants. However, the rodeo manager was eager to sell Big John because the Brahma bull had a bad habit. Big John always behaved well in the chute as the cowboy settled himself on the animal's broad back. But when Big John emerged from the chute, bucking and snorting, he habitually threw himself sideways against the wall of the chute, breaking the hapless rider's leg. Several cowboys had been disabled by Big John, and the owner happily sold him to us for a reasonable price.

We felt certain Big John was a manly bull indeed. Never would he spend his time smelling the flowers or hiding from shaggy buffalo cows. Surely Big John would demonstrate mating eagerness rather than mating indifference. But Big John also was a failure. He hid in the pine grove, terrified of the curious buffalo cows. Big John's hiding seemed to irritate the buffalo cows, perhaps because they were afraid mating season might pass unreproductively. An available bull was making himself very unavailable. Maybe the buffalo cows were demonstrating "the fury of a woman scorned" when they ganged up on him and killed him. At any rate, Big John, the terror of the rodeo, who lived a life of violence, died a violent death.

In the meantime little Vindicator matured into a fine young bull. Though not yet a huge he-man, he showed interest in the buffalo cows, and they seemed to accept him as an ally. Then one morning we found Vindicator, badly gored, his broken leg caught in the hay-feeder. We had to destroy Vindicator to end his suffering. Though we couldn't be certain what had happened, we believe Vindicator's death was an accident. Vindicator had grown up with the buffalo herd, and they seemed to accept him as one of them. Most likely, while crowding around the hay-feeder, Vindicator's hoof had gotten caught in the feeder. As he thrashed around trying to free his leg, the herd may have gotten excited, and in the panic and confusion, swung their lethal horns, catching the helpless bull.

Just a few months later, the buffalo cows committed another assault ending in death. Two years earlier we'd purchased a pair of young yaks from a game farm in New York State. A member of the oxen family, the yak is a distant relative of the buffalo. The yak originates in the mountains of Tibet, and for centuries Asians have domesticated them for beasts of burden and as providers of dairy products. As six-month-old calves, our male and female yak joined our buffalo herd and dwelled there peacefully, though they grazed on the fringes of the herd. The two yaks were inseparable, always together, often with their sides touching, as if they were joined at the flank. Slightly smaller than buffalo, the yaks had beautiful black hair which grew nearly to the ground, and long, bushy tails. They shed their fur each spring as buffalo do. The yaks and buffalo seemed indifferent to each other, but there was no antagonism. For two years they lived together in harmony.

On a bitterly cold December day, just a few months after the Brahma bull met his demise, Bill discovered the body of our yak bull hanging in a tall hay-feeder. Some distance away he spotted the female yak. Beside her was a newborn baby yak, looking much like a tiny French poodle. We could guess what had happened.

Buffalo cows are extremely curious. When a buffalo calf is born, each cow in the herd takes her turn approaching the new calf and giving it a quick, welcome sniff. Undoubtedly the newborn baby yak excited their curiosity, and they attempted to approach the new mother and her baby. Paternally protective, the male yak probably tried to fend off the nosey buffalo, and in so doing, he raised their ire. The irritated buffalo cows sent him to the happy hunting ground to join Big John and Vindicator.

Nature is sometimes cruel, red in fang and claw, but we were heartsick over the violent turn our experiment in crossbreeding had taken. We vowed to sacrifice no more bulls to our buffalo cows.

We decided to return to crossing domestic cows with

27

a buffalo bull. A friend who owned a travelling rodeo told us about thirteen longhorn cows for sale, and we purchased them. The rugged cows were strange-looking beasts, their heads sporting the very long, broad horns of the old Texas range animals. Many of the cows had Scottish Highland blood. Their reddish coats were long and shaggy, and we believed they would be winter-hardy in our northern climate. Wild and fierce in spirit, they seemed more like buffalo than domestic cattle.

When released from the stock truck, the longhorns galloped off in a cloud of dust and disappeared into a section of pasture containing tall, bushy pine trees. For days they stayed hidden, mere shadows skulking through the trees.

Two more cows joined the animals in our buffalo pasture, though not by planning. In the animal world buffalo seem to be very popular beasts. Whenever horses or cows get loose in the vicinity, they seem to wind up at our buffalo pasture. This is how we obtained Bertha, and her daughter, No-Name. Bertha was a Holstein cow, and No-Name, a Holstein heifer. "Heifer" means a female who never has had a calf. Escapees from a nearby dairy herd, the two black-and-white spotted cattle broke into our buffalo pasture one night and made themselves at home. The owner and Bill had to catch the fugitives, return them to their own pasture, and repair the broken fences. A few days later, Bertha and No-Name returned, irresistibly drawn by some animal attraction.

This time the exasperated owner said, "Look, Doc, I can't keep those two Holsteins home, now that they've seen your buffalo. Why don't you just buy them from me?"

We didn't particularly yen for Holstein cows, which are a dairy breed. Our crossbreeding project dealt with achieving an improved beef animal, and we hadn't considered using a dairy cow. Even so, they were big, healthy animals, and we agreed to buy them and let them roam with the buffalo. Bertha and No-Name made themselves at home, and we more or less disregarded their presence. They seemed of no importance. We were betting on the tough, wild Texas longhorn cows to cross successfully with our buffalo.

Two of the longhorn cows were pregnant at the time we purchased them. At Christmastime the first longhorn calf was born on a snowy, frigid morning when the thermometer plunged to twenty-below-zero. A little heifer, the calf was well-insulated with a thick coat of furry auburn hair. When Bill discovered her, she was still wet from birth and shivering. He rubbed her dry with an old blanket, and within an hour the little calf was warm and comfortable, unbothered by the extremely cold air.

Bill shook his head in amazement. "I think these longhorns are about as rugged as the buffalo. Now if they'll just socialize a little bit!"

When the longhorns had resided with the buffalo for six months, there was still no sign of fraternization. The longhorns grazed in one group, and the buffalo in another. Patience, we reminded ourselves. We must be patient. With thirteen longhorn cows, surely some of them soon would become pregnant with half-buffalo calves.

"Body and spirit are twins."
—Algernon Swinburne, 1880

•

Project
Crazy
Horse

4 Behind our home stretched a thirty-acre backyard pasture surrounded by an electric fence, one flimsy strand of wire charged with electricity. Our daughter, Beth, had always yearned for a horse. When she was twelve years old, and mature enough to care for a horse, we let her buy a huge Tennessee Walker mare named Pogo. A few months later seven-year-old Brenda acquired a fat little Shetland pony named Dandy. With dismay we saw that the electric fence was inadequate. Pogo was tall and Dandy was short. If we positioned the wire low enough to keep Dandy confined within the pasture, Pogo stepped over it. If we raised the wire, Dandy walked under it.

"We'll have to build a better fence," Bill told us.

He began bringing home loads of cedar posts and dozens of tall steel fence posts. When a truck delivered huge rolls of heavy woven wire, I grew suspicious. A horse fence could be a simple affair of three strands of barbed wire. "Woven wire is for buffalo," I told myself, as we labored building the new fence. I had a feeling that our thirty-acre backyard was being readied for buffalo.

Through his research work with the National Buffalo Association Bill had become fascinated with the special

31

traits and qualities of buffalo. He was convinced that the immunity mechanism of the buffalo held special qualities that could make a great contribution to the scientific world.

I'm not science-minded, and it was hard for me to grasp the idea. Patiently, Bill explained it to me. "Many people are allergic to horse serum," he said. "Organ transplant patients may have to receive serum for the rest of their lives to keep their bodies from rejecting the new organ. A non-allergenic serum must be developed. We've never found an incident of anyone being allergic to buffalo or buffalo products. Allergists routinely prescribe buffalo meat to patients they find allergic to domestic beef. This points to buffalo blood as being a good non-allergenic base for serum. Then, too, there's another black mark against horse serum. Horses have a very low resistance to some types of cancer. We can find no instance of a buffalo in the wild state ever having succumbed to cancer."

When Bill attended medical meetings and seminars around the country he mentioned his buffalo immunity theory to different immunologists. All of them listened with interest, agreeing that it was a logical theory which should be worked upon.

But how to go about it? Bill didn't know how to get his foot in the door of the ivory-tower, experimental science world. He wrote many letters and continued to discuss his theory with any scientists he met. Eventually some organ transplant researchers at a prominent university heard of Bill's buffalo immunity theory, and they expressed interest in investigating it. After many phone calls and exchanges of letters, the research plan was worked out.

Biweekly the director of the transplant study team would ship to us by Air Express a refrigerated vial of human white blood cells. We were to select one of our buffalo as the experimental animal, and inject these human white blood cells into him. The buffalo would receive injections of increasing amounts of human white blood cells at two week intervals. Blood would be drawn before each injection, and this blood would be tested to measure the amount of antibodies present. When the antibody level was as high as we thought we could achieve, the next stage would be to draw blood from this buffalo, probably at weekly intervals, or however often we deemed safe for the donor animal. Bill was to take this blood to his hospital laboratory where the blood would be put through a centrifuge to spin off the red blood cells. The plasma which remained was the desired product. We were to freeze these bottles of buffalo blood plasma and periodically ship them to the organ transplant team's laboratories for testing.

The proposal sounded simple to anyone who wasn't familiar with buffalo. But to anyone accustomed to working with free-spirited, fierce buffalo, it was fraught with complications. The buffalo is a wild animal, possessing great strength and endurance. They look clumsy, but they can wheel and charge with tremendous speed. Though a buffalo cow seldom weighs more than twelve hundred pounds, a bull may reach a ton easily, and some older buffalo bulls weigh three thousand pounds. Buffalo hate being confined, and they are anything but docile.

We would have to confine a buffalo in order to administer an injection and to draw blood from it. In the early stages of our preparations we worked with a Utah company which constructed equipment for cattle ranchers. We had them make us a steel squeeze chute especially designed for buffalo, with modifications for the buffalo's large head and shoulders. A squeeze chute is basically a steel-barred cage, with gates at both ends. Once the buffalo is in the squeeze chute, both ends are closed, and the swinging sides pulled firmly against his ribs, holding him reasonably immobile. To release him, one loosens the constricting sides, opens the front end, and the buffalo gallops away.

We installed the big squeeze chute at the ranch as a part of our wooden, loading-chute corral. The more we looked at our set-up, the more pessimistic we became. Bill knew he could get a buffalo into the squeeze chute once, to give him the first injection. But buffalo have long memories. Bill worried that he wouldn't be able to coax the animal back into the chute for the second scheduled injection two weeks later. And coaxing a buffalo is the best way. Using force with a buffalo means danger, both to the animal and to the handlers.

"Our part in this research project sounds a bit dangerous," I observed to Bill. "I think it calls for more rodeo skill than scientific prowess."

Bill agreed. "We've got to be in control of the animal so we can give injections and take blood at specified intervals. I've been thinking a lot about this, and I think the solution is to do it in our backyard, where the animals are handy for us. We have to conduct the scientific part on a strict schedule, and we must watch the animal closely for adverse reactions."

My eyes bugged. My backyard! "I have to turn my backyard into a bull-pen?" I sputtered. "Where will I hang out my washing? Where will the children play?"

"Oh, I don't mean to bring a big old bull over to the house," Bill pacified me. "I've been thinking that it'd be safest to use a young buffalo, one that's small and easier to manage."

Ordinarily I wouldn't appreciate turning my backyard into a barnyard, but I was so relieved that our backyard buffalo would be a small one, I agreed without protest.

One of our buffalo cows had given birth to a calf in early December, which is not the best time for calving, and fairly unusual. Most wild animals, including buffalo, bear their young in the spring. This is nature's proper timing as it spares the newborn animals the rigors of winter during their first vulnerable weeks of life. As the winter temperatures plunged lower, Bill worried about the little calf.

"I suppose he'll survive," he said, "but I'd hate to lose him. If I bring him to our backyard, I can make certain he has plenty of food and a windbreak when he needs it. If this calf seems strong and vigorous, he can be the first experimental animal in our research."

The little calf was just ten weeks old when Bill separated him from his mother and brought him to our backyard. The calf was fighting mad and struggling, so Bill put him in a box stall in the barn.

"We'll probably have to keep him confined to the stall for a couple days until he calms down. I don't want him throwing himself against our fence and hurting himself." Bill slipped into the stall and sat down on a bale of hay, talking soothingly to the frightened calf. He looked up at me and grinned. "This is Crazy Horse, and our buffalo serum project we'll call Project Crazy Horse."

I understood. Up to now, horses had been the donor animals in transplant serum production. Now it would be a buffalo calf, substituting for a horse, a Crazy Horse.

Slowly, Bill held his hand out toward the newly-named Crazy Horse. With a bellow the little calf lowered his head and slammed into Bill's ribs. Bill rolled out of the way, laughing, "You mean little cuss!" but I could see him gingerly feeling his bruised chest.

Again, Bill stretched a friendly hand toward Crazy Horse, and the little calf repeated his head-down charge, thumping Bill's legs. Fortunately, Bill was wearing an insulated snowmobile suit, which gave him some protection.

"Come on in and sit down," Bill urged me. "We want him to get used to us."

I declined. I was leaning over the gate into the box stall, and Crazy Horse would have to grow accustomed to me that way. I wasn't about to become a punching bag for a baby buffalo.

Within the next two days Crazy Horse put aside most of his hostility toward us. He recognized us as the source of his food and water, and he began eating from our hands. Bill dislikes keeping an animal enclosed in a barn, an unnatural and unhealthy confinement. We decided to free Crazy Horse into the larger space of our fenced backyard.

The moment Crazy Horse stepped from the dimly lit barn into bright daylight he gave a grateful grunt. Then he caught sight of Bruno, our St. Bernard. The two loped toward each other curiously. Bruno never had seen a buffalo nor had Crazy Horse seen so large a dog. They circled each other, sniffing. Having assured himself that Crazy Horse was O.K., Bruno lay down in the snow beside our back door. Bill and I watched, surprised, as the buffalo calf sauntered toward Bruno and lay down beside him. Crazy Horse was only slightly smaller than the St. Bernard, and they made a cozy pair.

The fluffy dog and the woolly calf soon formed an affectionate attachment to each other. Frequently they cuddled together beside the back door. If it began snowing hard, Bruno usually got into his huge St. Bernard doghouse. Within a few days Crazy Horse decided to try the doghouse, too. The first time I saw the buffalo climb into the doghouse after Bruno, I expected to see Bruno exit fast, but Bruno didn't mind sharing his doghouse at all. He had no prejudice against hoofs and horns. His shaggy new friend gave off warmth and was good company.

We built a wooden chute which would be used to restrain Crazy Horse when we administered injections and drew blood. We framed in a small plywood pen between our two barns and placed the restraining chute in the enclosure. The set-up was complete when Bill stretched two sections of fencing at the outer end. Here the fence was wide apart, but it converged into the chute. Once Crazy Horse was lured into the wide end of the funnel, we could block that end, and he had nowhere to go but forward into the chute.

The first vial of human white blood cells arrived by Air Express, Special Delivery. With no difficulty, we coaxed Crazy Horse into the chute, and Bill gave him the injection of white cells. For a few days Bill watched Crazy Horse carefully, fearing an adverse reaction. The little buffalo acted slightly sluggish, but showed no serious symptoms.

Two weeks later we received another vial of human white cells, and again Bill injected the cells into Crazy Horse with no ill effects. We drew blood for an antibody test before the third injection was administered a month later. This time Crazy Horse showed a mild reaction. As soon as we released him from the squeeze chute, he began to lick his lips constantly and shake his head. For two hours he remained dizzy and unsteady on his feet.

The laboratory workers were amazed at the skyrocketing antibody titre level Crazy Horse was showing. Buffalo did indeed have a unique and violent immunity response mechanism.

The fourth injection caused a pronounced reaction. Immediately upon leaving the chute, Crazy Horse's knees collapsed, and he fell. Struggling, he managed to get his forelegs under him, and he swayed off, dragging his hindquarters. For two hours he suffered this hindquarter paralysis. Even when the paralysis left, he was miserable. Disoriented and panting, he lay very still on the ground. His nose felt hot, and he would neither eat nor drink water.

At bedtime Crazy Horse was unimproved. Just after midnight Bill got up to check on the little buffalo, who had not moved. Bill worried over Crazy Horse's one hundred six degree temperature, since one hundred one is normal for buffalo.

Bill slept fitfully, and at four in the morning he rose, intending to give Crazy Horse an injection of cortisone to stop the reaction. However, he found that the buffalo's temperature had dropped to one hundred four degrees, and his eyes were clearing. Bill thought that Crazy Horse might live, and he decided against the cortisone injection as it would cut down on his antibody titre, that very important measurement we were trying to build through the white cell injections.

Within two days Crazy Horse returned to normal, much to our relief. We were getting attached to our experimental animal, an unwise emotion in research.

In June we began drawing blood at one week intervals. Bill took the blood to the hospital laboratory where it was centrifuged, then he brought home the remaining plasma, which we froze in our home freezer. Each time we collected four liters of frozen plasma, we air-freighted it, frozen, to the organ transplant research laboratory. The initial tests proved exciting. Crazy Horse had produced an antibody titre twice as high as that ever produced by a horse, and in just half the time.

Crazy Horse's near-fatal reaction made us realize it wasn't wise to have only one experimental animal.

"We really should have some more buffalo calves over here for this work," Bill suggested. Doubtful of my reaction, he gave me a wary look.

I shrugged. "Why not? When you have one buffalo in your backyard, I guess a few more won't be that much trouble."

Bill cleared his throat. "Well," he began, "remember that Crazy Horse was nearly three months old when we took him away from his mother and brought him over here. He was old enough to eat hay and grain. The calves I'm talking about are less than two weeks old and nursing from their mothers."

I looked up, glimpsing the future.

Bill nodded. "Yes, it means bottle-feeding them."

Though not a farm girl, from somewhere in my Iowa-bred past I called up a recollection of a metal pail filled with milk. From the lower part of the bucket there protruded a big rubber nipple. The calves walked up to the hanging bucket, sucked their fill of milk, and the feeding was completed. This didn't sound so difficult. Hanging a bucket of milk from a fence post a few times each day shouldn't take too much time. Besides, the children eagerly promised to help feed any buffalo calves we captured and brought to our backyard.

A few days later Bill brought home two young buffalo calves, crowded into a wooden crate. We put them in a box stall in the barn to wait for them to calm down. I hurried to a farmer's supply store to purchase a bucket with a nipple on it. The store manager suggested that we start, not with the bucket-with-a-nipple, but with huge half-gallon plastic bottles fitted with three-inch long nipples.

"You must start calves with these," he said, "before you can advance to the independent feeding with the buckets."

I returned with the huge calf-feeding bottles, and we spent the rest of the evening in the barn, trying to coax the two frightened and hostile buffalo calves to take the long black nipples into their mouths. We had no success, but hoped they would grow hungry and eager during the night.

By morning the calves were ravenous. When we rubbed warm milk on their muzzles, they licked their lips greedily. However, they refused to take the large rubber nipples into their mouths.

"You know," Bill said, "these nipples are huge compared to the teats of a buffalo. I can see how they would seem of normal size to a Holstein or Hereford calf, whose mother has large teats, but buffalo calves are accustomed to their mother's small nipples. I think regular baby bottles would seem more natural to these calves."

So it was we tried human baby bottles, and the two young buffalo drank lustily. Later in the day we freed them from the barn, and they joined Crazy Horse in the backyard. Now seven months old, Crazy Horse seemed huge compared to the two-week-old auburn calves.

We named the bull calf Boy Called Sue, referring to the song which tells how tough a young boy must be to overcome his given name of Sue. The little heifer we named Sisseton Sioux, in deference to the Indian reservation where Bill spent his early years. The two calves became a close pair, and usually we referred to them as "the two Sues."

The following week Bill brought home another calf. This bull calf was a little older than the first two, larger and wilder, so we named him The Wild One.

Now there were four buffalo in our backyard, three of which had to be fed bottles of warm milk several times a day. For six weeks, the calves remained so wild that they would not approach us voluntarily to drink from the bottles. We had to drive them into the cutting chute and pen them in before we could get them started sucking on the bottles. Once they started, they went into a feeding frenzy, and nothing could stop them. When we paused to refill empty bottles, the calves stampeded us, stomping on our feet and impatiently butting our legs. It was a relief the day they actually ran up to us when they saw us come out the back door holding the milk pail and baby bottles. Not having to chase them into the chute for each feeding saved a great deal of time.

When the irises around the barn began to bloom, Crazy Horse sampled them and found them to be delicious, especially the purple flowers, which he ate first. When these were gone, he moved on to the yellow iris. Until now Crazy Horse had stuck to eating grass, hay, and grain, but this sampling of flowers seemed to cause his taste to grow more cosmopolitan. His expanded eating horizons caused a big falling out with Bruno. One day when I placed Bruno's huge bowl of Gravy Train dogfood beside the doghouse, Bruno loped over slowly, as usual. In the past, Crazy Horse frequently had stood beside Bruno when the bushy dog ate, but this day the young buffalo sniffed this new sort of food. After a tiny nibble Crazy Horse decided that he really liked Gravy Train, and he lowered his shaggy head to eat. Aghast at this new development, Bruno growled and tore into the surprised buffalo. Recovering quickly, Crazy Horse lowered his big head and gave Bruno a frightful bunt in the ribs. Grunting, barking, and flying fur filled the yard as I ran for a broom and broke up the melee. The two opponents eyed each other grievously. A good friendship had gone awry, all over a bowl of Gravy Train. Never again did the two animals share the doghouse in a peaceful afternoon snooze

I had to give up hanging sheets on the clothesline. The little calves thought the flapping sheets were there for fun. They loved bunting the wet sheets, and the dark smudges left by their play meant I had to re-wash the sheets. There was also the possibility that a vigorous bunt might pull the sheet loose from its clothespins. With a wet sheet covering his head and blinding him, a frightened calf might hurt himself.

By autumn these darling little auburn calves had become dark brown adolescents. Though Crazy Horse was several months older than they, he was no larger. Immunizing him against human white blood cells and the repeated removing of so much blood had done strange things to his body. Though he was developing a hump and other characteristics of a mature bull, his growth was severely stunted. His skin grew wrinkled, and he began to look like an old, decrepit buffalo—strange, indeed, when one considered that Crazy Horse was not quite one year old.

As the nights grew frostier and dry leaves fluttered to the ground, Crazy Horse's aging process speeded up. Just before his first birthday, the young buffalo bull died, apparently from old age. We sorrowed over his untimely death, and felt guilty, knowing that Crazy Horse had been sacrificed to gain scientific knowledge. In spite of being great animal-lovers, we are greater people-lovers, and the hope that Crazy Horse had given up his life for the benefit of human beings made us feel it was worthwhile.

For the next year and one half Bill carried on confidential correspondence and discussions with Parker B. Francis III, President of the Puritan-Bennett Gas Corporation, in an effort to use information gained from Project Crazy Horse toward the establishment of a research project to develop an anti-cancer vaccine, using buffalo. Mr. Francis was a member of the Board of Directors of the American Cancer Society. Over the months of discussion he became as convinced as Bill was that an anti-cancer vaccine could be developed using the same techniques as those Bill used in the organ transplant serum production. The main difference would be the substitution of cancer cells for white blood cells used in Project Crazy Horse.

They referred to their new program for cancer vaccine as Project The Wild One. Their plans were kept confidential since Mr. Francis believed it was important to avoid offending any of the large medical research institutions, if they were not included in the project. Bill honored the confidentiality requested, and he remained silent even when he received letters of inquiry from some of these institutions.

Bill believes that we humans have a very high degree of immunity to cancer as compared to our immunity to other types of killing diseases. Before the advent of antibiotics, a bacterial pneumonia, peritonitis, or meningitis would kill a patient within a matter of hours. Though we have no successful anti-cancer drugs, it still takes cancer several months, and sometimes, years, to kill a person. This has to be because the human immunity mechanism continuously fights off cancer, though sometimes it isn't strong enough to fight off and destroy cancer permanently. In fifteen years Bill had seen two patients who recovered from cancer without treatment.

Bill explains that the immunity mechanism of an individual is closely related to, and responsive to the spirit of that individual. It is similar to the fight-or-flight response, where adrenalin is injected into the blood stream when an animal, or human, is enraged or in great fear. The immunity response is a slower response, taking hours, or even several days before peaking, instead of the split second response of the stress mechanism.

Bill described to Mr. Francis the uncommon immunity mechanism of buffalo. "Buffalo are unique," he explained, "in that they have either a complete immunity to cancer, or at least a very high degree of immunity. In the eight years I've been chairman of the Research Committee of the National Buffalo Association, I've seen only two cases of cancer in buffalo. Both of those buffalo were zoo animals, and you know the spirit of the animal had been broken."

Fascinated with these ideas, Mr. Francis later visited South Africa and discussed these theories with research scientists there. He was surprised to learn that some of the men in the heart transplant program there held the same ideas. These men were conducting studies on South African wild animals concerning their resistance to cancer. The thinking of these men coincided with Bill's, that the wild spirit of an animal influences his immunity response, and more especially, his high degree of immunity to cancer.

Bill and Mr. Francis gathered information enthusiastically. Then, tragically, Mr. Francis was killed in an auto accident. Bill's hopes of establishing a research program with buffalo anti-cancer vaccine were dashed.

We discontinued bottle-feeding the three young calves which we had been preparing for the anti-cancer vaccine project, The Wild One. They were eating sufficient quantities of hay and grain, and no longer needed the milk supplement. This was a great relief, as they now weighed nearly three hundred pounds each, and our toes were taking a frightful beating from their eager stomping.

*"Chasing the buffalo is better
than chasing the rabbit.
Even when you catch the rabbit,
you're still hungry."*
        —Indian saying

•

Buffalo
to the
Indians

5 Several newspapers and magazines carried articles describing our buffalo herd and Bill's unique research work with buffalo. This publicity brought on our involvement with Michigan Indians—the Chippewa Indians of the far north Upper Peninsula.

The Office of Economic Opportunity in our state capitol contacted Bill for advice and assistance on a new project. Jack, the O.E.O. representative, explained that the Indians of the Keweenaw Bay Reservation wanted to start raising buffalo.

For several years Bill had been working in an effort to get buffalo back to the Indians. As Vice-President and chairman of the Research Committee of the National Buffalo Association, Bill persisted in his attempts to get the Department of the Interior to live up to an agreement made in 1965, giving surplus buffalo from federal parks to American Indians. The Department of the Interior had not lived up to this agreement, and Bill struggled patiently to urge them into compliance.

He wrote letters to Senator Hart and Senator Griffin, our senators from Michigan, urging them to look into this flagrant disregard of a written agreement between the National Park Service and the Bureau of Indian Affairs. Polite, noncommittal letters came from the senators saying they "would look into the matter." Bill plodded along, urging governmental agencies to reconsider their methods of disposing of surplus buffalo. Our file grew several inches thick. Bureaucracy was good at returning letters, but it remained unresponsive to the needs of people.

Several times Bill talked by phone to Jack, the O.E.O. representative. Finally it was decided that representatives from the Indians' tribal council and Jack would come to our home to formulate plans for the Indians' entrance into buffalo raising.

They arrived on St. Patrick's Day, which was also our daughter, Beth's, birthday, while I was plastering a birthday cake with green frosting. I offered coffee and green birthday cake for refreshments. As the huge cake began to disappear, the frown on Beth's face turned to a scowl. Having an Indian powwow wasn't her idea of a proper birthday party. Soon she became interested in the discussion and her irritation faded.

The projected plan for getting the Chippewa Indians into the buffalo raising business called for an ultimate expenditure of $125,000 to $150,000. Jack explained the plan. Like most O.E.O. and Peace Corps workers, he was imaginative and idealistic, not a typical bureaucrat. Even so, he was bound with unavoidable paperwork and red tape in these government-funded projects. Jack suggested that Bill be hired as a part-time consultant for two years at $10,000 a year. The first phase was to involve a feasibility study, which was projected to cost $50,000, and would determine whether it was feasible for the Indians to attempt to raise buffalo.

Bill had been squirming restlessly in his chair as these proposals unfolded. Finally, he could stand it no longer.

"Look," he said, "when you get through with this feasibility study you're going to have spent a heck of a lot of money and you still won't have any buffalo. Great efforts will be made at filing reports and conducting studies.

46

You need experience raising a few buffalo before you get a lot of them. I've got better things to do with my time than fill out forms and answer questionnaires. I know that's the way bureaucracy works, but I can't stomach it. I want you guys to learn how to raise buffalo, not how to fill out government forms."

Bill shoved his chair forward and picked up a pen. "Let me make you a counter-proposal. I started with thirteen buffalo. That's a nice, round lucky number for us Indians. I'm willing to give you thirteen buffalo calves to get you started, if you'll pay for the shipping or do it yourselves. But I'm going to be an Indian-giver. These calves will multiply into a nice herd for you. In seven years you can give me back thirteen buffalo calves."

There was a long period of silence. The Indians were used to prolonged sessions ending with "Make out a request form and we'll see if we can process it through proper government channels." The two tribal council members blinked and gazed at each other uneasily.

Bill picked up a paper grocery bag and began to write on it with a brown marking pen. "I'll set up the agreement in writing," he offered.

So with a handshake and an agreement scribbled on a brown paper bag the matter was settled.

That summer the Chippewas put up hay to use during the ensuing winter. With O.E.O. funds to purchase fencing materials, they fenced forty acres of pastureland. By late fall they were ready for buffalo. We reserved all the buffalo calves born that summer for the Chippewa Indians at Keweenaw Bay, a finger of land which thrusts into the frigid waters of Lake Superior. During that summer and autumn we stayed in close contact with the tribal council, advising them about the needed strength of their fences, and notifying them of the birth of each additional calf. The Chippewas grew enthusiastic about future projects based on having their own buffalo herd. They expected the herd to become a tourist attraction. If they drew a large number of tourists, they could sell more handicraft and souvenir items. When their herd increased sufficiently, they planned to build a buffalo-burger restaurant where they would cook and sell buffalo meat. Just as in the old days when the Plains Indians used every part of each buffalo, the Chippewas intended to use the hides for leathercraft items and the horns and hoofs for souvenir products, such as ashtrays and powder horns.

On the morning of December 30 Bill called me from the hospital. "Pinkie, we're having a big New Year's Eve party tomorrow. The Indians have left L'Anse with a truck and should arrive in Stanwood this evening. We'll load the calves tomorrow morning."

During the night a heavy snow moved in and by morning eighteen inches of snow smothered the ground. A ten-below-zero dawn greeted us. We dressed in our warmest clothing and highest boots.

Upon arriving at the buffalo pasture, we saw several cars and trucks filled with television cameramen and reporters. They hurried to get their cameras set up for the round-up. As they stamped their feet to keep warm, the reporters talked among themselves.

"Indians and buffalo. I like that."

One of the reporters interviewed Fred Dakota, the chief of the tribal council. With his horn-rimmed glasses Fred looked like a young university student except for his colorful feathered Indian bonnet.

The reporter questioned Fred about tribal plans for buffalo. Finally, he asked, "Mr. Dakota, have you ever tasted buffalo meat?"

Without hesitation Fred retorted, "Heck, no. The greedy white people shot all the buffalo long before I was born." Fred explained that in the days long ago Indians and buffalo were a natural association, like ham and eggs. Then the insatiable buffalo hunters nearly annihilated the vast herds which the Indians relied upon for food, clothing, and shelter. The starving Indians had to abandon their way of life and attempt to survive without their buffalo. Still, an old Sioux legend persisted among the tribes, a legend which said the buffalo were not really gone from this earth, but were hiding in underground caverns, and

48

that one day the shaggy herds would come thundering out of hiding and once again cover the earth.

"Our buffalo aren't flowing out of caves," chuckled Fred, "but we don't care where they come from. We're just grateful to get some buffalo."

"But why do you Indians want buffalo?" one reporter persisted.

A twitch of amusement flashed across Fred's face as he replied, "We Indians have a saying, 'Chasing the buffalo is better than chasing the rabbit. Even when you catch the rabbit, you're still hungry.'"

The reporters would have liked to see the Indians grab bows and arrows, jump on horses, and, with war whoops, gallop into the herd to cut out their buffalo calves. However, the Indians humbly admitted they knew nothing about handling buffalo. They offered to assist wherever they could and were assigned positions of opening and closing corral gates at the proper times.

The brunt of the dangerous round-up proceedings fell upon Bill, our son Bruce, two of Bruce's school friends, our ranch foreman, Bob, and his son, and some brave friends from the village who volunteered to help. Most of the calves were only six-months-old and not yet weaned. Buffalo mothers are extremely protective. Separating a calf from its mother is a real challenge. One must think fast and move fast, and moving fast in eighteen inches of snow is like trying to run through knee-deep water, something you usually do only in nightmares. The deep snow didn't slow the buffalo a bit, and the bitter cold made them violent and fast. The men were so numbed by the cold that the idea of getting gored by a charging buffalo somehow didn't seem quite so horrible as when one thinks of these dangers while in the safety of his bed.

Television cameramen got good action sequences for their New Year's Eve news broadcasts as the buffalo thundered through the corrals, snow spewing into the air from their skidding hoofs. One at a time, calves were separated from their mothers and directed into the stock truck which was backed against the loading chute. It was a long, all-day process, and when daylight neared an end, only seven calves had been loaded.

Fred Dakota shrugged. "Well, at least we got seven this trip. We'll just have to come back another time for the rest."

The truck left, heading north for L'Anse, a twelve-hour drive.

We returned home, cold and weary, but grateful there had been no injuries, either human or animal. With steaming hot toddies for Bill and me, and hot chocolate for the children, we curled up cozily in our living room to watch the evening news, flicking channels to pick up the buffalo round-up on each station.

Bruce pointed to one scene of action. "That's where that old cow just about nailed me," he commented.

Shuddering, I sank deeper into my arm chair, glad that the buffalo round-up was over for the time being.

At noon the next day Fred Dakota called to say the truck had arrived back at the reservation at sun-up. The young buffalo had been unloaded, having survived the trip well. However, three of the calves already had broken out of the pasture, he reported. The Indians were going to try to round them up. Fred said their thermometer read twenty-below zero. We felt sorry for the inexperienced Indians having to handle buffalo on the loose. Fortunately, the escapees were only six-month-old calves, weighing no more than three or four hundred pounds, and there would be no angry mothers to deal with. Bill and I figured the Indians would have little difficulty corralling the wandering buffalo calves.

We were wrong. Five days later the Indians were still pursuing the fugitive buffalo, which had worked their way several miles from their intended pasture. They were moving toward the Iron Mountain Range, where it would be extremely difficult to capture them. Finally, the Chippewas contacted the Department of Natural Resources people for help with tranquilizer guns. The newspapers had a heyday with article headings: "Buffalo Loose, In-

dians in Pursuit''; ''Indians Call Paleface Hunters'';
''Palefaces Round Up Buffalo.''

With snowmobiles the hunters were able to approach
the fleeing calves and by using tranquilizer guns, im-
mobilize the animals long enough to get them loaded on a
truck. At last the three vagabond calves were returned to
the pasture the Indians had prepared, now with reinforced
fences.

The young calves thrived in their very northern, frigid
climate, proving that it was feasible to raise buffalo in
very cold regions. This, of course, was no surprise to us
since we knew that buffalo thrived on the frigid plains of
Saskatchewan and Northwest Territories just south of the
Great Slave Lake.

The publicity which accompanied our giving buffalo to
the Chippewa Indians brought on Bill's next involvement
in Indian affairs a few months later. Under construction
was a huge wastewater management system, a new concept in disposing of sewage. Vast amounts of federal
money were being used to develop this experimental project in an effort to clean up Lake Michigan. Most cities
near Lake Michigan treat their sewage at disposal plants,
then dump it into the lake, steadily polluting this magnificent body of water. The new wastewater system would end
all this by piping the sewage, not to the lake, but inland,
where it would be held and treated in monstrous reservoirs
and ultimately sprayed on thousands of surrounding acres
of barren, sandy soil in a giant farming operation.

Work on this multi-million dollar project was over
half-completed when we received a phone call one day
from a woman who was attempting to rally all the Indians
in the area. She was most upset.

''An outflow pipe of this system will disgorge a thirty-
six-inch stream of water and inundate an ancient Indian
burial ground and village site,'' she explained. ''I think it
would be a crime to ruin these historic mounds.''

The woman had tried to persuade the wastewater
authorities to move the pipe a short distance, but they insisted their plans couldn't be changed at this late stage.

"It's up to you Indians now," she said. "I'm contacting all the Indians and Indian organizations I know of to meet tonight at the township hall and protest this rigid attitude of the wastewater planners." We agreed to attend the meeting.

That evening our two older children had school activities to attend, but Bill and I headed for the Indian gathering accompanied by our youngest daughter, Brenda, who proudly wore her "Indian Power" button which the Chippewas had given her.

At the ramshackle frame building which serves as the township hall, we discovered the muddy parking lot was overflowing with cars, mostly dilapidated pick-up trucks, which Indians refer to as "Indian convertibles."

As we stepped into the hall we were met with the stale odor of a seldom-used building, and the babble of voices from over one hundred Indians and a couple dozen white people. I was amazed. I hadn't realized there were that many Indians in western Michigan. There were several older Indian people, sitting stoically, arms folded, appearing terribly dignified. Perhaps forty angry young Indian men and women stood around looking militant and defiant. The room was nearly filled with metal folding chairs, and more were set up to handle the crowd.

The meeting began with an amateur archeologist reading a paper by a professional archeologist explaining the value of the Indian village which was threatened. The site had been excavated in 1931 by amateur diggers who uncovered the remains of a young child which dated the mounds as part of the ancient Hopewell culture. The letter reported that there was an extensive Indian village area which had not yet been examined and should not be destroyed.

Another well-meaning archeologist stood up and reported that at this site she had seen a fire hole which dated back many centuries. In this hole, she said, fires had been burned constantly to guide the Indian hunters home to their camp. Other local diggers told of finding ancient dugout canoes, a knoll which had been the great council grounds, and bones and jars which appeared to be about thirteen hundred years old.

As these archeologists presented their cases they glanced serenely toward the Indians with the knowledge that the political and social clout of a learned university archeologist would save the day for the Indians. They were aware of the sentimentality of the Indians concerning their ancestors but knew this would have no effect of slowing the builders' bulldozers. The archeologists knew that politicians would fear the threat of attack and ridicule from scientists. The archeologists believed themselves to be on the same side as the Indians, and by preventing the destruction of an historic site, they were doing the Indians a big favor.

Suddenly, a young militant Indian jumped up, shaking his fist at the archeologists. "We Indians are not going to stand for this, your digging up our people's graves! You must stop this disruption of sacred land! I'm calling upon Indians in this country to let white people know we will not stand for it. We fought white people once before. We can do it again!"

An angry roar grumbled through the audience.

"Right on, baby! Custer had it coming!"

Many of the young people gave the closed fist, straight arm gesture of Indian Power. The archeologists sat stiff and bewildered, confused that their sincere concern had thrown them into the "bad guy" category. Having come to the meeting to help Indians, they found themselves being attacked as grave robbers and destroyers.

"Yes, white eyes!" came a shout from the back of the room. We all turned to stare. A very drunk Indian man wearing a toothless leer gummed the words, "How'd you like us to dig up *your* bones, baby?"

Everyone laughed, and tension lowered. Even so, Brenda and I slouched lower in our folding chairs, uncomfortably aware of our very blue eyes.

The indignation of the Indians raged on. "We have fifteen thousand young people in the American Indian Movement now, and one thing we will do is dig up one of your people for every one of our people you dig up!" cried one young man. "We're going to start in Arlington Cemetery. We're going to rob graves all over the country until you quit digging up our people and let them sleep in peace!"

One of the braver archeologists stood up. "At least we all agree that this village site and burial grounds must not be destroyed. The Hopewell culture was very advanced. In these mounds we find shells from the Gulf of Mexico, mica from the Carolinas, obsidian from the Rocky Mountains. There is a great deal of cord-marked pottery, and a one-thousand-year-old enclosure which must be investigated. Just last year an arrowhead found there was dated as "archaic," which puts the site back into the very earliest Indian habitation of the area, some twelve to thirteen thousand years ago."

Without rising to his feet, an older Indian called out sharply, "They'd never try to dump sewage on an old Lutheran graveyard!"

This brought on another loud rumble of Indian anger, and the archeologist sat down quickly.

On a metal table at the front of the room the hapless archeologists had arranged a display of Indian bones and pottery which they had dug up. A middle-aged, portly Indian man strode up to the table, and, hands on hips, he glared at the display. His heavy jowls trembled. "I just shake all over in anger," he said slowly, "when I see my ancestor's bones treated in this disrespectful, sacrilegious manner."

The crowd murmured agreement. A young Indian girl voiced her protest. "No one asks *us* what we're like. Instead, they're always digging up the ground to find out what we're really like. Dumb white people!"

The county commissioners in attendance and the wastewater director had been getting more and more nervous, fidgeting in their chairs. Every time the crowd grew noisy, their eyes darted about as if looking for the escape exit.

An Indian woman rose and suggested that the Indians

54

should go through the courts to stop the destruction of the burial ground and village site. "Let's do it the white man's way," she said. "We'll get an injunction and stop them cold."

This was too much for the wastewater director, who jumped to his feet, his face pale. This was a multi-million dollar project. He dared not risk letting a handful of insignificant Indians stop his earthmovers and construction equipment for even a day.

At the beginning of the meeting the wastewater director's attitude had been unbending—the outflow pipe could not possibly be moved. Now, at the words "court injunction" his whole outlook changed. He felt certain that the pipe could be moved in one direction or another, so it wouldn't pour wastewater on an historic site. He suggested that a committee of Indians be set up to study the blueprints and maps along with the wastewater authorities. He requested a meeting at the courthouse the following Monday to settle the outflow pipe location to everyone's satisfaction.

Two or three Indians were appointed when someone said, "We want The Buffalo Doctor on the committee." Bill nodded his assent and strode to the front of the room to join the forming committee.

This Indian vs. White confrontation ended peaceably. The committee and the wastewater authorities found another location for the outflow pipe, and the historic site was saved. The new direction of the drain ditch made it three-quarters of a mile shorter and saved the project thousands of dollars.

*"Oh, give me a home
where the buffalo roam."*
   —Brewster Higley, 1873

•

*Buffalo
in our
Backyard*

6 Our three backyard buffalo calves grew into large, mature-looking buffalo. Now when they rolled in their buffalo wallow beside my back door, great clouds of dust rose, challenging my housecleaning abilities. Sometimes I was startled when a black, shaggy head appeared in the window, its nostrils leaving two moist prints on the glass. The Wild One, always somewhat larger than Sisseton Sioux or Boy Called Sue, was maturing into a beautiful young bull. His magnificent black head reminded us of a young version of Black Diamond, the buffalo carved on the buffalo nickel.

At times the buffalo were a nuisance. Our son, Bruce, was an avid pilot, and when he was seventeen, he bought an old tail-wheel Aeronca Champ. He had a summer job at the airport, but he spent his off-hours constructing a landing strip in our pasture. While he waited for the grass seed to sprout on his strip, he battled the young buffalo. They loved rolling in the soft, bare dirt, and Bruce was kept busy filling in and raking buffalo wallows.

At last the grass grew thick, covering the bare dirt, and Bruce was ready to bring his plane in for his first landing in our backyard pasture. Uneasy over this maiden landing at our home-made airport, I stationed myself in the backyard and nervously studied the southern sky for a sign of Bruce's white-and-red plane. Suddenly the plane was there, coming in low. Bruce buzzed the runway, then circled the house. Though my heart thumped madly, I waved cheerfully as he swept past the house. Again, he buzzed the runway and circled the house.

Puzzled and worried, I wondered why he didn't land. Then I knew. The buffalo! The buffalo were lying on the runway.

"Girls!" I shrieked. "We've got to get the buffalo off the runway so Bruce can land!"

I grabbed a broom, Brenda jumped on her minibike, and Beth climbed onto her horse. The three of us charged upon the unsuspecting buffalo. In confusion, they stampeded up and down the runway until we finally got them turned toward the house. They ran into the safety of our backyard, their tongues hanging out from exertion. We were so intent upon chasing and corralling the buffalo, we didn't see Bruce land, and were unaware of the plane until it put-putted up to the fence beside the house.

Wearing a look of disgust, Bruce climbed out of the cockpit. "I thought I was going to run out of gas before you got those buffalo off the runway!"

I sighed. Motherhood is full of challenges. I did learn my lesson, however. From then on, whenever I heard a plane circling, I grabbed my broom like a Halloween witch and prepared for a wild dash of buffalo herding.

With three buffalo roaming freely through our backyard, our lawn looked more like a stockyards than a grassy expanse. Buffalo chips freckled the whole landscape. I consoled myself with the thought that it was a temporary way of life, like diapers and trips to the orthodontist. Then I learned that we were to have some additional cloven-hoofed guests.

At last, after all our failures and disappointments in crossbreeding buffalo with cattle, there was a new hopeful pregnancy. We had thought the thirteen Texas longhorn cows were our best potential for crossing. None of them as yet showed any signs of pregnancy. Instead, the cow pregnant with a half-buffalo calf was Bertha, the uninvited, intruding Holstein who had run off from her dairy herd to join our buffalo.

"I don't know when she'll have the calf," Bill said, "but I want to bring her to the backyard where I can keep a close eye on her condition."

Bob, who was feeding the herd for us that winter, agreed to load Bertha into his truck and bring her to our backyard.

"While you're bringing Bertha, why don't you bring Good Cow, too?" Bill suggested. Good Cow was one of our original buffalo which we'd purchased in Iowa. Soon after the birth of her first calf, Good Cow developed a strong attachment to Bill. She loved to have him scratch her, and she followed him about like a devoted puppy dog. Because of her friendliness, Bill was especially fond of Good Cow. He thought she would enjoy dwelling in our backyard where Bill was near at hand to spend more time with her.

When the black-and-white Holstein and the brown buffalo were unloaded from the truck, the three young buffalo eyed the newcomers warily. Unaccustomed to seeing a full-grown buffalo, they shied away from Good Cow. The Wild One was just beginning to realize he was a bull. Though he ignored Good Cow, he became immensely attracted to the bulging, pregnant Bertha. His interest seemed to be protective rather than sexual. Wherever the black-and-white Holstein went, The Wild One always kept close by. Though The Wild One never had fathered a calf, he acted just like a proud, protective father-to-be.

Bertha adjusted quickly to her new pasture and showed no ill effects from the truck ride. Good Cow, however, didn't display the same adaptability. Always serene and affectionate in the past, Good Cow disliked our backyard pasture from the outset. Restlessly, she spent her days pacing the fence line, staring at the world on the other side of the fence with a yearning glare. She seemed to consider her new home a prison, and she devoted her energies to walking the perimeter, searching for an escape route. On occasion, she condescended to let Bill scratch her, but the magic had gone out of her attachment to him. He was just an old flame who no longer could kindle any sparks.

Bill kept a close watch on Bertha. As her abdomen grew larger with the growing calf, she remained healthy, showing no signs of fluid retention. Early in April Bill was scheduled to go on an annual fishing trip. He hesitated leaving for fear Bertha might develop complications, or even go into labor. After a long mental struggle, he decided to chance going. Bill left me with a long list of detailed instructions. Daily, I was to check Bertha's ankles for signs of swelling, and study her flank and abdominal area for any noticeable change in size and configuration. "Now, if she goes into labor, call a veterinarian. Don't try to deliver the calf yourself," he ordered.

I swallowed a hysterical laugh. Deliver the calf myself! My experience with cows was confined to drinking milk. I'd never so much as seen a calf born. "I'll call a vet," I promised, although we both knew this was a hollow promise. Veterinarians who care for large animals are rare in our part of the state, and difficult to get hold of. Most likely I'd have to call nearby farmers to find a volunteer midwife.

Dutifully, I checked Bertha's ankles while Bill was away, and to my everlasting gratitude, she neither retained fluid nor went into labor.

Bill returned on a Sunday afternoon. Immediately, he hurried out to the pasture to examine Bertha. "She looks fine," he reported, "but I think her time is close. I'm glad I'm back."

His return was timely. The very next morning as we were dawdling over after-breakfast coffee Bill began staring intently toward the grove of tall white pine trees at the far corner of our pasture. On the edge of the grove we could make out the distant shape of Bertha, repeatedly kneeling on her front legs and then rising again.

Holding the field glasses to his eyes, Bill focused on Bertha. "My gosh," he cried, "she has a huge bag of waters hanging out of her! She's in labor! Let's get out there!''

Quickly we grabbed a hunting knife, a stout rope, and a camera and hurried out to the pine grove. Still intact, the bag of waters looked like a sixteen-inch balloon bulging from beneath Bertha's tail. Dirt and pine needles coated the bag, indicating that Bertha had been in labor for some time. Between contractions, she lay down, but with the onset of each contraction, she rose and humped her back, straining to deliver the calf. The Wild One, having attached himself to Bertha, stood nearby protectively. When the cow lay down, he stood directly over her. The young bull's instincts told him that she was vulnerable to predators, and he assumed a watchful, guarding attitude.

As Bill and I approached Bertha, she struggled to her feet, trying to get away. We stood very still, and promptly the laboring cow lay down. Slowly, Bill moved toward her. The Wild One stared intently at him.

"Grab that steel fence post over there," Bill whispered to me. "Now stay close behind me with it. We may have to use that post to fend off The Wild One if he charges us."

Kneeling, Bill stretched out towards Bertha's rear end. With his hunting knife he slit the bulging bag of waters. With a great gush, amber fluid spurted out. Bertha began to rise, but then sensed relief and relaxed into a comfortable position. She seemed to understand that she needed help. Two tiny hooves protruded from the cow's vagina. Bill grasped the slippery hooves. Bertha started to get up, but a contraction began, and she lay down, straining and pushing. Bill dug the heels of his cowboy boots into the soft earth and pulled on the protruding hooves.

A low grunt came from the watchful buffalo bull, and I raised the fence post at him in what I hoped was a menacing gesture.

As Bertha began to get another contraction, Bill tied a rope to the little legs and pulled. There was some progress. The hooves emerged farther, and we could make out a tiny nose resting on the forelegs. Bill needed more leverage, so he wrapped the rope around his back and placed his

61

boots against Bertha's hips. With the next contraction Bill pulled while Bertha strained, and the head and forelegs protruded farther. After several more contractions the calf slid out with a loud gush, accompanied by much yellowish fluid. Exhausted, Bertha lay still.

Quickly, Bill cleaned the membranes away from the newborn calf's nostrils and began rubbing and massaging the slippery animal. The calf lay perfectly still, unmoving, as Bill began artificial respiration. At last a hind leg kicked, and the newborn heifer gasped and began to breathe.

"It's okay! It's alive!" Bill and I grinned at each other.

"It's barely kicking," I worried.

"Naw, she's fine," Bill said, stroking the wet pile of dark fur. "That's a good name—Barely Kicking. Barely Kicking von Holstein."

The young buffalo bull stayed his distance, watching, less anxious now that Bertha seemed to be resting peacefully, free from pain. As I snapped pictures in the shady pine grove, Bill rubbed the newborn cattalo, and quietly repeated over and over, "Barely. Barely." In the first few moments after birth, the calf usually is conditioned to the sound of its mother's voice. Bill hoped to condition Barely to the sound of his voice, so she would be tame and respond to his calling her.

After awhile Bertha heaved herself to a standing position. For a moment she stared doubtfully at Bill, who was stroking her new calf. Then, seemingly assured that he meant no harm, she strolled off aways and humped up her back. With a grunt, she expelled the large afterbirth, then calmly turned and began to eat it. A wave of revulsion swept over me. Cows, and buffalo, are strictly vegetarians, and it seemed unnatural to see a cow eating something besides grass and hay. Then I remembered that this was a self-preservation instinct. Traces of calving must be cleaned up. Otherwise threatening predators might be attracted to the scene. A newborn calf is wobbly and vulnerable during its first days of life.

After disposing of the afterbirth, Bertha returned to her calf. Bill and I backed off a distance and watched mother and child get acquainted. Bertha's long tongue began cleaning the little calf. Even when Barely rose for the first time on shaky, uncertain legs, Bertha continued her bathing licks. The little calf was tipped off balance and collapsed under the pressure of her mother's tongue. These were the important moments of imprinting, when the mother is teaching the calf, "I am your mother. I will take care of you and feed you and guard you. You must stay close to me." Later when the calf begins to nuzzle its mother, and finally begins sucking milk, the cow lets her calf drink enough to know that milk is good, but she moves away before the calf can drink its fill. In this way she trains the calf by enticing it to follow her so it can get more milk.

On her second day of life Barely's legs were strong, and she got around well. Now that her coat was dry, we could see that she was solid black. A large calf, square and sturdy, she showed promise of maturing into an extremely large animal.

Out in the pasture Bill cavorted with the little heifer and laughed heartily when she bunted him playfully. He whispered "Barely" into her ear, scratched her, and leaped about in the fashion that calves do when they play together. Barely pranced and jumped, then lowered her head and butted Bill. This playful game later turned out to be a big mistake.

Every wife knows that there's an unwritten law which goes: "When your husband is out of town, everything goes wrong."

Just let the man of the house get five hundred miles from home and right away the garage door sticks shut, imprisoning your car. The children get sick, the furnace ruptures a vital part, thunderstorms strike nightly, and there's a house burglary down the street. I don't know *how* inanimate objects, germs, and weather know that the little woman is alone and vulnerable, but they know. And so do our buffalo.

When Boy Called Sue, Sisseton Sioux, and The Wild One neared two years in age, they became dissatisfied with their life-style. Boy Sue began pushing against the pasture fence, thrusting his horns beneath it in an apparent escape effort. We suspected that he was unhappy over the sex ratio of his threesome, two bulls and only one heifer, far from the ideal ratio of ten cows to one buffalo bull. Perhaps Boy Sue felt cheated, and he wished to scout the neighborhood in search of more buffalo heifers. Hoping to discourage a break for freedom, I piled tree branches and broken lawn chairs over the gaps in the fence wire that Sue had stretched.

The backyard buffalo seemed to have gotten wind that Bill was far off in Washington, D.C. attending a urology seminar. At five thirty in the morning the phone rang. It was neighbors one-half mile down the road. "Some of your buffalo just ran through our yard," they said.

"Thmmanks," I mumbled sleepily, figuring this was the worst nightmare ever. I struggled out of bed and to the window. Out in the pasture I checked off: the horse, Bertha, Barely, Good Cow . . . , frantically, my eyes searched the pasture. There was not a sign of Boy Sue, Sisseton Sioux, or The Wild One. They *were* gone.

I woke the children. "Get dressed fast! The buffalo are out!" Pulling blue jeans over our pajamas, we hurried to collect coffee cans full of grain. These would be the enticers to lure our buffalo home.

We found The Wild One first. He was peering into a bedroom window, while the other two buffalo milled about closeby. The occupants of the house stepped onto their back porch uneasily. "We'd help you round them up," the man apologized, "but we have to leave for work." He gestured toward a stout board-fence corral. "Would you like to put them in the corral for the time being?"

I had planned to Pied Piper the three buffalo back home, urging them to follow us with our cans of grain. Now I could see they were too riled up. Soon school buses would be starting out on their routes, and children would be standing along the road, waiting. I dared not chance trying to lead our escapees home.

Gratefully, we accepted his offer of penning them in. He swung open a large gate, and Bruce and I entered, waving the grain cans enticingly. Licking their lips hungrily, the three buffalo followed, and we had them enclosed. We hurried home where the children hastily cleaned up for school and dashed off.

My feet were muddy and cold. Sticky grain had worked its way down my neck, and I itched. I looked at my watch. Not yet seven thirty in the morning. I'd been up for two hours and not so much as a cup of coffee. Three of our buffalo were off "down the road." Oh, misery!

I thought of Bill dozing peacefully in his hotel room in Washington. A vision of his serene, sleeping face passed before me, and an ornery impulse struck. My reasoning was, "I'm awake and miserable. Why should he be sleeping?" So I telephoned him.

He answered the phone groggily, and I wailed out my woes. Bill didn't sound upset, though I'd expected him to be. But he takes for granted the coping with buffalo problems. Brave and self-assured in handling buffalo, Bill forgets how cowardly I am.

"Leaver has a truck, doesn't he?" Bill yawned. "Why don't you phone him? He'll help you load the animals and get them home."

Late in the morning I got hold of Leaver, an elderly man who has worked with animals most of his life. I didn't even try to keep the tearful waver out of my voice. I suspected Leaver might be one of the old school who enjoyed helping damsels in distress.

"Don't you worry, little lady," he soothed. "I'll be there about one o'clock, and we'll get your buffalo back for you."

When Leaver arrived with a truck and two helpers we drove to the board corral. There was no sign of our buffalo. Then I saw movement within the dark shed. The animals had entered the cool shed to escape the sun beating down on the corral. We backed the truck up to the shed door. Now we had them penned. Their only way out was to get into the truck. We waited awhile, hoping they might mosey into the truck out of curiosity, but I suspected we couldn't be so lucky.

Someone had to enter that shadowy building and "shoo" the buffalo out. Male chivalry stopped here. No volunteers stepped forward. Their attitude was, "They're *your* buffalo, lady, and you know them better than we do."

Squeezing through the small space between truck and doorjamb, I waited for my eyes to adjust to the dim light.

"Okay, you guys," I barked. "Into the truck! Right now! No horsing around!" There was a tremor in my voice which I prayed the buffalo couldn't detect. My bravado was shaky, but the buffalo mustn't sense that.

The two Sues moved docilely toward the truck and jumped in. I tried to look cool, but actually I was amazed at their obedience. I looked expectantly at The Wild One, silently begging him to follow them. Instead, he planted his hoofs and shook his massive black head. I rattled the grain can enticingly, but The Wild One retreated farther into the dark recesses of the shed. Slowly, I moved toward him, off to one side, hoping to get behind him and then drive him toward the truck at the opposite end of the shed. As I inched behind the two-year-old bull, he turned his big head toward me, throwing me a disdainful look. My neck hairs prickled. I was cornered. Now he could turn and crunch me against the rear wall.

Dredging up a hoarse, fish-wife voice, I howled, "You get out of here! Get on that truck! Right now!"

More from surprise than respect, The Wild One trudged toward the truck and hopped in. Outwardly, I suffered from rubbery knees, but inside, I felt like John Wayne. If only Bill could have seen my act! He would have been so proud! It was my finest hour. I had buffaloed the buffalo.

But my elation was short-lived. With Bill out of town, the law of "Husband away, everything goes wrong" remained in effect.

The children and I had managed to repair the fences, foiling any future buffalo escapes, and I anticipated a quiet Saturday morning. Brenda went outside to feed her ducks, while I tidied up the kitchen. Through the open window I heard an eerie, gargling sound. Frowning, I tipped my head, listening. What on earth was that noise?

Brenda came streaking toward the house, screaming, "Barely's choking to death! She's strangling!"

Beth and I tore out the back door, heading toward the choking sound. Bruno, our St. Bernard, galloped past us, his nose twitching with sensed danger.

Our prized cattalo calf had stuck her head through a section of woven wire fence behind the smaller barn, and she was trying to force the rest of her body through the hole, which was large enough to admit only her head. Barely wasn't actually choking, though the wire did press against her throat as she tried to struggle forward.

"If she'd just back up, she'd be free!" Beth cried.

"We'll have to pull her out backwards!" I ordered. I climbed over the fence to push against her head and instructed Brenda and Beth to pull backwards on her body. Though just a young calf, Barely was too much for us with her flailing legs and thrusting body. She wanted to go forward, and the three of us weren't strong enough to make her go backwards.

"The wire cutters!" I yelled. "Get them, and I'll cut the wire!"

Beth raced toward the garage.

In the melee Bruno got the mistaken idea that Barely was trying to hurt us, and he joined in the pandemonium, barking and nipping at Barely's legs. I was swatting and howling at Bruno as Beth returned with the wire cutters.

Our fence wire is a heavy-duty, extra-thick wire, and usually I need all the strength of both my hands to cut a piece of wire. But with the fear of Barely's hurting herself and the tumult, I snipped strands of wire, one-handed, as easily as cutting paper. The third snip opened the hole wide enough for Barely to force herself free, and she tumbled through the fence at my feet, with Bruno still barking and nipping. I grabbed Bruno by the scruff of his neck.

As I looked up to see Barely running to the safety of her mother, I gasped in terror. Not twenty feet away, her shaggy head down, was Good Cow, charging straight at me.

"Run, girls!" I yelled, grateful they were on the other side of the fence. I whirled backwards into the ten-foot square holding chute behind me, tripping and stumbling over the terrified Bruno. A small crate five feet high stood in the middle of the holding chute, and I scrambled atop that wobbly perch just as Good Cow burst into the chute. I saw a stout board swing and smash the angry buffalo cow right between the eyes, but it didn't slow her a bit. Dust flying, Good Cow churned into the small chute, bumping the crate I was balanced upon. It rocked crazily while I tried to figure out if my fate was to be goring or stomping to death. Good Cow made a tight turn around my crate and back out the narrow opening of the chute, in pursuit of a white flash. It was Bruno she was after! Not me at all. Bruno could take care of himself. He'd be all right.

"Is everybody okay?" I called shakily. Two pairs of eyes peered down at me from the roof of the small red barn, where the girls had taken refuge.

"Oh, Mom," Brenda began to cry. "I thought you were killed!"

"I thought so, too, honey, for a minute," I panted. "But Good Cow wasn't after me, really. It was Bruno she was after. She thought he was trying to hurt Barely."

Of course, the moment Bruno saw Good Cow charging toward him, he had twined himself around my ankles. Good Cow probably had no anger against me, but with Bruno wrapped tightly to my legs, if she'd smashed into him, I'd have gotten it, too. Her intentions toward me might not have been deadly, but the results would have been fatal.

I swung the gate shut to keep the buffalo out of the backyard, and saw that Bruno had escaped Good Cow by crawling under the fence. Still breathing hard, the girls climbed down from the barn roof. Beth picked up a six-foot long, very thick board.

"I hit Good Cow with this, Mom, just as she was going into the chute after you."

"I know. I saw it, and I sure thank you for trying to help."

"But it didn't even slow her down! And I hit her so hard, right on the forehead!"

"Their skulls are awfully tough there," I said. "Sometimes even bullets won't penetrate the forepart of their skulls."

From that time on the girls and I were terrified of Good Cow, and we refused to get close to her. Though we acknowledged that her charge had been directed at Bruno, the frightening memory of her charging toward us at full gallop made us distrust and fear her. And she sensed our fear. She was the boss, and we didn't argue with her. Bill and Bruce still had her respect, but to her, the rest of us were sniveling cowards. She had us buffaloed.

"What is Life?
It is the flash of a firefly in the night.
It is the breath of a buffalo
in the winter time."
    —Crowfoot 1890

•

Little Joe
the
Buffalo

7 When Barely Kicking von Holstein was just six days old, Little Joe entered our lives. Bill first encountered Little Joe on a warm Sunday afternoon in April. He'd been called to the hospital on an emergency, and after seeing the patient, Bill walked out to the buffalo pasture to check on the animals. Cow-With-One-Good-Eye was not with the herd. Bill tramped into the woods searching and listening. In a dense clump of quaking aspen he came upon the missing buffalo and her newborn calf, still wet from birth.

Immediately, Cow-With-One-Good-Eye walked a short distance from her calf, trying to entice Bill toward her and away from the calf. Bill remained at the edge of the woods, seating himself on a fallen log.

The little bull calf struggled up onto wobbly legs and tottered toward his mother. Looking for warm milk, he began to nuzzle around her belly, but the mother moved a few steps farther away. She was intent upon getting the calf to follow her away from Bill.

Cow-With-One-Good-Eye was in the process of passing her afterbirth. Buffalo cows usually go some distance from their calves to pass the afterbirth, but Cow-With-One-Good-Eye was in a quandary. With a human being so

71

close, she hated to separate herself from her calf. At last when she had coaxed the calf nearly one-hundred feet from Bill, the little calf lay down in some dry leaves. The mother moved off a short distance and expelled the afterbirth, after which she ate it to avoid attracting predators. The afterbirth also furnishes the cow with a rich source of protein for the first few days after giving birth. During this period she is busy tending her newborn calf and can't graze well.

Upon returning to her little red calf, Cow-With-One-Good-Eye coaxed him to follow her into a grove of pine trees which afforded thick cover.

That evening when Bill returned home, he reported happily that our first calf of the season had been born. "A little bull calf," he said, "born to Cow-With-One-Good-Eye." Cow-With-One-Good-Eye is just what her name says—a cow with a blind eye.

It was three days later before Bill again found time to roam through the pasture, checking on his beloved buffalo. Off on a distant hillside far from the herd, he spotted Cow-With-One-Good-Eye. He was perplexed about this, wondering why she remained so far from the herd. Normally, buffalo cows separate themselves from the herd when they give birth, but within a matter of hours they coax their newborn calves to follow them back to the safety of the group. Bill headed toward the far off hillside to check on this unusual behavior.

As Bill approached the mother and calf, Cow-With-One-Good-Eye tossed her horns threateningly and dug her hoofs into the turf, danger signals that a buffalo is preparing to charge. Her little auburn calf had been lying in the deep grass, but at Bill's approach he heaved himself onto his legs. With a sinking feeling, Bill saw that the calf's left hind leg was broken, dangling at a crazy angle. The tiny bull calf attempted to limp away, fell, and struggled up again, trying to bear some weight on the fractured leg. Bill winced to think of the pain that little calf was enduring, all without a sound. The leg would have to be set. And to do this, of course, the calf must be taken away from his protective mother.

Hoping to run her off, Bill ran at Cow-With-One-Good-Eye, yelling and cracking his long bullwhip. The bluff didn't work. The fearful mother lowered her head and began to charge toward Bill. Quickly Bill swung the bullwhip, cracking her across the nose. This stopped her, and she turned, her nose bleeding from the whip's lash. She glared at Bill defiantly. The devoted mother wasn't going to leave her injured calf. Bill didn't wish to hurt her. He retreated to gather reinforcements to help him.

Another doctor, an anesthesiologist, lived on a farm not far from the buffalo pasture. Bill remembered that this doctor had a tractor with a front-end loader, a sort of scoop which could be raised or lowered. He thought this might be just the right piece of equipment for abducting a buffalo calf.

The doctor's two teenage sons drove the tractor to the ranch and through the south gate, while Bill led the way with his pickup truck. They had to cross two swampy areas enroute to the hillside and the injured calf, and twice the truck and tractor became mired in the soft earth. At last they reached high ground and approached Cow-With-One-Good-Eye with the tractor.

The bucket of the tractor's front-end loader would lift nearly twelve feet in the air, out of the reach of the angry buffalo cow. Bill explained to the boys what they must do.

"Dave, you climb into the loader. I'll try to distract the cow. Then, Mark, you lower the front-end loader so Dave can grab the calf. Raise him up fast! As quick as you can, because she'll go after the calf!"

The boys agreed and tensed, preparing for the rescue.

Bill began cracking his bullwhip to attract the attention of Cow-With-One-Good-Eye toward himself. At the proper moment, when the angered mother's attention was solely occupied with Bill and his whip, Mark lowered the front-end loader, and Dave scooped the little calf into his arms. The painful jostling brought a hoarse bleat from the calf, and Cow-With-One-Good-Eye whirled toward the sound. Head down, she charged at the rising bucket, but it had lifted far above her. The boys slowly backed the tractor away as Bill continued to crack the bullwhip to keep the enraged mother away from the tractor.

Fortunately, the injured calf made no more sounds, and the puzzled mother returned to sniff the spot where her calf had been. She carefully searched for a scent in every direction, but because he had been raised up into the air, there was no trail to scent.

While she was occupied in searching, the boys drove the tractor up to Bill's pickup truck. Bill lifted the calf into the cab and immediately taped some boards onto the broken leg to provide a splint and support the leg. The moment the leg was stabilized in the splint, the little calf quit struggling and fell asleep.

In the cab of the pickup beside Bill, the calf slept soundly the whole way home. Now that the broken bones were supported and not grating, the little buffalo was free from pain and could sleep. Bill figured the poor thing hadn't had any rest since the moment of his injury. This was our first experience with an injured calf, and we had to assume it was because of Cow-With-One-Good-Eye's blindness in one eye. Very likely the little calf had been lying on his mother's blind side, and she had stepped on his leg accidentally.

That evening when Bill arrived home and climbed from the truck cradling a baby buffalo in his arms, we all ran out to meet him. Tenderly he laid the calf in the grass, and we crowded around, gently touching the soft fur. The little buffalo remained amazingly calm.

Beth stuck her index finger into the calf's lips, and he began to suck vigorously on her finger. "Oh, he's really hungry!" she cried.

While the girls and I searched through the garage for an old baby bottle, Bill and Bruce began replacing the temporary splint with a more effective one. Bill reduced the fracture, lining up the bones properly. Wrapping the calf's leg tightly with folded newspapers, he taped on strips of wood lath which were two inches longer than the calf's hoof. This provided a makeshift walking cast, preventing the little buffalo from touching his hoof to the ground and thus, bearing weight on the fracture site. There was no point in applying a plaster cast. The April mud puddles and rain would collapse plaster in a short time, so Bill used layers of adhesive tape.

After some searching, I found an old baby bottle and filled it with warm milk.

"Let me feed him," Bruce begged. "I'd like this calf to be mine. I'll be going away to college next fall, and this is my last chance to raise a buffalo calf." As soon as the rubber nipple touched the calf's lips, he raised his head eagerly and began sucking the warm milk.

"With that broken leg I doubt that he was able to stand up to nurse," Bill said. "I imagine this is his first nourishment in a couple days."

The little buffalo had finished the bottle and was sucking air. "Should I give him more?" Bruce asked.

"No." Bill squatted down and felt the furry belly. "Buffalo calves eat frequently, but not too much at one time." An impish twinkle in his eyes, Bill went on. "Since you want this one for your calf, Bruce, you'll have to feed him during the night. He'll probably need a bottle a couple times during the night, especially since he's so undernourished right now, and he needs calcium to get those bones healing."

Bruce agreed. "Okay, I'll spread newspapers on the floor, and he can sleep beside my bed." Bruce stroked the soft muzzle of the little calf, who was now dozing contentedly. "I'm going to call him Little Joe," he said. "Little Joe the Buffalo."

Though it was late in the evening Bill wanted to be certain he had aligned the bones properly. He called the x-ray department at the hospital and told Howard, the x-ray technician, that he was bringing in a patient.

Bill and Bruce drove Little Joe to the hospital and parked outside the emergency room door. Bruce cradled the little calf in his arms, and Bill tossed a sheet over the calf before they walked through the emergency waiting room. The waiting patients stared anxiously, assuming the draped form was a child. Fortunately, Little Joe didn't struggle, or poke a telltale hoof out of the covering sheet.

Howard, the technician, chuckled over his unusual patient, as he carefully took x-rays from various angles. When developed, the x-rays revealed excellent reduction with perfect alignment. If the cast could hold that alignment, there should be excellent healing.

The next morning Bruce awoke bleary-eyed. "I had to feed Little Joe three times during the night," he groaned. "And then this morning, what a mess! All over the newspapers!"

It was a clear, warm spring day, so we carried Little Joe out into our backyard where he could be healed by the natural fresh air and sunshine. To our surprise, Little Joe managed to get around very well with that clumsy long cast on his leg. He moved about the yard, sniffing and pricking his ears. Then suddenly, he became aware that he had strayed far from Bruce, and, three-legged, he came loping back to Bruce's side. To Little Joe, Bruce was his mother.

Within a few days we decided that Little Joe could survive without middle-of-the-night feedings, as he was filling out well, and his ribs no longer protruded. Late each evening Bruce fed the little calf, then put him in a stall in the barn. Each morning, before school, Bruce let Little Joe out of the barn and fed him his breakfast bottles. During school hours Bill or I fed the little calf, but for several weeks Bruce performed most of the loving care and received most of Joe's affection in return. Actually, Little Joe liked all human beings. He was people-oriented. But he was most fond of Bruce.

After a few weeks Bruce got caught up in the flurry of high school graduation activities and he had less time to spend with Little Joe. The calf needed anywhere from five to seven bottle-feedings a day, and I began to take over the major share of nursing. Slowly, Joe's affection shifted to me. In his eyes, I became his mother.

Little Joe followed me everywhere, clumping along on

his walking cast. As I hung clothes on the line, Little Joe stood beside me, nuzzling the wet clothes in the basket, or bunting those on the line. When I raked the grass, he was there beside me getting in the way.

From the very beginning Little Joe loved to come in the house. If we were in the house, he wanted to be there, too. We had to race him to the back door if we wanted to get inside without his squeezing in along with us.

By the time Little Joe was a month old, the wooden splint supports on his walking cast had worn down flush with his hoof, and when he ran he was bearing some weight on the fracture. Bill figured the fracture must be healing, but he wanted to make sure the alignment had remained perfect, so again, Little Joe was taken to the hospital for x-rays. This time he was too big to carry, so the portable x-ray was brought out onto the loading dock. While admiring nurses and personnel crowded around, the technician took x-rays of Joe's injured leg. Results showed excellent healing and alignment and a good callous formation around the fracture site.

Bill removed the dirty, makeshift cast, and set to work cleaning Little Joe's leg with alcohol, after which he rubbed in olive oil. Though free of the cumbersome cast, Joe continued to walk three-legged for a few days. When standing or walking slowly he put weight on his injured leg, but if he wanted to run fast, he reverted to his long-used three-legged gait. Each day he used the leg more, and within a week he was jumping and hopping on all four legs, exactly like a normal, uninjured calf.

First thing in the morning Little Joe always was ravenous from his long night's fasting. We no longer put him in the barn at night. Instead, he had adopted the doghouse, using it for shelter from rain, and occasionally sleeping in it on damp nights. This proved frustrating to Bruno, who was left without shelter. Bruno seemed to have forgotten his cozy days of sharing his doghouse with Crazy Horse.

When the children began swimming in our backyard pond Joe swam with them, obeying his urge to follow his loved ones everywhere. Buffalo are strong swimmers, and Little Joe paddled around the pond with little effort. He wasn't popular when he emerged from the pond and shook water at everybody. After shaking, he always lay down in the sand and wallowed, collecting sand on his coat as protection against insects.

In the summertime we spend most of our daytime hours in our backyard, and Little Joe was happy with all the companionship. When Brenda jumped on the trampoline with her friends, Joe stood there and watched. When we sat in lawn chairs, reading or sunning, Joe lay beside us. Often the girls grew irritated with Joe when they tried to take sunbaths. Dressed in brief swimming suits, they spread a blanket on the grass and stretched out to grow tan. Soon would come the wail, "Mom! Call Little Joe and get him away from here. He's taking up the whole blanket and putting me in his shadow!"

On rainy days we let Joe come into the house for his bottle-feedings. It was better than getting drenched outside in the downpour. Guests enjoyed giving Little Joe his bottles. Their eyes always twinkled with fascination, and we knew they were thinking, "Boy, wait until I tell the guys at the office that I fed a buffalo a bottle of milk!"

At first we kept Little Joe and Barely Kicking von Holstein apart. We were afraid that the exuberant Barely might hurt Little Joe's leg. When Little Joe seemed sturdy and healed, we decided to introduce them. Barely was curious and friendly, but when her friendliness got too persistent, Joe ran to the safety of a human being's legs. Joe preferred people.

People spoke softly and were gentle. Barely exhibited no gentleness, and her voice was fearsome. Like a normal cow, Bertha emitted a deep, prolonged "moo." Buffalo make a low, abrupt grunt. Half-cow, half-buffalo, Barely spoke in a loud, raucous "bah" eruption, resembling a purposeful, deep belch. As she grew older, her voice became louder and lower. It was sort of a silly sound, but also frightening. The loud bawling seemed threatening in its strangeness.

Barely had no hump as yet, but even buffalo calves don't begin developing a hump until toward the end of their first year. Her tail seemed to be a half-way compromise between the very long tail of a cow, and the short tail of a buffalo. As a young heifer calf, Barely didn't look too different from an ordinary domestic calf. Her voice and her tail were the main clues to her mixed ancestry.

That summer Barely grew rapidly, an important trait of cattalo. Though only six days older than Little Joe, Barely was twice his size. She continued her playful bunting of Bill. One day she gleefully blasted into Bill, tossing him eight feet through the air. Talking to himself, Bill limped into the house to examine his injured leg. A blood vessel had been torn, and Bill's whole thigh was turning an ugly purple and black. Bill touched his sore leg sheepishly. "I think I'm doing something wrong with Barely. I can't have her throwing me around like this. Think what she could do to me when she weighs a ton and a half!"

I agreed. For some time I'd been avoiding any close contact with Barely. She was too rough for me.

Bill quit cavorting and wrestling with Barely and began trying to discipline her. Every time she tried to bunt him, he swatted her hard on the nose. This got her under control, and prevented future bruises, or worse, but Barely never could be trusted. This childhood game of "bunting" always lingered in the back of her brain.

At summer's end we were able to cut Little Joe's feedings to three per day, since his capacity had increased. He gulped nearly a quart and a half of milk at each feeding. Sucking voraciously and impatiently, Little Joe tolerated no pause during his meal, such as refilling a baby bottle. Consequently, in preparation for each feeding, we filled five baby bottles with milk so there would be no interruption. Besides hating interruptions, Joe was very particular about the temperature of his milk. If the milk were too cold or too warm, he bunted the bottle in agitation, and curled his body around your legs, stomping on your toes. Cowboy boots were the best footwear for feeding Little

Joe. They gave more protection than tennis shoes or sandals.

Little Joe's auburn baby fur had darkened to the brown heavy coat typical of mature buffalo. As Joe grew larger and developed such greedy feeding habits, I began to dread feeding time. As my toes became bruised and sore from his eager stomping, I complained that Joe was old enough to eat hay and grain. "Surely he can survive without milk," I argued.

"We want to keep Joe gentle and tame," Bill reminded me. "By continuing the bottle-feeding, he'll grow more attached to us."

I rubbed my throbbing toes, wondering if we really wanted an affectionate buffalo.

Gradually, Bill began to feed Joe more frequently than I. Little Joe behaved perfectly when Bill fed him. Sucking contentedly, the little buffalo closed his eyes and enjoyed Bill's motherly ministrations. Following the final bottle, Bill always scratched and rubbed Joe, chatting happily with his growing pet. Joe's share of the conversation consisted of reaching up to suck on Bill's chin.

When I complained that Joe didn't behave when I fed him, Bill said, "That's because afterwards you don't fondle him and let him suck on your chin." A buffalo's tongue is as rough as a wood rasp. There's no facial cream in the world soothing enough to battle the ravages of a buffalo tongue on tender skin.

"I'll pet him, I'll brush him, I'll feed him, but he can suck on *your* chin," I retorted.

The post-feeding ritual between Bill and Little Joe progressed until Bill could say, "Joe, give me a kiss," and Joe would stretch up affectionately and press his lips against Bill's chin.

When frigid weather arrived, we cut Little Joe's bottle-feedings to twice a day, and this continued throughout the winter. When I fed Joe, to save my toes and my disposition, I usually stood on top of our picnic table out of his reach. People driving past sometimes stopped and called out, "Can I help you?" They thought I was treed by a buffalo.

Little Joe still adored coming into the house. Always a gentleman, in the house Joe moved carefully. He seemed to be housebroken as he never had an accident. He had one hang-up, however. Joe couldn't bear to see newspapers and magazines littering our coffee table. With a few sweeps of his beard, he cleared the top of the coffee table, brushing the magazines to the floor.

Barely was very fond of Little Joe, and she liked to stay close to him. When we fondled and scratched Joe, she approached and stood nearby, bawling her raucous noise. When we took Little Joe into our house, Barely peeked in the window enviously. She seemed to sense that Joe was getting something she didn't get, though she never figured out that her boisterous, threatening attitude kept us aloof.

Though not yet one year old, Barely was as large as her Holstein mother. A slight hump on her back showed her buffalo heredity, as did her thick, soft winter fur.

After all the failures we'd suffered in trying to get a cattalo calf, Bill was tremendously proud of Barely. Whenever he gazed out over our backyard pasture at the animals, he smiled serenely. Out there grazed two of his fondest dreams—a cattalo heifer and a tame buffalo. We were leading a rewarding life, and the future looked even more promising. But then came the phone call. Once again the Indians needed Bill's assistance.

"Brother! My voice is become weak.
You can scarcely hear me.
It is not the shout of a warrior,
but the wail of an infant."
    —Choctaw chief

•

Getting Involved

8 The evening of March 5, 1973, Bill received a phone call from a local man, a stranger to us. "Is this The Buffalo Doctor?" he asked. "We need your help."

His name was Ben, and he explained that he and some other Indian people had gathered two truckloads of food down in Detroit. They wanted to get this food to the Indians at Wounded Knee as soon as possible. Ben described how they had called the Indians holding the village of Wounded Knee. The woman they spoke with was crying. She said that they were all terribly hungry. Babies could be heard crying in the background, and the woman explained that the babies were hungry, especially for milk. The woman begged them to send food quickly.

Ben explained that the trucks would arrive in Muskegon by dawn the next morning. "Could you hire a pilot to fly this food in?" he asked. "We have to get it there quickly. Our people there are desperate for food. We don't have the money right now, but we'll get it somehow and pay the pilot one way or another."

"I think I can arrange something," Bill said. He took Ben's phone number and promised to call him back.

Bill gazed across the living room at me, his dark eyes thoughtful. "They want me to get a pilot to fly a planeload of food to Wounded Knee."

For the past few days newspapers and television had been covering the Indian protest at the hamlet on Wounded Knee Creek. Being busy with our bottomless muddy roads and the problems of transporting the children in and out to school, I hadn't paid close attention. I was familiar enough with Indian history to know that Wounded Knee had a tragic past. On that rolling Dakota prairie in 1890 nearly three hundred hungry and helpless Sioux, most of them women and children, were massacred by four Hotchkiss guns, each spitting a bullet a second. The torn and frozen bodies had been thrown into a mass grave on a hill. Later, a picturesque white church was built beside the horrendous giant grave. Currently, according to the news media, armed and defiant Indians were turning the little white church into a dining hall and fortress.

"Hello, Bob," Bill was speaking into the phone. I knew that Bob was a pilot friend of our son's, an amiable, pleasant man who drove huge semi-trucks for a living, and flew his precious Piper Cub for pleasure. "I've got to find a pilot to fly a load of food to the Indians at Wounded Knee," Bill said. "Do you think Jack would do it?"

Jack was another pilot. He made his living by flying charter flights and freight runs. Bob thought a minute, then advised that he didn't believe Jack would do this for fear of endangering his flying service. "There's a pilot in Grand Haven who might do it," Bob suggested. "He's an excellent pilot who's had some daring flying adventures. Why don't you call him? His name is Paul Davids."

Bill phoned Paul Davids. "This is Dr. Cummings, The Buffalo Doctor. I just received a phone call from some Indians who have two truckloads of food they want flown into Wounded Knee, South Dakota. Are you interested in flying it in?"

There were a few moments of silence at the other end of the phone before the surprised pilot blurted, "You've got to be kidding!"

"No, I'm dead serious," Bill answered. "Do you want to go, or don't you?"

The answer was definite. "You're damn right I want to go. When do we leave?"

Bill explained that the trucks of food would arrive at the Grand Haven airport by six the next morning. "By the way, how much are you going to charge for the trip?"

Paul said the usual charge would be about six hundred dollars. "I suppose it's hard for the Indians to come up with that much, isn't it? I probably could do it for expenses of three hundred dollars," he offered.

"I can't be sure the Indians can raise that kind of money, but I'll guarantee to pay the expenses if they can't," Bill said. "I'll see you in the morning, Paul. I'll be down at your hangar about five-thirty."

Bill hung up the telephone and cast a searching look across the room at me. I'm sure he expected me to begin pleading with him not to get involved. Instead, I shrugged and smiled at him. I knew this was something Bill had to do.

Understanding that he had my support, he grinned and picked up the telephone. "I have some phone calls to make."

First Bill called another surgeon. "Would you cover my patients for me for a couple days, Frank? My brother in South Dakota has been shot in the leg, and I have to go out there," Bill explained, wondering how long it would take Frank to make the connection between "shot in the leg" and Wounded Knee.

Next he phoned his office nurse and, repeating the same story, asked her to cancel the office patients he was scheduled to see the next day.

Bill called Ben and reported that arrangements were all made. The pilot and plane would be ready to leave by six the next morning. "Ben, will you get word to the Indians at Wounded Knee that we're coming, so they won't shoot us down?"

"You're going, too, Doc?" Ben asked.

Bill answered that he couldn't ask a pilot to run the

85

risks and hazards without going with him. It is the way of the Sioux that you do not ask another man to do what you would not do yourself.

Bill stared thoughtfully into space, his hand poised over the telephone. "I think I'd better call Don Hight to find out how the people out there in Dakota feel about the Wounded Knee situation, and what the weather's like out there."

Don Hight, a rancher friend of ours, was also a fellow buffalo-raiser, though on a much larger scale, with over one thousand head of buffalo on his vast South Dakota ranch adjoining the Rosebud Indian Reservation. Over the years we have known many western ranchers, and generally, ranchers are about as sympathetic to Indians as cats are to mice. Don, however, was a hard-working, fair-minded sort, and we believed he had a certain sympathy for Indian problems because he'd worked hard with the Indians on the Rosebud Reservation trying to help them establish a hide tanning plant. Don's livestock—buffalo, cattle, Texas longhorns, and bucking horses,—often strayed over onto the Rosebud Reservation, and the Indian cattle wandered onto his ranch.

Bill rubbed his chin, thinking. "What we really need to do is set up an airlift of food into Wounded Knee, sort of like the Berlin Airlift. It seems silly to continue to fly food all the way from Michigan. We ought to be able to get the food nearby in South Dakota and fly it in with a series of short hops. I think I'll call Don."

When Don answered Bill's call the two buffalo raisers spent a few minutes discussing the perils and joys of their shaggy beasts, then Bill explained that he was thinking of going out to Wounded Knee to see what was going on.

"Doc, I think you ought to keep your nose out of it," Don advised. "We get along well with our own Indians here in Dakota. They don't give us any trouble. It's the outsiders comin' in and raisin' hell out here who are givin' us problems. These outsiders stir up our Indians and make them dissatisfied."

"What's really going on at Wounded Knee?" Bill asked.

"That situation is going to get worse before it gets better, Doc. They're goin' to end up doin' some shootin' and somebody's goin' to get hurt. You can't do any good out there."

Bill chuckled. "Well, then, I assume that if I go out to Wounded Knee, I'd be welcome at your place on the way out, but I'd better not stop at your place on my way back from Wounded Knee."

There was a long pause while Don thought that over, then he laughed. "Hell, Doc, we've been friends a long time. You're different. You're welcome any time. But don't stick your nose into this situation out here. It doesn't concern you."

The two men chatted awhile, discussing the weather and meat prices before saying good-bye.

Bill turned to me and grinned. "I guess I can't use Don's grass landing strip for a Wounded Knee airlift as I'd hoped. If he'd been sympathetic to the Indian cause, I thought we could spend two or three days flying in enough supplies so food wouldn't be a problem. I just can't believe the F.B.I. is really serious in their efforts to starve out the people in Wounded Knee. I don't believe our government would do that."

"You know, I just thought of something," I smiled. "Bruce is just going to die when he learns what excitement he's missing here."

Bruce is the pilot in our family. A freshman in college, he was presently in Daytona Beach, Florida, with his roommate and another boy, searching for adventure during their ten-day spring break.

Beth and Brenda wandered into the living room to find out what all the telephoning was about, and we tried to explain the situation to them. Beth's red hair bobbed with enthusiasm. "Let me go, too, Dad, please."

Bill explained to her that the purpose of the flight was to carry enough food to relieve the suffering out there. "If you went along, we'd have to leave behind over one hundred pounds of much-needed food.''

Though disappointed, Beth accepted this as reasonable.

We had to start considering details, and I thought of the first hitch. ''You're going to need money for food and gas,'' I reminded Bill. ''I have less than five dollars in my purse.''

Brenda jumped up eagerly. ''I have money Dad can use. I have sixty dollars!'' she cried, rushing to her room to get her money. For two years Brenda had been saving for a ten-speed bike. Proudly, she handed Bill her money.

It was two-thirty in the morning before we had everything ready for the trip. Wearily we crawled into bed and set the alarm for four thirty.

Before dawn Bill ate a hearty breakfast, struggled into his snowmobile suit, and stuck a clean pair of socks in his pocket. When we turned on the yard light, we were dismayed to see that a heavy fog had rolled in during the night.

''You can't take off in this,'' I protested.

''The fog probably will burn off after the sun comes up,'' Bill said.

Bill filled a large cardboard carton with frozen buffalo meat from our freezer. Buffalo meat should be a real treat for hungry people. He also took his black doctor bag. Though he had no way of knowing if the Indians trapped in Wounded Knee needed medical assistance, he made sure he had a supply of antibiotics, pain medication, and insulin.

When Bill arrived at the small Grand Haven airport and parked beside Paul Davids' hangar, he saw that the Indians already had arrived with one truckload of food. Their other truck had broken down enroute, so the Indians had piled most of the food into the functioning truck and continued.

The red-white-and-blue Cessna 182 stood half in and half out of the hangar. Paul was at work unbolting the back seat from the four-place plane. With the back seat removed, more food could be stashed aboard. Bill leaned through the door to help.

The Indians stood about, murmuring and talking among themselves, their black eyes sparkling over their achievement of initiating this food lift to a group of their people in distress. Most of the Indians were family people. Several small children tore screeching about the hangar, investigating the exciting paraphernalia of aviation. There were two militant-looking young men, one sporting long braids and the other wearing a beaded headband.

Shortly after seven o'clock I drove the girls and some neighbor children to school since school bus service had been discontinued because of our mucky roads. Avoiding the impassable sections of soupy mire was especially difficult because of the thick fog. I couldn't see thirty feet ahead of my car, but I dared not drive too slow or I surely would get stuck. My heavy station wagon slid and plunged along, the ruts grating against the undercarriage. With a tremendous feeling of relief we slogged onto the blacktop road. The children cheered. We'd made it out again!

At the school when Brenda climbed from the car, she turned to me happily. "I can hardly wait to tell everyone that today Dad is taking food to Wounded Knee for the hungry Indians there!"

I smiled, wondering how her teachers would take this piece of show-and-tell.

I stopped at the post office to pick up our mail and was surprised to find a package from New Mexico from a friend we hadn't seen in twenty years. Thrilled with an unexpected present, I opened the package right there in the post office. I lifted out a beautiful Navajo sand-painting depicting an Indian medicine man wearing a white buffalo robe. At the bottom of the carton was another small package which I unwrapped and found to be Dee Brown's book, *Bury My Heart at Wounded Knee.* Goose bumps rose on my arms. What a strange coincidence that this should arrive this morning. I studied the sand-painting thoughtfully and felt the goose bumps recede. It had to be an omen. A good omen. I've got to show this to Bill before he leaves, I decided.

Slowly I drove through the dense fog to the airport.

Bill and Paul were just beginning to load the food aboard the plane. I introduced myself to the Indians standing around and stared gloomily at the fog, which as yet showed no sign of lifting. Wondering what sort of food the Michigan Indians were sending to the South Dakota Indians, I poked through the cartons on the hangar floor. There were dozens and dozens of cans of peaches, pears, and soup, large cans of beans and coffee. There were big bags of flour, rice, sugar, and powdered milk. Especially strange to me were the huge fifty-pound brown bags labelled "pinto beans." I wasn't sure what pinto beans were, but there were so many of them I concluded Indians liked pinto beans. One cardboard box contained a five gallon can of cooking oil, surrounded by several cartons of cigarettes. Behind this box towered a huge clear plastic bag filled with twenty rolls of toilet paper. Toilet paper—an obvious necessity, but never would I have thought of it. When reminiscing about his childhood in South Dakota, Bill had told of the Sears Roebuck catalog which served as their "bathroom tissue," and was valued because it was better than grass and leaves. Only people who have lived without comforts can truly appreciate and value such mundane items as toilet paper.

While I was still musing over the toilet paper I noticed another thoughtful item—a large box of Kotex. Some Michigan Indian woman's practical mind had considered the comforts of the women at Wounded Knee. Only a woman would have thought of sending sanitary napkins. But I never would have thought of them. My life has been too easy, I realized. There are too many things I take for granted.

Bill and Paul continued loading the food, placing the heavier items on the bottom, and distributing the weight evenly behind the front seats and toward the back of the plane. Paul wanted to keep weight forward in the airplane so the center of gravity of the aircraft would not be too off balance. When all the food was loaded, the fog remained, with zero visibility.

One of the younger mechanics asked Paul, "Did you consider making a parachute drop of this food?"

Paul nodded. "Yeah, I considered it at first. But so much weight would be involved in packing the food to withstand a drop, that we wouldn't be able to take in a fraction of what we have here. And if we didn't get the stuff packaged good enough, hell, there'd be pinto beans spread all over the reservation."

"Do you think you'll get into trouble making this trip?" the young mechanic wanted to know.

"I called Gary, my lawyer," Paul answered, "to make sure my plane insurance would cover the trip. He assured me that since this is a chartered flight, my insurance is okay. Say, by the way, Doc, Gary said he'd sort of met you a few years ago. There was some kid really mangled up by a motor boat, and Gary was the one who took him in to the emergency room. I guess you took care of the kid?"

"I remember that!" Bill nodded grimly. "I had to take six hundred twenty three stitches to sew the fellow up. His heart stopped during surgery, and we had to give cardiac resuscitation to get it going again. He recovered fine, though, and six months later he was a paratrooper."

We all crowded into Paul's small office, which was a partitioned section of the hangar, where we drank coffee and waited for the weather to improve. This was my first opportunity to evaluate Paul. I was anxious to see what sort of person he was, since Bill's life was to be entrusted to him. A tall, muscular man in his early forties, Paul's good-natured, easy grin made you like him at once. There was an adventurous twinkle in his eyes, but everything concerning his airplane and flying was dead serious.

As he called Chicago to get an up-to-date forecast on the fog, I studied Paul's small office. His desk and filing system were immaculate and orderly. Two threadbare davenports provided the seating arrangements. Other pilots and mechanics from around the airport dropped in and helped themselves to the coffee from the commercial coffee-maker. Paul's office was obviously a favorite hangout. The other pilots were envious over the proposed trip. One pilot offered to fly his plane, too, if funds could be gotten to finance food and expenses. Bill made a couple phone calls but was unable to locate anyone in a position to donate money.

In one corner of the office there was a square cardboard box with a small door cut in one side. As we sat there chatting, a small but very pregnant black cat emerged from the box, stretched, and stared boldly up at Paul. Quickly, Paul opened a can of chopped tuna and filled the cat's dish, murmuring soothingly to the waiting cat.

"It's a stray cat," the woman-pilot sitting beside me explained. "It came here about a month ago. Paul can't do enough for that cat."

One of the visiting pilots asked about Wounded Knee. "What's the problem out there, anyway?"

The tall Indian with braids, silent until now, spoke up. "The situation on the Pine Ridge Reservation has become unbearable. The tribal government is corrupt, the Bureau of Indian Affairs is unresponsive to the needs of the people. Things are bad out there. Some of the old people away from the settlements had to eat dog this past winter. No human being should have to eat his own dog to survive."

In shamefaced silence we sipped our coffee, all of us terribly aware that our country was still troubled with the problem of "the haves" and "the have-nots."

Paul broke the silence. "You've worked at helping Indians, Doc. What do you think can be done to change things?"

Bill sighed. "The Indians on most of the reservations need more protein in their diets. They need meat. For five years I've been writing to Congressmen, the Bureau of Indian Affairs, the Department of the Interior, the Department of Agriculture and the news media, trying to establish the policy that surplus buffalo from the federal parks be given to the Indians. This was agreed upon in writing by the National Park Service in 1965. The Indians could use the surplus buffalo for meat and to build buffalo herds on their reservations. My efforts have accomplished nothing.

"In the eighteenth and nineteenth centuries the buffalo were the source of life for the Plains Indians. I think buffalo could be of great help to modern Indians, too. Indians on reservations need meaningful work, work that they know is a contribution to mankind. If the federal government would establish some research projects on the reservations, the Indians would be involved in meaningful work."

"What sort of programs do you mean, Doc?" one of the Indians asked.

"There are big nutritional differences between buffalo meat and domestic beef, but studies along this line have just scratched the surface. For four years we've worked with South Dakota State College, where Dr. Rust is interested in these striking differences. With only haphazard small samples of buffalo meat furnished her, Dr. Rust found that buffalo meat has a higher concentration of essential amino acids. It has more unsaturated fatty acids and less cholesterol. She found that buffalo meat has qualities similar to the meat found in a goose's wing, qualities which make a goose capable of long, sustained flights. The study of nutrition should be an important program, since large portions of our world are populated by undernourished people.

"If there were buffalo herds on Indian reservations, these animals could be used in research programs for the development of buffalo vaccines. The work that Pinkie and I did developing a serum from buffalo to use in organ transplant patients was strictly a backyard operation. This work should be conducted on a bigger scale, with a good scientific setup. The unusual and intriguing qualities of buffalo blood can broaden to other types of vaccines. I'm especially convinced that a cancer vaccine could be produced with these methods, and a remote area such as can

93

be found on Indian reservations is ideal for this type of research.

"Another project ideally suitable to Indian reservations is work in crossbreeding buffalo and domestic beef to establish a hardy breed of beef suitable for the northern beef ranges of Wyoming, Montana, the Dakotas, and Canada."

"Can you cross buffalo and cattle?" the woman pilot asked.

Bill leaned forward eagerly. "We've spent the last eight years working at crossbreeding. Finally, we have one success—an animal that is an excellent example of what we're shooting for. We call her Barely Kicking von Holstein, as she has a Holstein cow for a mother, and a buffalo bull for a father. She's a very rugged animal with heavy winter fur which sheds in the spring. She has demonstrated a rapid early weight gain which is very important in the beef industry. Her carcass is large and full."

Paul asked, "Are you the only one who's done this crossbreeding?"

"No," Bill answered. "Back in 1890 Dr. William Hornaday approached Congress with a proposal of developing a new strain of range cattle by crossing buffalo and beef. Out west he had seen some examples of these hybrid animals, and he was impressed by them. Then the Canadian government spent fifty years at their Wainwright station studying crossbreeding, but gave it up and destroyed the herds in 1965. Their work was mostly a nature study. They didn't make any effort to select good bulls and breeding stock to develop a stable new strain. Right now the Russians are working on crossbreeding American buffalo with cattle to develop a hardy strain for Siberia. Crossbreeding different strains can produce magnificent results. Back in the early part of this century the King ranch crossed Brahma cattle with their ordinary range cattle and developed the Santa Gertrudis, which today is a valuable, prized beef animal for the southern ranges. Our northern beef ranges need a new, rugged type of animal, and I think adding the buffalo characteristics is the answer."

One of the Indians commented, "Most Indians really like working outdoors and with animals."

"Right," Bill agreed. "A buffalo crossbreeding project would be right up their alley—if we could just get the government to give them some buffalo, that is."

"Why won't the government go along with giving their surplus buffalo to the Indians?" asked Paul. "What's the problem—bureaucracy and red tape?"

"That's right," Bill replied. "Bureaucracy is a social cancer that grows and consumes and kills, if we don't control it. If we let the bureaucrats oppress the Indians, the bureaucrats will gain power and soon oppress all of us, just like in Nazi Germany.

"In our situation the federal parks say the buffalo are part of an ecosystem. The surplus buffalo die of starvation. The maggots eat the carcasses. The birds eat the maggots. The fox eat the birds. The fox dies and fertilizes the earth and grass. The buffalo eat the grass.

"I say the Indian was part of that ecosystem. Instead of letting the buffalo die of starvation, let the Indian eat the surplus buffalo. Let the parks feed the Indian dung to the maggots. This would keep the cycle in the ecosystem intact."

The tall Indian gave his braid a toss. "Right on! We've been getting nothing but dung from the bureaucrats for years. We'd be happy to give them back some of our dung!"

Bill went on. "Bureaucracy seems to be terribly unresponsive to the needs of people. I have a file several inches thick from my correspondence urging governmental agencies to reconsider their methods of disposing of surplus buffalo. But I just can't seem to get past bureaucracy. The last straw came about ten days ago. I thought perhaps the news media could be a catalyst in stirring up public opinion for getting surplus buffalo to the Indians.

"The local paper wanted to do a feature on Little Joe, our tame yearling buffalo that we've bottle-fed. Little Joe loves people and loves to come in our house. I agreed with the reporter and photographer that they could do a photo-feature on Little Joe if they'd promise to slant the article to the need for surplus buffalo from the parks to be given to Indians on reservations. They took a lot of pictures, but the article came out as a full-page photo-feature about a kooky doctor who has buffalo in his house. I guess newspapers are looking for sensationalism, something that will sell papers, rather than in promoting a good cause.''

A short, dark Indian woman spoke, her eyes glowing with emotion. ''It's too bad we have to resort to demonstrations and violence to bring about changes. But bureaucracy and the establishment aren't easy to change through reasonable, peaceable methods.''

The other Indians nodded agreement sadly.

Her voice rising, she continued. ''I don't like violence. We Indians aren't a violent people. But by God, we've been under the white man's heel for over a hundred years. How long must we crouch weakly, waiting to be stomped out? We're a patient people, but our patience has brought us nothing but poverty, hunger, and poor health. I say, more power to the impatient Indians at Wounded Knee!''

''Right on!'' the Indians cried.

A pilot from another hangar stuck his head in the office door. ''The fog's lifting to about ten feet, Paul,'' he announced.

We all trooped out into the hangar to see the progress in the weather. It wasn't flying weather yet, but the lifting fog raised our hopes.

The pregnant black cat padded silently across the hangar toward the open door. A little Indian boy about four years old scampered after the cat and awkwardly scooped her up.

With a quick lunge, Paul grabbed the boy and eased the cat from the youngster's clutches. Paul gave the boy a stern look. ''Don't pick up the kitty!''

I smiled serenely. Bill should be safe with Paul as his pilot. Any man who is over-protective with a stray, pregnant cat must be a good man, I reasoned.

The air was growing warmer, and I knew I must get

home before the frost thawed our rutted road. The cold air at night hardened our roads a bit, but by mid-day the slight firmness left. I would have to leave without seeing the plane safely airborne.

I kissed Bill good-bye, muttering a nonchalant "be careful," when what I really meant was "God go with you." With Bill leaving for the unknown, it seemed important to keep it casual.

"I appeal to any white man to say
if he ever entered Logan's cabin hungry
and he gave him not meat;
if ever he came cold and naked
and he clothed him not?"
  —Logan, Mingo Chief, 1774

•

Wounded
Knee
Airlift

9 At last the sun burned off the remaining fog, and at eleven-thirty in the morning the little red-white-and-blue Cessna taxied away from the hangar and onto the runway. After the takeoff run, the moment the wheels left the ground, Paul realized the plane was overloaded. The plane climbed very slowly, and when Paul began to make his thirty degree turn the controls were mushy. Paul knew he must avoid any quick maneuvers or the plane would stall. In a straight climb they gained altitude and after leveling off at flight level, the plane gained sufficient airspeed.

"We're okay," Paul reassured Bill, "but with this kind of load we can't do any fancy flying."

Their flight course took them down along the east coast of Lake Michigan and across the south end of the lake over Chicago Heights and on west. Weather remained good until they approached the Mississippi River near Clinton, Iowa. On the far side of the mighty Mississippi they could see what appeared to be a cloud bank.

"Looks as if we're going to have to fly instrument," Paul said. "I think I'll set down at the Clinton airport and file a flight plan with the F.A.A."

Half-way across the river, rain and wind began pelting

the plane, and zero visibility clouds swallowed them. Paul radioed the Clinton airport, which reported zero visibility. With Clinton socked in, they couldn't land there.

Paul turned the plane back east and with relief they slid out of the clouds and landed at the small airport at Savanna, Illinois. There they gassed up the plane, and Paul filed his flight plan for instrument flying with the F.A.A.

Again, they headed west across the Mississippi River into the dense cloud bank. Huge raindrops pelted their windshield and plunked heavily against the fuselage. The heavily loaded plane waddled and bumped along in the stormy air.

The weather was terrible all the way across Iowa, and the two men spoke little since Paul was busy watching his instruments. Thoughtfully, Paul showed Bill how his instruments were helping him navigate, and how to use the instruments. Bill was receiving a memorable lesson in instrument flying. Paul pointed out the system of OMNI beacons spread across the country, which are to instrument pilots what lighthouse beacons are to ship's captains. In a plane equipped with OMNI radio, the pilot can tune in on the frequency of an OMNI station that is marked on his air map. If the plane is within range of that OMNI station, the pilot's OMNI radio will tell him exactly what direction he is from the station, and whether he is headed toward or away from it. By getting his exact direction in compass degrees from two OMNI stations, the pilot can locate on his air map where these two lines cross. "The intersection of these two lines is the plane's position at that time. This is the basic concept of air instrument navigation," Paul explained.

From Des Moines west Bill did the navigating. When they emerged from the clouds at the Missouri River, Bill proudly pointed out that they were just south of Omaha, Nebraska, exactly as he had calculated.

By late afternoon they realized they couldn't reach Wounded Knee before dark. Since Paul was planning a pasture landing near the little church at Wounded Knee, daylight was crucial for selecting a proper landing site and bringing the plane down safely.

"I guess we won't make it tonight," Paul said, "but we'll get as close to Wounded Knee as we can. Then in the morning we'll have just a short hop to Wounded Knee, and we can get back home tomorrow night."

At dusk the Cessna 182 landed at O'Neill, Nebraska. A poster advertised the nearby Townhouse Motel, and sleep and food sounded wonderful to the hungry, weary men. While an attendant gassed up the plane, Bill called the motel, and a station wagon was dispatched to the airport to pick them up.

As soon as they'd checked into their motel room, Bill tried to telephone Ramon Roubideaux at Rapid City, South Dakota. Roubideaux was the attorney for the Indians at Wounded Knee, and Bill was anxious that the Indians be informed that their plane would be coming into Wounded Knee at dawn. Bill and Paul didn't want to be shot down. A few days earlier newspapers had reported that low flying planes were being shot at by the Indians. There was no answer at the lawyer's home.

The two men ate supper in the motel restaurant and returned to their room where they stretched out on their beds, watching television and talking. By ten o'clock Paul simply closed his eyes and was asleep.

Bill snapped off the television so it wouldn't bother Paul, but he lay there wide awake, staring into the darkness. The whole experience was so strange for Bill that excitement pushed sleep far off. Besides, he still hoped to get hold of the lawyer in Rapid City. In the dim light he continued to dial the Rapid City number for the next hour, but got no answer.

Finally he decided that a drink might help him relax and sleep so he left the room and went to the motel bar. There he chatted with the patrons, trying to get the feel of how the Nebraska people felt about the Wounded Knee situation. One man who was with the Department of Agriculture claimed to be open-minded, saying that he didn't take sides. However, when Bill mentioned that he had been raised on an Indian reservation in South Dakota, and was part Sioux, the conversation dribbled to a close, and the man left.

Bill returned to his room after midnight and again placed a call to Roubideaux. This time a child answered the phone. Bill asked to speak to his father or his mother.

The boy explained that neither was there, they both were attending meetings. He said his name was Mark, and he was twelve years old.

Bill sighed. He would have to count on the child to get the message through. "Mark, do you understand that your father is a lawyer, and that he's working for the Indians at Wounded Knee?" he asked.

"Sure," answered Mark. "He's down at Pine Ridge right now, negotiating for the Indians there."

"Well, Mark," Bill went on, "we have a planeload of food which we plan to land at Wounded Knee about daybreak. It's very important that the Indians find out we're coming, and that none of the white people learn about it. Can you keep a secret like this?"

"Oh, that," said Mark. "It's been all over town this afternoon. Everyone says a planeload of food is coming into Wounded Knee. Everyone thought it would be there today before dark, but since it didn't arrive today, they're expecting it tomorrow."

Surprised, Bill asked, "Well, if it's all over Rapid City, how about the Indians? Do the Indians at Wounded Knee know we're coming?"

Mark thought so, but wasn't sure.

Bill asked Mark to try to get hold of his father at Pine Ridge and let him know they would fly in at dawn in a red-white-and-blue plane.

When Bill hung up the phone, he shook his head. This seemed to be a mission run by innocents and babes. Our twelve-year-old Brenda had financed the flight, and now their safety in the morning depended upon twelve-year-old Mark delivering a message.

There was nothing more he could do, so Bill lay down and soon fell asleep. At three-thirty in the morning the

102

telephone rang, bringing their wake-up call from the manager at the desk, who had promised to drive them to the airport. The manager was an especially accommodating man who thoughtfully asked them if they wouldn't like breakfast before they flew out. "There's an all-night truck stop between here and the airport," he offered. "I can take you over there for breakfast."

Bill and Paul washed quickly without taking time to shave. At the truck stop they both ate a huge western breakfast, meat, potatoes, and eggs. The motel manager seemed very curious abut their destination, but was polite enough to avoid too pointed questions.

Paul had brought along masking tape to cover the numerals on the airplane. As they walked toward the plane, Paul told Bill that he had decided against using the tape to mask out the identification of the plane. It would be a grave violation of F.A.A. regulations, he explained.

The grass taxi-ways were muddy from the rain the day before. "How about kicking a little mud on the under-body of the plane, and splashing some over the numerals?" Bill suggested.

The two men looked at each other, then glanced back over their shoulders. The thoughtful motel manager remained in his parked car, his headlights shining on the plane. The manager was polite to the last, now furnishing them lights in the darkness of the airport. There was no way they could do anything unusual without arousing suspicions of the manager.

Paul taxied onto the runway, pulling up at the end of the runway for completion of the final check-list and a run-up of the engine before take-off. Even yet, the motel manager remained parked, either out of curiosity to see the take-off, or to furnish light, which really wasn't needed.

With the engine revved to full power, the plane tore down the runway, but reluctantly refused to leave the ground. With the heavy load and the increased altitude of three thousand feet, the plane couldn't seem to get airborne.

"How long is this runway?" Paul hollered. "We're going to run out of runway!"

As Bill struggled with the map in the dim red lights of the cockpit, trying to read runway lengths, he felt the plane leave the ground. Looking down, Bill saw, just two feet below, the green lights marking the end of the runway. They were out of runway with only two or three feet of altitude. The stall buzzer was still buzzing, warning that they were in danger of stalling. There was nothing but blackness ahead on either side. It was too dark to see the ground.

The Cessna slowly roared upward. At an altitude of a few hundred feet, they spotted lights of a town, and as they climbed higher, they saw scattered tiny lights from ranches. Bill found it hard to tell the difference between a star and a point of light on the ground. Paul pointed out that in western country, if there is no moon, there can be a real problem orienting yourself without instruments.

They headed west, took a two hundred and eighty degree heading slightly north so they would cross into South Dakota directly south of Wounded Knee. They spotted the lights and airport beacon at Gordon, Nebraska, and cruised on, descending to an altitude of about five hundred feet so roads and creek beds could be seen for landmarks. The sky was becoming considerably lighter, especially in the east, and now they could see the ground.

"I think the sun will come up in about ten minutes," Paul said.

Shortly, they saw a small settlement with a church. "That's it, I think!" Bill cried, pointing. But a re-check of the air map showed curved roads leading north out of Wounded Knee, and the roads of this settlement were straight.

"That's Pine Ridge, Doc!" Paul cried. "Let's get away from here!"

The forces opposing the Indians at Wounded Knee were headquartered at Pine Ridge. This amounted to cruising over enemy territory, and the two men held their breath, fearing they might get shot out of the air.

Paul pointed the nose northeast. Immediately they sighted the creek bed that wandered through Wounded Knee. Climbing to a higher altitude, they could see a little white church surrounded by foxholes and bunkers. On the perimeter of the valley, about a mile from the church, were parked the ominous shapes of federal armored personnel carriers. This was obviously Wounded Knee.

Circling low over the village, they buzzed past the church. Trails of smoke rose from two trash barrels, a hopeful sign that the Indians might be expecting a plane, and had started fires so the smoke would indicate wind direction for landing. As the plane roared past the church at about fifty feet of altitude, two Indians standing at a corner of the church building pointed toward the road.

"They want us to land on that blacktop road in front of the church," Bill shouted over the engine noise.

Paul shook his head. "Those road signs beside the road are too close. I'm afraid our wings might clip 'em," he said. "That grassy pasture on the other side of the road looks better. That's where we'll go in."

A creek lined with trees bordered the east edge of the pasture. Paul would have to drop the plane down quickly after passing over the trees, as the pasture did not provide a comfortably long landing space. The pasture surface looked reasonably smooth, though the grass was long, and there were occasional skeletons of dry cornstalks peeking out of the grass.

Paul circled. "Let's take one more look at it."

As the plane roared over the trees, Paul cut his engine. Bill jerked his head toward Paul, surprised.

"Hang on!" Paul cried. "We'll set down now!"

Just past the trees, Paul did a very gentle slip, straightened the plane, and the wheels touched ground.

The moment the wheels contacted the ground, the men realized this was no smooth pasture, but a frozen swamp, littered with knobs of icy sod. The Cessna rocked, bounced, and bumped, careening forward at high speed because of the heavy load of supplies.

As the plane rushed onward, its speed slowing only slightly, an awful sight loomed in front of them. Dilapidated, leaning fence posts crossed the pasture directly ahead of the speeding plane.

Paul shouted, "Hang on! We're going to crash!"

*"When our perils are past,
shall our gratitude sleep?
No, here's to the pilot
that weathered the storm."*
    —George Canning, 1802

•

Broke
My Plane

10 Paul pushed hard left rudder and left brake. The heavily-loaded plane began to slide, finally turned to the left and skidded sideways, lurching to a stop, the white wing tip just inches from a rotting fence post.

With a happy snort, Paul thrust his right hand to Bill for a victory handshake. "We did it! We're down!"

Paul patted his little Cessna affectionately and laughed. "She goes sideways nice, doesn't she?"

Several Indians were running down the incline from the church toward the plane, followed by a mud-plastered panel truck and four cars loaded with armed Indians. Gun barrels bristled out of every car window, as in a South Dakota pheasant hunt.

Nearly twenty Indians approached the plane. The apparent leader, a man with long braids pulled back severely, directed the men to set up guard. Quickly the Cessna was surrounded by Indians bearing carbines, twenty-two rifles, and shotguns.

"Set up the line. Let's get this plane unloaded," the Indian leader ordered.

The men began to maneuver the muddy panel truck through the sagging fence up to the airplane.

107

Paul climbed from the plane and shook hands with two unenthusiastic young men. He pulled a small camera from his jacket pocket and began snapping pictures. A young Indian called to Paul, "Hey, how about this, dude?"

Paul pointed the camera toward the voice and found himself facing the barrel of a shotgun aimed at him. Paul grinned weakly and put the camera away, suspecting the man meant, "Do you want me to click you, too?"

Several Indians formed a fire-brigade line between the plane and the muddy van. Bill stood in the doorway of the plane to hand the supplies out to the line of waiting men. As he lifted the first bag of powdered milk toward a waiting Indian boy, the youth grasped the bag clumsily with his left hand because his right hand was clutching a shotgun. As the boy reached toward the bag, the barrel of the shotgun jabbed Bill in the stomach.

Bill suspected the shotgun was loaded and that the eager boy probably had his finger on the trigger. Bill grasped the barrel and pointed it to one side. "Come on, Ace," he said. "Let's put the gun down for a couple minutes until we get the food unloaded. Then you can go on with whatever you're doing."

The leader came rushing up. "Jesus Christ, you guys! Let's watch those guns! Put the firearms down."

Bill laid the boy's shotgun on the ground under the plane's fuselage and continued handing out the packages. Within eight minutes the plane was unloaded. All the food was in the panel truck and the doors of the truck closed when some reporters came rushing up, their eyes still heavy with sleep.

The Indian leader called to them, "No pictures, you guys, no pictures!"

Paul had finished inspecting the plane. Though there was some denting in the tail, the elevators worked, and there seemed to be no serious damage. "Let's get out of here," he said.

They revved up the engine on their taxi run to the other end of the pasture. The smoke from the trash barrels stirred only slightly as there was very little breeze.

After the instrument check, Paul said, "We're ready, here we go."

The lightened plane bounced across the frozen, bumpy pasture. Bill held his breath. It seemed the plane would never leave the ground. Finally, a jolt jarred the plane, and they bounced into the air. Immediately Paul put the nose down slightly, and slowly the airspeed and altitude increased. They cleared the telephone wires, but as the Cessna sped past the church Bill found himself looking *up* at the steeple.

The sun hung about one degree above the horizon. The eastern sky blushed bright orange.

Bill leaned back, relaxed and happy. The food was delivered. Of course, there was the nagging worry that perhaps the photographers had gotten pictures of their plane taking off. Perhaps when the pictures were developed, the identification numbers of the plane would show up readably. Well, Bill figured, they would have to land to get gas somewhere on their return trip. When they gave their call numbers to land at a controlled field, they would learn whether an "all points" bulletin had been issued for their plane.

Paul's forehead pressed against the side window of the cockpit. "That was a hell of a jolt we got taking off. I'm worried about our landing gear. I've got a wheel on my side. How about on your side, Doc?"

Bill gulped and craned his head to look. With relief, he replied that he had a wheel, too.

"Then it's gotta be the nosegear," Paul groaned. "I'll take us down so we can pick up our shadow on the ground. Maybe we can tell if our nosegear is still there."

When they picked up the plane's shadow racing them along the rolling prairie, the welcome outline of their nosegear showed up on the shadow. "It's still with us," Paul sighed gratefully, as he began examining the instrument panel. All the instruments were slanted forward, loosened from their mountings. Paul began tapping the altimeter. The needle that reads in hundreds was broken off, however, the needle indicating thousands still functioned. "Damn, the altimeter's broken!" he said. "We're putting down at the nearest airport. Which one is closest?"

Bill studied the map. "Ainsworth, Nebraska, is our nearest one."

Bill knew that he must abandon his hopes for a continued airlift of food to Wounded Knee because of the damage to the plane.

As they approached Ainsworth there were no planes in the pattern or in the area of the old triangular World War II pilot-training base. It appeared nearly abandoned, but they spotted a windsock. Paul got the wind direction and picked his runway. Without cutting his engine, Paul made a power landing so he would have as much control of the plane as possible. Since there might be unknown damage, he wanted to be prepared for anything. As the wheels touched the runway and the forward momentum of the plane slowed, Paul realized that the plane's nose wouldn't come down. The long-unused concrete block runway was very rough, and Paul struggled to keep the plane straight. Because the nosegear was jammed in an extended position, control of the plane on the ground was extremely difficult. When at last Paul got the plane stopped, he turned toward the gas pumps located in front of a group of hangars.

A man leaning against a gas pump was studying their damaged plane warily.

"Let me handle this one, Paul," Bill said. Shakily, he climbed from the cockpit and leaned against the tail-low fuselage, gulping deep breaths of air as if he were about to be sick.

The skeptical onlooker, obviously a pilot, sauntered up to the tail assembly and began plucking cornstalks and weeds from the tail and landing gear. Arms folded, he looked over the obscenely extended nosegear and the dented fuselage under the tail section. Running his hands along the fuselage, he searched for telltale wrinkles that would indicate unseen stress in the plane's structure. Next he stepped back a distance and studied the lines of the plane from both front and side views. At last he gave Bill a quizzical look and mumbled, "Good morning."

Bill took another deep breath, cleared his throat and began his cover story. "I'm just a student pilot, and we've been up to Murdo, South Dakota, to a friend's ranch to do some huntin' and for me to get some practice in grass field landings. When I took off, I hit a cattle trail and banged up this nosegear. We thought we'd better get to an airport with a runway where we could put her down and repair her." Bill figured this story would explain the damaged plane swathed in weeds and cornstalks.

The man seemed to accept the story. Out-of-season hunting is common in the West, but it's not polite to question strangers about it. "That must have been some take-off," he said, and offered to help them get the plane repaired.

A replacement for the broken fork on the hydraulic mechanism of the nosegear was needed. After removing the broken fork, Paul telephoned suppliers in Omaha, Denver, and finally located the part in Chicago. The Chicago dealer said he could ship the part on a Greyhound bus for arrival the next day.

Paul groaned. "I've got an identical nose fork lying in my hangar in Grand Haven. We could get Dale to fly it out to us, but it would cost us three hundred dollars for his gas, and he probably wouldn't get it here until tomorrow."

"There's a lot of surgery scheduled for me to do tomorrow morning," Bill said.

Both of them were nervous about the radio blaring through the hangar. Frequent news bulletins announced current activities at Wounded Knee, and at each newscast Bill and Paul feared they would announce the description of a small plane that flew supplies into the village. If what they had done was considered a crime, they didn't want to be caught and prosecuted in the West, where any infraction of minor rules by Indians or Indian sympathizers is prosecuted with vigor by law enforcement bodies. Both men were eager to get out of the West and back home.

The pilot who had met them upon landing ran a crop-dusting service, and his hangar was well-equipped for repair and maintenance of aircraft. The man was busy reinforcing a pesticide tank. Paul asked if he could use some of his equipment and some scrap metal for patching up the nose fork enough to get them home.

"Help yourself," the man motioned and returned to his work.

The two men had to pattern, hack saw, drill, and fit a heavy steel splint for the fork. Every time a news bulletin came over the radio the pilot and the surgeon hammered and sawed with enthusiastic clamor, hoping to blot out the announcement.

When the fork was splinted Bill and Paul took it out to the plane where they put the nosegear back together. They gassed up the plane, paid the pilot, and thanked him for the use of his tools. Before taking off, they decided to test their repair patch by pushing down on the tail section of the plane to raise the nose and extend the hydraulic nosegear. When they released their pressure on the tail, the nosegear was jammed again. The plane's nose would not lower from its upward pointing attitude. The repair job hadn't held. The whole thing would have to be dismantled and done again.

Back inside the hangar with the fork removed, they found a piece of right-angle steel that looked promising. With much sawing and drilling this steel piece surely would hold the fork without binding the mechanism. Paul set to work fashioning the repair piece.

Bill borrowed the crop duster's car and drove into town to buy some food. He chose favorite foods: sardines, liver sausage, crackers, and orange juice. Almost as an afterthought he bought a bottle of scotch to be opened if and when they made it safely back to Grand Haven. When the flying was all done, Bill figured they would welcome a drink.

Upon returning to the hangar, Bill found Paul putting the finishing touches on reassembling the nosegear with the newly-splinted fork. They tested the new splint repeatedly, and this time, it functioned perfectly.

Again, they thanked the crop duster for his hospitality, and with great relief, took off, heading east. The weather was sparkling clear and cold, completely different from the soup they had flown through on the way west. Paul resumed his on-the-spot flying lessons for Bill while the two of them hungrily devoured the sardines, liver sausage, and crackers.

His full stomach and the routine, clear-weather flying made Paul bored and sleepy. Bill tried to keep up an interesting conversation to prevent Paul's dozing off. The flying instructions continued until Bill was flying the plane. Relaxed and enjoying himself, Bill piloted the plane for several minutes. Drowsily, Paul's head nodded lower, and his eyes closed.

A feeling of panic crawled across Bill's skin as he realized he was flying the plane alone, his real pilot asleep. "Paul!" Bill cried. "Don't go to sleep on me! I'm not a brave wild blue yonder guy. I'm really afraid of flying."

Paul blinked awake. "You looked pretty cool to me on this trip. We've had some pretty hairy moments, and I never sensed you were afraid."

"I know, and this really surprises me." Bill thought of flying instrument through zero-visibility on the way west, the nip-and-tuck take-offs in the overloaded plane, the dangerous landing and near crash at Wounded Knee, the take-off that damaged the nosegear, and the landing at Ainsworth with the broken nosegear. "I've always been afraid when flying, except on this trip. To me, this trip was a job that had to be done. Sort of like the Eskimo who goes out in the Arctic night for food. He knows the dangerous polar bear is out there, but he also knows that if he doesn't go out, his family surely will starve. He has to go, so he dares not be afraid."

Midway during their flight home it was necessary to gas up the plane. Waterloo, Iowa, was chosen as the refueling stop. As they approached the Waterloo airport, Paul radioed the control tower and received landing instructions. The men prepared the plane for landing, which would be the moment of truth on their repair job of the nosegear. Very gently Paul touched the plane down onto the runway. As the plane slowed, the nosegear remained in its attention-drawing obscene nose-high attitude, still locked in its extended position. Paul tried braking action, but the nose remained up and off the runway. Just as the men gave up hope that the gear would lower, the plane bumped against an uneven spot in the runway. The nosegear unlocked and lowered properly, and Paul casually taxied up to the gas pumps.

While the plane was being refueled the men went into the office for coffee. In the lounge room the radio was crackling out news bulletins concerning Wounded Knee, but there was no mention of a plane taking supplies to the Indians.

The last leg of the flight from Waterloo, Iowa, to Grand Haven was routine. Paul continued the flying instruction, and although saturated with flying, Bill dared not show it for fear Paul would grow sleepy again and leave Bill, terrified, flying the plane alone.

Bill had called me from Iowa while they were refueling, saying they should arrive home at the Grand Haven airport about five that afternoon.

I telephoned two of the local Indian families who had organized the gathering of the food and told them the good news. They said they planned to go to the airport to greet the returning airlift.

Since the school buses couldn't negotiate our muddy roads, the girls had to walk home from school that day, four and one-half miles. As soon as they'd rested up and cleaned the mud from their shoes, we left for the airport, about fifteen miles from our home. All the way we scanned the skies for sight of the returning plane.

*"I would rather see a sermon
than hear a sermon."*
    —Rose Shalifoe, 1973

•

The F.B.I.
Gets Its
Man

11 When we arrived at Paul's hangar there was still no sign of an approaching plane. I pushed open the hangar door and was startled to see the red-white-and-blue Cessna parked inside. Bill grinned down at me through a three-day growth of beard.

"Welcome home!" I cried and kissed him through the scratchy stubble. I'd managed to remain calm while he was gone, but now that he was safely back, my hands shook as I thought of the risks and dangers he had undertaken.

"When did you get back?" I asked.

"We just got in."

Already several mechanics and pilots had gathered in the hangar, and everyone was asking questions at once.

"Should we put the seat back in?" a young mechanic asked Paul.

"Does the radio gear still work?" one of the pilots wondered.

Paul was busy with a roll of paper towels, wiping hydraulic fluid from the fuselage.

One of the pilots watched Paul's cleaning work. "Looking for bullet holes?" he asked.

Paul grinned. "Nope, we didn't pick up any bullets. No arrowheads either."

"There were a lot of guns out there, though," Bill added.

"Did you actually get into Wounded Knee?" I asked.

Bill's dark eyes sparkled. "Right by the church." He held up his paper cup in salute. "Have a sip," he offered.

I took a swallow of what I thought was orange juice. It was well-laced with scotch. Bill motioned towards Paul's office. "Orange juice and a bottle of scotch in there. Everybody fix yourself something. I'm not going to be bartender. I've done my work for today."

We all moved into Paul's office, where I almost sat on a toy mouse lying on a sofa. Paul surely took good care of that stray black cat.

"Tell us about your trip," an older pilot asked.

Paul scratched the blond stubble on his chin and grinned ruefully. "Damn, that place was rough! I've been into some bad fields, but that one was a baddy!"

"What about the landing?" the woman pilot asked.

"The powerlines were lining up, but interspersed were some direction signs on the shoulder of the road, and the road wasn't that wide. I thought the field looked good. I dragged both the road and the field. The field didn't look too bad. So I made my set-up and I came in. The damn thing looked all right. I've been in rough fields before, but this was the roughest damned field I've ever been in in my life. I'm on the binders trying to hold the damn wheel back, you know. I got on fairly short and I figured around a one thousand foot strip, but there was a fifty foot trailer lying longwise on it, so we might have six hundred feet. But then there was this fence in the middle of it."

The pilots and mechanics groaned in sympathetic agony.

Paul continued. "I'm rolling, going like a bat out of hell, and I see fence posts. I jammed on the left brake, and it came around sideways." He made a loud screeching noise for sound effects. "We go sideways right up to the fence." Paul laughed. "It goes sideways real nice."

"Was the ground froze?" Dale asked.

"Froze," Paul said. "That was the problem. I horsed that thing off on take-off at twenty degrees flaps, and we're squealing and squeaking, but we get out of there. And I said, 'we're going in to the first airport we find. We'll get some gas and get the hell out of there.'"

In response to a timid knock at the office door, Paul pushed the door ajar. Two dozen Indians were gathered in the hangar.

Rose, the matriarch of the clan, spoke. "Welcome home. When did you get back?"

"Just about twenty minutes ago."

There were about a dozen little Indian children in the group, and they all crowded around Bill, hugging and kissing him, their adored hero. With my small camera I began snapping pictures. One of the women touched my shoulder and whispered, "Save some film for the doctor when he opens his present."

Chief Shalifoe, the clan patriarch, was moving through the crowd toward Bill. The Chief held a long brown box in his arms.

Very dignified, Chief Shalifoe stood before Bill. "This is from the Indians of Muskegon. From us to you, with our thanks."

Bill opened the narrow cardboard box. We all gasped. Inside lay a beautiful full Indian headdress.

"My mom and dad made it," the young Indian woman sitting beside me whispered.

Carefully, the Chief removed the headdress and opened it up so we could see the beautifully worked pink headband, the long fluffy white feathers surrounded by trailing pink feathers at the top of the headdress. Two streamers of white rabbit fur dangled from the front. With great dignity, the Chief placed the bonnet on Bill's head.

Bill looked stunned and deliriously happy. Nothing could have pleased him more or made him more proud.

"And now the pilot," the Chief said. Paul, too, was crowned with a similar full headdress, made with red instead of pink and white feathers.

117

I insisted upon taking a snapshot of the two men in their new bonnets. As the two returning heroes posed for the picture, the little Indian children clustered around them, hugging their legs, and staring up at them worshipfully.

Rose, the graying, stately wife of Chief Shalifoe, spoke. "Today we've seen what a little handful of people can do if they just care about their fellow human beings. It has been like a sermon. And I would rather *see* a sermon, than hear one."

It was a happy time for everyone. We felt like good samaritans. A hungry woman, a stranger, had said, "Our children are hungry. Our babies are crying for milk." And all of us, a mere handful of people, mostly strangers to each other, had managed to feed the hungry. We parted, heading for our own homes, sharing the feeling that we had contributed to the comfort of our fellow men.

As soon as we arrived home, the girls wanted to see their father's beautiful chief's headdress again. They stroked the soft feathers and fur and asked Bill to put it on for them.

Proudly, Bill posed in his chief's bonnet.

"You really look big and tall in that, Dad," Beth commented.

"With the Sioux, that was one of the purposes of this sort of chief's headdress," Bill explained. "It makes you look larger than you are, more formidable. This huge impressive headwear was a sort of bluff, a way of buffaloing your enemy. Some species of prairie birds and owls use this same psychology by fluffing out their feathers when approached by an enemy. With their feathers and tail ruff extended, these birds appear larger than they are and more threatening. The American Indian war bonnet is the most colorful and spectacular item of headwear of any people in the world."

Bill explained that this sort of Indian headdress originally had been worn only by the Plains tribes. Forest-dwelling Indians, which include most of the Eastern Indians, would have had great difficulty maneuvering

118

through dense woods while wearing a spreading feathered war bonnet. Nowadays Indians from all over the country have adopted the colorful chief's headdress as a symbol of being Indian.

"Of course, tourists expect Indians to look like Hollywood and television Indians," Bill added, "and the picturesque war bonnet is the most effective way of looking Indian." Bill grinned at us. "Don't I look more Indian with this headdress on?"

"You look just like a brave Indian, Dad," Brenda said. "But you earned your headdress. The Indians gave it to you kind of like a medal."

"Exactly," Bill agreed. "In the old days each feather in a headdress was won by performing a brave act or deed. A headdress containing many feathers was comparable to a soldier's uniform being covered with medals."

"What did an Indian have to do to earn each feather?" Brenda asked.

"Indian warriors put great emphasis on counting coup," Bill replied. "'Coup' is the French word for blow, and the Indian considered it a braver act to touch an enemy than to kill him. For instance, once the Indians acquired guns, the man who shot an enemy did not count coup for doing this. It was the first warrior who rode up and touched the fallen enemy who could count a coup. And contact with a live enemy was considered the supreme act of bravery. You know, the Indians weren't really vicious killers. War, to them, was a game in which they hoped to frighten the enemy. The field of war was an arena for them in which they could prove their bravery and manhood. Basically the Indians were a gentle people."

"I doubt if the pioneers on the wagon trains thought they were gentle," I commented.

"Pinkie, you have to remember that the white people were invaders, taking the Indians' land and shooting his livestock, the buffalo," Bill reminded me. "If a bunch of squatters began setting up tents and trailers in our front yard, and slaughtering our buffalo for food, I doubt if we'd welcome them with gentle kindness. At first, you know, the Indians did greet the white man with friendliness. Christopher Columbus said the Indians were a peaceable, gentle, smiling people, that in the whole world there wasn't a better nation. And if it hadn't been for the help and kindness of the Indians, the Pilgrims never would have survived. The Indian accepted the arrival of the white man, believing there was plenty of room in this huge land for everyone. The Indian just had no idea of how many thousands and millions of white people would be arriving. When the Indian finally realized what a threat this white population explosion presented, then he began to resist further expansion of white civilization. But, of course, it was too late then. The flow of white migration was endless. White people literally overran the continent. There was no way the Indians could turn back the hordes of people."

I looked at my watch and was startled to see how late it was. "Say, you girls get to bed. Look how late it is and you have school tomorrow!"

Reluctantly, the girls shuffled off toward their bedrooms. I looked at Bill's red, tired eyes, and added, "You should be in bed, too. You've hardly had any sleep for the past two nights."

Bill nodded, stifling a yawn. "I know, but I'd like to see the eleven o'clock news and find out what's happening today at Wounded Knee."

The news from Wounded Knee proved frightening. The government issued an ultimatum. Everyone, the government ordered, must leave the village of Wounded Knee by six the following evening, or else. It was the "or else" that was terrifying.

"Surely the government won't storm the village!" I protested.

Bill shook his head sadly. "They just don't understand how desperate those people are. A desperate people are willing to die. They haven't that much to lose."

Just then across our television screen flashed a picture of a red-white-and-blue Cessna taking off from a pasture at Wounded Knee. The voice from our television set announced that a small plane had landed today delivering ammunition and supplies. Then the news switched to other subjects.

"Ammunition!" I squealed, staring in horror at Bill.

Grim white lines circled Bill's mouth. "Could you read the numbers on the plane?" he asked.

"No, it was moving too fast, but if they stopped the action, I'm afraid the numbers would be clear. Why would they say you took in ammunition?" I stormed. "Why do people always suspect the worst?"

Bill rubbed his eyes. "We don't have to be afraid of the truth, and there wasn't any ammunition or any guns, so let's not worry about it. Let's get to sleep. I have a heavy load of surgery to do in the morning."

I set the alarm for six, and we fell asleep exhausted, only to be awakened at four fifteen in the morning by the phone call from the F.B.I.

As Bill and I sat in silence, waiting for the F.B.I. to arrive, we wondered what was keeping them. They'd said they were at the sheriff's office and would be right out. Suddenly we remembered our muddy roads.

Our home is one mile from any paved, hard-surface road. Annually with the spring thaw and rains the bottom goes out of our roads, and they become a quagmire. For ten days the roads approaching our house had been marked with "Road Impassable" signs.

"Do you think the F.B.I. can get through?" I asked Bill.

Forty-five minutes passed from the time of the phone call before we saw car headlights swing into our driveway.

Bill opened the door to three clean-cut young men in business suits. He greeted them hospitably. "Come in and have some coffee."

One, the leader, stepped in, but the other two pointed to their mudcaked shoes and spattered trousers and said they'd wait outside.

"Oh, that's okay," I babbled. "We've been living with mud for two weeks. It's too cold to wait outside."

Their eyes coolly appraised our living room as they stepped inside. The leader introduced himself and thrust out his identification card for Bill's examination. The other two agents continued their surveillance of our living room.

I always had pictured ourselves as quiet, conservative, family-people, but now, seeing our home decor through the eyes of an F.B.I. agent, my heart sank. Bill and I were admirers and collectors of Indian art and crafts, and our walls were covered with our collection of Indian beadwork and photographs of Indians we admired. My eyes followed theirs to our fireplace, where a white buffalo adorned the mantle, and to the six-foot-tall redwood Indian statue beside the television set. I groaned inwardly. They surely would take us for kooks.

Again, Bill offered coffee, and again, they refused. I could see that our hospitality was embarrassing to them.

In a borderline sharp voice, the spokesman said, "Doctor, we want you to go with us to the F.B.I. office in Grand Rapids. We want to talk to you."

"Can't we talk here?" Bill asked.

"No, we'd like you to go with us," the leader answered.

It was very quiet for many seconds. Bill and I were stunned at this unexpected request.

Bill frowned. "Does this mean I'm under arrest?"

"Yes, it does, doctor," the agent replied. "And I would like you to read this paper informing you of your rights."

He handed Bill a sheet of paper. Side by side Bill and I sat on the davenport, laying the paper on the coffee table in front of us. My heart was thudding hard against my ribs, and I stared at the typed letters on the paper, trying to force my brain to turn these letters into English words. When Bill slid the paper closer to me, I noticed his hands were trembling. I forced myself to concentrate on what the paper said. Finally I realized it was a waiver of one's rights to remain silent, and to be questioned without the presence of one's attorney. Television policemen always rattled off these words to a newly-arrested person, I remembered.

"Do you wish to sign this, doctor?" the agent asked.

Bill handed the paper back to the agent. "No, I'm not going to sign that."

"All right, doctor." The agent took the paper. "Shall we go?"

"Can I call my lawyer first?" Bill asked.

The agent nodded his permission.

Tom, our lawyer, was a pleasant young man who had handled legal matters for us when we sold some property. While Bill dialed Information to get Tom's home telephone number, I glanced over at the two agents waiting beside our front door and smiled weakly. An effort at some sort of conversation seemed proper.

"Did you have any trouble getting here?" I asked. Our nearly impassable roads had been my chief thought and frustration for many days.

The shorter, darker agent nodded ruefully. "We got stuck. Had to be towed out."

I smiled sympathetically. "I've had to be towed out twice in the past week."

"What's the best way out of here?" he asked.

I began giving advice to head south, since in that direction there was only one really bad spot. Then I stopped, remembering. "Well, if my husband is going to be with you, he can show you the way," I said. It didn't occur to me until later that they might not want to trust Bill's directions since he was an accused criminal.

Bill finally got through to our lawyer. "Tom? This is The Buffalo Doctor. Some F.B.I. agents are here in my home, and they've arrested me."

There was a long silence. I pitied poor Tom, trying to shake off sleep and assimilate this bizarre information about his respectable doctor-client.

Bill looked up at the chief agent. "He wants to know what the charges are."

The agent explained that he wasn't sure of the exact

charges yet, but it had something to do with interfering with federal officers on an Indian reservation.

Bill handed the phone to the agent. "Well, here, you tell him."

The agent talked to Tom briefly, saying something about the riot act and other legal jargon which we didn't understand. Then he handed the phone to Bill.

When Bill hung up, he turned to me to explain. "Tom will go down to Grand Rapids in a little while. He says for you to stay here since you'll have to get the money to post bond for me. He'll call you when he knows how much money you'll have to get. He says the charge is a federal felony."

"But the banks won't open until ten o'clock," I said. "I won't be able to get any money until ten." I was trying to overcome panic, but my thoughts jerked ahead in spasms instead of flowing smoothly. It would be five hours before I could get any money to free Bill from their clutches, and it would take me yet another hour to drive to Grand Rapids with the money.

The leader looked at his watch. "We've got to go now."

Bill remained seated. "How long is this going to take? I'm scheduled to do three major surgeries this morning. Do I have to cancel them?"

The agent replied that he didn't think it would take too long.

Bill explained that very shortly his patients would be receiving their pre-surgery medication. He asked if he could call the hospital and order a "hold" on the medication. The agent gave permission to place this phone call.

After hanging up, Bill rose, rubbing the three-day growth of dark stubble on his chin. "May I shower and shave and put on some clean clothes?" he asked.

"No. We'll have to go now, doctor," the agent insisted.

I saw Bill's jaw tighten with irritation as he said, "All right." He moved toward the kitchen to get a pack of cigarettes. The two younger agents in the doorway stepped

124

forward nervously, calling, "Doctor! Oh, doctor!" Their apprehension hit me like a blow to the stomach. Obviously they thought Bill was a dangerous criminal. They didn't want him out of their line of vision. Then the other half of the one-two punch hit me. These three men must be carrying guns! Three armed men were standing in my living room. They had arrested my husband and were taking him off into the night. But this is the United States of America, I told myself. I have nothing to fear. Even so, the ache in my stomach was the pain of fear.

Bill slipped into his western-style sheepskin overcoat. One of the agents opened the door, and the chilly March air rushed in. Aghast, I stared at Bill's bare feet, clad only in loose moccasins. Bill shrugged, meaning, "What can I do?" His brown eyes were calm and reassuring as he kissed me good-bye.

My hand trembled as I closed the door against the black cold air. Car doors slammed, headlights glared briefly against the window, and the car sped off. I was alone with my nightmare. But I wouldn't awaken to find life normal. The nightmare was real. Bill truly had been arrested by the F.B.I. and taken off into the night.

My teeth began to chatter, and I bit hard on my knuckles to force away panic. I must do something. But what can I do at five in the morning? Lawyer. That's it. I'll call the lawyer.

On the notepad beside the phone was the young lawyer's home phone number where Bill had scribbled it. Fumbling nervously, I dialed the number.

"Tom, this is Jean Cummings. They just left with Bill. They took him away." I cleared my throat, trying to get rid of the high-pitched wail.

"Okay," he said. "Now, I'm not a criminal lawyer, so this is out of my field, but I think it's a felony offense. I'll get hold of the criminal lawyer in our firm, and we'll go to the federal building in Grand Rapids. That's where they took him, didn't they?"

"That's what they said."

He continued his instructions. "As soon as I find out

what kind of bond they're going to set, I'll call you so you can get the money together. It will have to be a cashier's check issued from a bank. Then you can bring it over to the federal building."

I apologized for waking him, but he assured me we were proper in calling him.

"I suppose you're wondering what this is all about," I began.

He stopped me. "Let's not talk now. Your phone may be tapped. We'll talk later. I'll call you."

I hung up the phone and stared at it in horror and disgust. Our phone might be tapped! Oh, come on. That was done only to people in organized crime, racketeers and spies. I'd never had even a traffic ticket.

On wobbling knees I moved into the kitchen and glanced at the clock. Only five-fifteen. A whole hour before I should awaken the girls for school. Slumping down at the kitchen table, I poured a cup of coffee. I needed both hands to hold the cup steady to my lips.

"Father! You have said we are in your hand,
and that by shutting it
you could crush us to nothing.
Are you determined to crush us?"
    —Cornplanter, Seneca Chief

•

Running
The
Gauntlet

12 Upon leaving our house, Bill was instructed to get in the back seat of the unmarked Ford. One of the agents sat beside him, and the other two climbed into the front seat. Just walking from our house to their parked car had chilled Bill's bare ankles. He felt himself shivering with cold and thinking of the horrible stories he'd heard about life in Nazi Germany, where the gestapo came in the night and took people off to concentration camps. Nighttime arrests were usual in police states, but it seemed unthinkable that our beloved F.B.I. had adopted the tactics of the gestapo and NKVD. Maybe they think I'm a hardened criminal, Bill thought, and catching me like this, sleepy and not completely dressed, puts me at a disadvantage.

Bill guided them through the muddy sections of the road, and they made it through to the four-lane highway to Grand Rapids.

The agent sitting beside Bill in the backseat conscientiously explained, "You don't have to talk if you don't want to, and you don't have to talk about anything you don't want to talk about."

Bill nodded absently. He was preoccupied with his aching cold feet.

"Am I to understand correctly, doctor, that you raise buffalo?" the agent asked. This seemed to be a neutral conversation opener.

Raising buffalo is a subject dear to Bill's heart, and he found himself telling the agents about the attributes of buffalo and describing some of our work with buffalo. Talking at least kept his mind off his frightening predicament and his miserably cold feet.

When they arrived at the federal building the driver maneuvered the car into the basement and brought it to a halt in the F.B.I. parking section. The two agents in the front seat quickly jumped from the car and opened the back door next to Bill. This reminded Bill that he was an apprehended criminal, someone who required close surveillance. Do they think I'm going to try to escape? he wondered. Why do they think I'm such a dangerous criminal? I've been a practicing surgeon for fifteen years. I'm a family man, a respectable citizen with no arrest record. As for Wounded Knee, all I took was flour, pinto beans, buffalo meat, toilet paper and Kotex . . .

Bill's thoughts were interrupted as the security elevator arrived at the seventh floor which housed the F.B.I. offices. He was led through an unmarked door into a large room, bounded by smaller rooms, a reception room, conference room, and arsenal. He noticed a Telex telephone machine for transmitting printed material via telephone, fingerprinting equipment, and a large coffee urn.

As Bill was led through the large room, he heard a shout, "Hi, Doc!" From a small room at his left he saw Paul Davids sitting with two F.B.I. agents. Paul's jovial face brightened, and he waved again, "Hi, Doc! Where was that place we landed in Nebraska? I can't remember the name of it."

Bill moved on without showing recognition. He thought it prudent to wait for the arrival of his lawyer before committing himself to anything at all.

He was steered into a far right hand room. One of the agents offered to take his coat, but Bill chose to huddle in his sheepskin rancher coat. What with his icy feet and the stress and lack of sleep over the past three days, his whole body ached with fatigue and chill.

"How about a cup of coffee?" an agent asked.

Bill agreed gratefully, and they moved into a smaller room where they poured coffee and sat down to sip it. The agent explained again that Bill didn't have to say anything, but that they could just chit-chat. For awhile, they talked about buffalo. The conversation got around to whether Bill had any relatives in South Dakota. Bill admitted that he had relatives living in South Dakota.

The agent started to ask if these relatives were involved or injured at Wounded Knee, but his question trailed off. "I suppose you don't want to talk about that."

"No, I shouldn't." Bill poured himself a second cup of coffee.

Bill turned to the agent. "Let me ask you something. What do you think of this ultimatum the Department of Justice has issued, ordering the Indians to leave Wounded Knee by this evening?"

"Law and order have to be maintained in this country," the agent replied. "We can't let people carry on criminal acts. The public has to be defended."

Bill leaned toward the agent. "Wounded Knee is a tiny village in the middle of nowhere. Nothing ever happens there, not since the last massacre of Wounded Knee did anything exciting happen. The winters are long, boring, cold and miserable. These people do well to survive there. Now all this excitement and attention at Wounded Knee presents a carnival atmosphere for them. Even their holding hostages was a play-acting thing. When they said the hostages were free to go, the so-called hostages didn't leave. They couldn't have been very frightened for their lives."

The agent shifted in his chair. "Our government can't permit this type of lawless behavior. We'd have complete disorganization in our government with the loss of law and order."

"Sure," answered Bill, "we're all for law and order. But the problem is how far will you go to establish law and order? The man from Washington says he's going to send tanks and armored personnel carriers into Wounded Knee at six o'clock tonight. There are many innocent women and children in Wounded Knee. Are you going to kill women and children in order to maintain law and order? After the big scandal over My Lai, where our army killed women and children, would our own F.B.I. do this to our own people here in America? It's unthinkable."

"I'm glad it's not my decision to make," the agent sighed.

Bill pressed on. "By threatening these people at Wounded Knee, you just heat up the mess. You're going to get into a massacre situation, just like the first Wounded Knee. If the Justice Department says it's going in at six o'clock, they're going to believe you. They might decide to attack you at five o'clock. I don't think the authorities are taking the Indians out there seriously. These men have nothing to lose. They're prepared to die for the Indian people. If you push them, they'll show you how to die. It would be a tragedy that would always be a blot on the record of the F.B.I. By the way, why is the F.B.I. involved in Wounded Knee? I thought it was an investigative organization. I wasn't aware that the F.B.I. was also a law enforcement body."

The agent explained that by Act of Congress the F.B.I. had been designated as a law enforcement body on certain Indian reservations. The feeling was that the F.B.I. could work with the Bureau of Indian Affairs police force better than local or state law enforcement bodies.

Bureaucracy always fails the Indian, Bill mused. It was a pity the F.B.I. hadn't used its power to investigate the corruption in administering Indian reservations, and to bring justice to the reservations. Now there was an armed confrontation. The simmering pot was boiling over.

Another agent came into the room, and the first agent excused himself. The new agent, another clean-cut young man, initiated conversation on general topics, then asked if Bill wouldn't like to talk about his flight to Wounded Knee.

130

"I really don't think I should commit myself until my lawyer gets here," Bill answered, trying to be courteous. "But I don't mind discussing the situation at Wounded Knee. I believe you men of the F.B.I. are dedicated, intelligent Christians. I understand a significant number of you agents started your careers studying for the priesthood?"

The young agent nodded agreement. "Quite a few of us had that inclination as young men, and then switched to the Bureau."

"Since most of you, then, are sincere and loyal Christians, can you be openminded in dealing with non- Christians? Many Indian people are non-Christians, and I've always found that deeply religious Christians hold prejudices against people who don't believe in Christianity. A big problem between Indians and Christians is that Indians practice and live the simple teachings of Christ, but they don't worship Christ. Too many Christians worship Christ but don't practice and live His teachings. Instead, they use Christ in an effort to influence their neighbors."

"We have freedom of religion in our country," the agent argued. "It's guaranteed by our Constitution."

"I doubt if Brigham Young believed we had freedom of religion," Bill smiled. "His religious beliefs called for the practice of polygamy, but our country passed laws prohibiting having more than one wife. The Mormons had to use subterfuge to practice their beliefs, and risk imprisonment if they were caught. This doesn't sound like freedom of religion to me. Mr. Hoover proved that the F.B.I can be influenced by prejudice. He wouldn't permit black people to become agents during his many years of reign over the Bureau."

The agent didn't reply.

"Do you think the Justice Department should storm the church at Wounded Knee, and root out those so-called insurgents?" Bill asked. "There's a lot of women and children there who will get hurt."

His eyes snapping, the agent leaned forward. "It's the

women and children there that really get me. What sort of cowards are those Indians who will hide behind the skirts of women? Why don't they act like real men?''

"For one hundred years," Bill answered softly, "Indian women and children on the reservations have shared with the men the poverty, slow starvation and young death. To them it's perfectly natural to share the risk of death in the church at the hands of the F.B.I. or federal marshals. Our country hasn't had any qualms over causing these individuals a slow, crippling death by starvation. Yet everyone grows queasy and feels it's improper to provide a quick, honorable death by bullet. The Indian faces dying every day. He sees death in the eyes of his potbellied, undernourished children.''

They moved to another room, and another replacement agent sat down with Bill. The pattern kept repeating itself, with new agents taking over being with him. Bill understood that he was being interrogated in a very soft-sell manner, always courteous and polite, but persistent.

Bill was reminded that he was an apprehended criminal when he rose to go into the coffee room to refill his cup. This moved him out of sight of the agent, who quickly jumped up, spilling his own coffee, saying, "Just a minute, Doc!" In spite of the polite courtesy, Bill was under strict surveillance, and any sudden moves on his part evoked quick reaction.

Agents continued taking turns conversing with Bill, changing guard about every ten or fifteen minutes. They encouraged Bill to relax, and eventually he tilted his chair back and propped his feet on the work table, a posture he claims is healthful for one's feet and legs. Bill's bare ankles and patched moccasins embarrassed the neatly dressed agents. They gazed uncomfortably at the homely patchwork job, then shifted their look elsewhere.

Bill noticed there was a flow of activity in the director's office, with agents going in and out constantly. When the district director of the F.B.I. out of Detroit arrived, nearly all the agents crowded into the director's office. Another new arrival attired in a precise black suit

132

received considerable obeisance from the local agents. Later, Bill learned that this man was a special agent from Washington who had been flown into Grand Rapids to deal with the two men who flew the Wounded Knee airlift.

When this man took his position as interrogator, Bill was amused by his naive questions concerning farming and buffalo. The special agent was obvious in his questions, trying to get Bill talking about Wounded Knee. "You guys sure had a ride for yourselves, didn't you?" he prompted.

Bill didn't respond.

Next the man asked some questions about flying.

Bill smiled ruefully. "I've always been afraid to fly. I'm a real coward in a plane. My hands perspire with fear."

The district director from Detroit took his turn next. Briskly and without sitting down, he began, "Now, doctor. You know your business and we know ours. For several hours you haven't told us a thing. I think you're a good man, and probably this is all a big mistake. If you'll just give us an explanation of how this got started, and what happened, we can all get out of here. You know, doctor, in this business we find that people who are innocent talk to us. Those who are guilty tell us to talk to their lawyer. Soon now we'll be charging you, fingerprinting you, and taking you before the magistrate for a bond hearing. You should know that we have information from South Dakota that you carried a bazooka and armor-piercing shells into Wounded Knee, as well as food supplies. This is a very serious charge. If you'll just explain to us what occurred, maybe we can get you out of here."

So that was the problem! If the American Indian Movement leaders at Wounded Knee were in possession of a bazooka and armor-piercing shells, the government forces were not safe in their armored personnel carriers. This would be a threatening and serious situation. The F.B.I. agents and marshals dared not storm the church until they were sure there was no bazooka in the area.

"I can see your concern for the situation," Bill replied,

"and your concern for the F.B.I. men in South Dakota. My problem is, I don't know how I can give you assurance that there was no bazooka or armor-piercing shells delivered into Wounded Knee. Many people slip in and out of Wounded Knee. If you don't mind, maybe I can call my lawyer and see if I can talk with you."

The director agreed, and Bill phoned his lawyer. Tom said he was just leaving to pick up their firm's criminal lawyer, and they would arrive at the F.B.I. offices in less than an hour. He advised Bill to say nothing until they arrived.

The original agent who had brought Bill to Grand Rapids came over to Bill's chair. "We'll have to get the fingerprinting out of the way now," he said. On the way to the fingerprinting room, Bill caught another glimpse of Paul through an open door. He realized they were being kept apart purposefully so they couldn't compare notes.

The fingerprinting equipment was all set up, and finger by finger, Bill's prints were pressed on the arrest card. As the agent filled in the statistical data on the card, he questioned Bill about his address and date of birth. Bill's place of birth, Rosholt, South Dakota, revealed his ties with Dakota. The agent continued with the routine questions: "Any previous arrests?"

Bill shook his head "no."

"Are you known by any other names, any aliases?"

Again, Bill said, "No."

The agent looked at Bill thoughtfully. "Well, I don't know, doctor. What about 'The Buffalo Doctor'?"

Bill smiled. "I never considered that an alias."

The agent wanted to be correct, so he dutifully wrote on the arrest card, "Alias The Buffalo Doctor."

Following the fingerprinting ritual, Bill asked if he could go to the restroom. Several agents collected around Bill for the trip to the bathroom, which was out in the hall corridor, past the elevators.

As soon as he stepped out into the corridor, Bill realized why so many agents were accompanying him. The hallway was filled with people from the news media, reporters and television cameramen. The moment they caught sight of Bill, they began shouting questions.

"Why did you do it, Dr. Cummings?"

"Will you make a statement, Doctor?"

"What are things like out at Wounded Knee?"

The encircling F.B.I. agents pushed on to the restroom. In the bathroom mirror Bill looked at his reflection and groaned. He looked like a dangerous criminal—haggard eyes, three-day growth of beard, all topped off by a head of tousled, uncombed hair.

The agents ran interference through the clamoring reporters back to the F.B.I. offices, where they slumped gratefully into chairs, feeling they had just escaped from Bedlam. The local director had a suggestion for the next trip to the restroom. He advised slipping through his office and out a back door to the restroom on the floor below.

Now that the reporters actually had seen Bill, they realized that The Buffalo Doctor truly was being held by the F.B.I., and they became more aggressive. Each time the outside door opened, several heads crowded forward to peek inside. The agents suggested that Bill sit with his back to the door in case a photographer managed to pop his camera through the open door and snap an unbecoming picture.

At last our lawyer arrived with Neal, the criminal lawyer from his law firm. The two lawyers and Bill were led into the fingerprint room where they could confer in privacy. Bill never had met Neal before, and he introduced himself to the short, husky lawyer who was to defend him.

Neal nodded brusquely. "Okay, Doc, I want you to tell me everything about everything. What you've done, and what you haven't done. I'm a criminal lawyer and I'll be defending you. Tell me the complete story."

"It began Monday night," Bill said, "with this phone call from a man, asking me to help get some food to the people at Wounded Knee."

"Carry on, and dread nought."
    —Sir Winston Churchill, 1939

●

The Show
Must
Go On

13 Bill told the young lawyer the complete story of the flight to Wounded Knee and emphasized that they had delivered no munitions, bazooka, or armor-piercing shells. Of course, he couldn't say whether someone else had or had not taken in a bazooka.

After listening to the whole story, Neal stood up. "Okay, now I have to talk to them."

Neal knocked on the F.B.I. director's door and entered, closing the door behind him. After a short time he returned, seated himself beside Bill, and spread out a yellow notepad. "I want you to tell me exactly what you took in there," he instructed Bill.

Listing all the items he could remember, Bill described the size of the bags and any brand names he recalled.

When the list was completed, Neal brusquely cross-examined Bill. "How can you be sure there weren't guns and ammunition hidden in a sack of flour or in a bag of dried milk?" he demanded.

Bill described how he had handled each article twice, once when he handed it to Paul while loading the plane, and again when he handed it to the Indians at Wounded

Knee. "I'm a surgeon," Bill said. "My hands are very sensitive. I'm sure none of the bags contained hidden items."

Once again Neal conferred with the director. After a lengthy session he returned and explained, "Now we just have to wait. The F.B.I. here in Michigan is really going to bat for you. They're convinced you're a reputable citizen and not a conspirator attempting to overthrow the government." The problem was that the authorities in South Dakota didn't believe that. They had demanded a $25,000 bail bond. Neal and the local agents were trying to convince the Dakota authorities that this was way out of line.

"Relax, Doc," Neal advised. "We may be here several hours while they dicker over your hide. But it's worth it if we can get that bail reduced."

By now it was nearly ten in the morning. Tom, the lawyer we had originally called, excused himself to telephone me to let me know about the amount of bail money I must secure.

My telephone had been ringing constantly for over an hour. Newspaper reporters wanted to find out what The Buffalo Doctor had done, had he really been arrested, where was he being held, what were the charges? I gave them only minimum information, though I hated sounding evasive, and thus, guilty. My hands trembled violently as I tried to cope with all the telephone calls. There was another problem upsetting me. I was scheduled to be the guest speaker at the Rotary Club luncheon at noon. I kept telling myself "I can't possibly do it," yet I couldn't bring myself to call the program chairman and tell him I couldn't do it. Backing out at the last moment seemed unforgiveable, and what reason would I give for not speaking?— "My husband has been arrested by the F.B.I.?" The words caught in my throat—I couldn't face saying those awful, but truthful words as yet.

When I answered the phone and heard Tom's voice, it was a great relief. "They're still demanding $25,000 bond," he explained, "but I'm sure it will be reduced considerably. That's ridiculously high. How much cash can you get your hands on?"

138

"Two thousand dollars is all we've got," I answered.

"Okay," Tom said. "Go to the bank and get two cashier's checks made out for one thousand dollars each to bring over here to the federal building. Now, just in case they won't reduce the bond, bring the deeds to the buffalo ranch with you. The property deeds would be security if you have to come up with $25,000 bond. You won't need to come until about two-thirty this afternoon. That's about when they'll be holding the arraignment and bond hearing. Just come up to the seventh floor of the federal building."

"How's Bill doing?" I asked. In my imagination I kept seeing my exhausted, red-eyed husband sitting in a hard chair with a bright light pouring on him, the old third-degree thing.

"Oh, he's fine," Tom assured me. "He's drinking about his tenth cup of coffee right now. He's doing great. Don't worry. By the way, he wants you to be sure and give your speech to the Rotary Club this noon. He says to tell you it's his wish that you go ahead and do it."

"That's been worrying me," I admitted. "But if I give the speech, can I get over to Grand Rapids by two-thirty?"

"Sure," Tom said. "Rotary meetings are always over by one or soon after. You can make it in time."

The moment I hung up the phone, it rang again. It was Jim, a black doctor and friend of Bill's, who had just heard of Bill's arrest. "Do you need some money?" he asked. "How much bail are they asking?"

I was very touched by his offer of money as he had recently suffered a great deal of persecution and troubles of his own. "They're asking $25,000 bond so far," I answered.

He whistled. "They think they have a real big criminal, don't they? That burns me!"

I thanked him for his concern and explained that our lawyer believed the bond would be reduced.

"Let me give you a little advice, Pinkie," Jim offered. "Tonight when Bill's back home safe and the kids are in bed, talk to each other. It's very important. During a tragic upheaval you both need support, and you can give it to each other. Talk. Be sure and talk.''

The news of Bill's arrest had not yet been on radio or television. Later, I learned how Jim had heard the news. As he was leaving for the hospital that morning, his car wouldn't start, and he had to call a tow truck. The driver of the tow truck commented to him, "I wonder what's going on with Dr. Cummings? About four-thirty this morning I had to tow out a car of F.B.I. agents who were stuck in the mud. They said they were on their way to Dr. Cummings' house."

The day before, I had prepared an outline of the speech I planned to give to the Rotary Club. Now I tried to look over my outline, but my mind wouldn't focus. I put on a black sweater and skirt, which must have been my psyche's way of donning mourning, ran a comb through my hair, and filled a briefcase with our property deeds. I stopped at the bank to draw out our two thousand dollars and put the cashier's checks in my purse.

At the Rotary luncheon I discovered I couldn't eat. There was no way I could make myself swallow. I felt just as if there had been a death in the family. Sitting beside me at the speaker's table, the poor program chairman was distraught. I'm sure he feared I was going to faint or embarrass him. I had felt it necessary to tell him about Bill's arrest so he could choose whether he wanted an accused felon's wife as a Rotary luncheon speaker.

Somehow I got through the speech. I tried to concentrate on the light and funny aspects of the buffalo-raising business. I dared not get too serious for fear I might choke up and cry. The large group of business and professional men laughed and seemed to be entertained by my cheery presentation. I'm sure they interpreted the occasional quaver in my voice as due to stage fright. Not until the afternoon paper came out would they know why I really was frightened.

I arrived at the federal building in Grand Rapids shortly after two o'clock and, as Tom has instructed, went directly to the seventh floor. Wandering up and down the

140

deserted corridors, lined with unmarked doors, I searched for a door which would say "Federal Bureau of Investigation." I felt afraid and lonely as my heels clicked noisily on the terraza floors. At last on a plain solid door I spied a scrap of paper taped to the door. In pencil was scrawled, "F.B.I. offices."

Timidly I tapped on the door. A very tall, handsome young man opened the door a crack.

I swallowed. "I'm Mrs. Cummings, and I'm looking for my husband."

"They've taken him down to court," he told me. "On the floor directly below."

I caught my breath. Was I too late with the bond money? Had they put him in jail?

I found a stairwell and hurried down. Directly ahead of me I saw doors labelled "United States District Court." One door was ajar, and I saw that the courtroom was empty. From around a corner I heard the babble of many voices, and I turned in that direction. That corridor was jammed with news people and cameramen waiting outside a set of double doors labelled "Magistrate." That must be where they have Bill, I figured. Bracing myself, I began to push my way through the crowd. Some of the reporters stared curiously at me. I hoped they would think I was a lawyer since I carried a briefcase. Pushing open the door to the magistrate's court, I slipped inside. Immediately an F.B.I. agent sprang to his feet and stepped to my side. "Mrs. Cummings?" he said. "Your lawyer is over there."

My eyes fell on the black-robed magistrate sitting behind his huge bench. Standing before him, like two criminals awaiting a sentence, were Bill and Paul. I rushed up to Bill, and his haggard, pale face smiled a welcome. I'm not usually a demonstrative person, and I surprised myself by kissing Bill. Suddenly aghast at my audacity, I peeked meekly at the judge, fearing he might pound his gavel and charge me with contempt of court. Instead, he shuffled some papers and continued with the proceedings which were nearly complete.

Bill and Paul began signing some papers, and Tom

whispered to me, "They reduced the bond. Both men are being released on their own personal recognizance." The money and property deeds I'd brought weren't needed. Bill and Paul signed agreements to appear in court on schedule and were released on personal recognizance and one thousand dollar bonds.

The hearing was completed, but Bill and Paul had to go to another room for a second bout of fingerprinting and mug shots. The agents slipped us out a rear door of the courtroom to avoid the crowd of newsmen. While the fingerprinting was being done, Bill and Paul's lawyers joked and chatted with the F.B.I. men. I found it hard not to glare hostilely at the agents. My wounds were too fresh. I couldn't feel charitable toward armed men who came to my home in the night and whisked away my husband.

During the fingerprinting Bill was listed once again as an accused felon with an alias, "Alias the Buffalo Doctor."

Tom introduced Neal. "This is our criminal lawyer, the man who will be defending your husband."

"Where did you park your car?" Neal asked me.

When I explained that it was in the basement parking garage, he said, "Good. That's where we're parked, too. We'll go down there together. Now we've got to battle our way through that throng of newsmen. Don't say a thing. I'll do any talking that's done."

Neal ran interference, leading the way into the crowd outside the doors. The moment we stepped into the corridor, blinding bright floodlights flashed on and television cameras began to whir. Bill's grip on my elbow tightened, and we pushed ahead. Walking backwards directly ahead of Bill were two television cameramen, pointing their lenses nearly in Bill's face. In trying to get closer to Bill several newsmen bumped and jarred against me, and I stumbled, but Bill's firm grasp on my arm pulled me along beside him. All the reporters were shouting questions.

"What is the charge against you, Doctor?"

"What did you take to Wounded Knee?"

"How have you been treated?"

Following Neal's orders to keep silent, Bill merely shook his head and smiled grimly. At that moment I understood why accused criminals always look so "criminal" when you see them being hustled into court. In this grim situation you are stiff with shock and horror over your predicament. A polite smile doesn't feel appropriate. As the news people crowd around, bumping, and stepping on toes, you feel angry and resentful. Yet no irritation must show or you look mean and guilty. I tried to assume a placid, uninvolved facial expression and made an effort to keep from wincing whenever an elbow or shoulder jabbed against me.

At last we reached the elevator and gratefully stepped on. At this point we had to turn and face the glaring lights, cameras, and reporters still calling out questions. The elevator doors began to close but stopped part way and began shaking, making a terrible clatter. I nearly panicked, thinking the elevator was about to fall. Bill thrust out a fist and gave the shaking door a hefty whack. The doors opened wide, then closed properly, blotting out the lights and cameras. As the elevator began to descend, a newsman shouted, "What do you think of the elevators in the federal building, Dr. Cummings?" In a rush of withheld emotion we laughed merrily, and the laughter from the crowd of reporters echoed down the elevator shaft.

In the basement parking area Tom and Neal gave us some farewell advice. "Go home and get some sleep. You both need it. Don't make any statements or talk to any reporters. Just tell them they'll have to talk with your attorneys."

On our drive home Bill told me how Paul had been arrested. Six F.B.I. agents with machine guns had surrounded his home, and three more agents awakened Paul's wife and went in. Dead tired and feeling the effects of several drinks, Paul awakened in a belligerent mood. We shuddered to think what might have happened if Paul had assumed they were a gang of thieves and had come at them swinging. An older, experienced agent called "Soupy" worked at calming Paul and preventing him from trying to slug it out with the unwelcome visitors. After his arrest, Paul was taken to the F.B.I. offices in Grand Rapids, where he talked freely without trying to call his lawyer. He related the whole story of his flight to Wounded Knee.

When Bill and I arrived home we were amazed to see that Beth and Brenda had established a system for recording the constant telephone calls and messages. They had rigged up their tape recorder into a telephone-bugging system and were recording all the phone messages so we could review them and return the calls. By now the afternoon papers were out, and everyone in western Michigan knew that The Buffalo Doctor had been arrested. Friends called voicing their concern, and offering their moral support. Newsmen continued to telephone asking Bill to make a statement.

When the girls saw us, they were greatly relieved, and Beth pointed at the telephone. "You take over, Mom. I've had it!"

The girls were furious and enraged over their father's arrest. They ranted about this being a police state, that the F.B.I. was just like the gestapo, and that life wasn't fair. Bill and I sat down at the kitchen table with them and tried to explain. We emphasized that the F.B.I. men had been good to Bill, that they were sincere men doing their job of protecting our country. We reminded them that police must arrest individuals who are suspected of committing a crime.

"How can it be a crime to give food to the Indians?" Brenda demanded. "Anyone who would keep food away from hungry people is bad!"

Bill told them that the F.B.I. had information that he and Paul had taken in guns, ammunition, a bazooka and armor-piercing shells. "If we had done this," Bill said, "this would indicate that we were revolutionary men, and it would put the law enforcement people out there in a very precarious position."

"Well, didn't you tell them that you just took in food?" asked Beth. "Wouldn't they believe you?"

144

"No, they have to collect evidence and facts. Law men can't just take you by your word," Bill answered.

I looked down at the list of phone messages Beth had written in a notebook. Nearly all of the calls were from wire services and newspapers. "Bruce hasn't called, has he?" I asked.

He hadn't, and this worried me. Our son and his two friends were driving home from Florida. I hated the possibility of Bruce hearing the news of his father's arrest over the car radio. But with no way of knowing where he was, we would have to wait for him to call us.

"I don't want to go to school tomorrow!" Beth fumed. "It was terrible today. I don't know how they found out so fast, but by fourth hour, all the teachers were coming up to me saying, 'Is your father okay? Is he in jail?'"

Brenda piped up, "You know what happened to me? A teacher asked me what happened, and she got the whole story out of me. I guess I just thought, oh, well, why not?"

Bill and I laughed. For years Brenda had kept her teachers amused with her show-and-tell stories about our family. We never had any secrets from Brenda's teachers.

"I was so mad at the F.B.I.," Beth added, tossing her red hair back indignantly, "that when I got to school and saw this cop who patrols our corridors, I just wanted to go up to him and kick him in the shins!"

"Keep cool, Beth," Bill smiled. "Say, did you feed the buffalo grain, or did you just give them hay?"

"I just gave them hay," she answered. "They seemed so jumpy and upset that I got out of there quick."

The girls wanted to know what was going to happen next.

"I'm to have a hearing in federal court March 16," Bill said.

"Oh, can we go, too?" the girls begged.

We agreed. Since the destiny of our family was involved, we believed it would help them understand if they participated in the proceedings.

Bill glanced at his watch. "It's almost time for the six o'clock news. I'm worried about what's going on out at Wounded Knee. They've given the Indians a deadline of 'Be out by sundown tonight or else the government will come in with their tank and armored vehicles.'" He flicked on the television set, and we all sat around on the floor.

"Do you think they'll say anything about Dad on television?" Brenda asked.

I sighed. "I wouldn't be surprised."

Brenda's eyes grew large.

Bill shushed us and pointed toward the screen where a news announcer was saying, "We have film reports on two west Michigan men who helped the Indians at Wounded Knee and now they're in trouble."

The newscaster reported that many women and children were leaving their home village of Wounded Knee, South Dakota. "There have been reports," he said, "of possible agreements between government officials and the Indians at Wounded Knee. But the deadline is still set for six P.M. when the Indians have been ordered to give up their positions. The crisis is still reported grave, and there has been some evacuation of women and children, but the militants are determined to carry out many of their threats if negotiations fall through." He reported that the Indians had been holding meetings.

The image on the screen faded and was replaced by the haggard, grim face of Bill moving through the crowd in the federal building corridors, surrounded by reporters. I was moving along with him, blinking and confused, and behind me I could make out Tom, trying to keep close to us.

The newscaster was saying, "Two west Michigan men were arrested by F.B.I. agents and charged with interfering with federal officers at Wounded Knee. The duo, a Muskegon doctor, and a charter airline pilot, allegedly flew supplies to Indians who were occupying Wounded Knee. Dwain W. Cummings, a Muskegon osteopath, and Paul Davids of Coopersville, owner of Davids Aviation

146

of Grand Haven, allegedly boarded this Cessna 182 aircraft Tuesday noon, loaded with nine hundred pounds of beans, staples, and other foodstuffs."

On the screen flashed a picture of Paul's neat little red-white-and-blue Cessna parked in its hangar. The voice continued, "Then they took off for Wounded Knee. On the way they were said to have stopped in Nebraska for the night, arriving at the Indian-occupied town early Wednesday morning, where they landed in an empty field. They encountered no federal agents as they unloaded the plane with the aid of several armed Indians. According to unconfirmed sources, Cummings and Davids immediately took off again after unloading, but had to land again to repair the plane's nosegear. The pair arrived back in Grand Haven about five yesterday afternoon. About one-thirty this morning federal agents who had traced the numbers on the plane arrested the two at their homes. They were arraigned today before Federal Magistrate Stephen Karr, who set March 16 as a hearing date and released Cummings and Davids on personal recognizance bond. Neil Welch, chief of the Michigan F.B.I., explained."

The scene shifted to that of Mr. Welch, being interviewed by a dozen eager newsmen, all calling questions to him. He was saying, "The charge as indicated in the federal complaint filed in Rapid City, South Dakota, charges these two men with flying from Grand Haven, Michigan, to Wounded Knee, South Dakota, and bringing them certain supplies, support items, including foodstuffs."

Several of the newsmen asked at once, "Were there explosives?"

"These are food supplies as indicated in the federal complaint," Welch said, "and the other supplies I don't . . . "

Again, the newsmen all babbled, "Did they take explosives?"

Appearing to cut the interview off, Welch said, "I have no further details at this time."

147

The newsmen continued to badger him about explosives, and he finally added, "The charge does not include or preclude explosives. It deals strictly with supplies and foodstuffs."

The television screen again reverted to pictures of Bill working his way through the packed corridors in the federal building, and the announcer continued, "The forty-five-year-old Cummings is part Sioux Indian. He owns a buffalo herd in Stanwood, Michigan, and part of the cargo is said to have been buffalo meat. Neither Cummings, who was clad in moccasins, nor his pilot Davids would comment for reporters. If found guilty of willfully obstructing federal officers in the performance of their duty during a civil disorder, the pair could be sentenced to up to five years in federal prison and a ten thousand dollar fine. And next, the news of sports."

"Explosives!" I blurted out. "What were all those insinuations about explosives?"

Bill shrugged. "They're just digging. Trying to get some news. Boy, I sure looked awful, didn't I?"

A three-day growth of beard could make Norman Vincent Peale look like a desperado, I thought.

Bill groaned, "Well, I'd planned to shower, shave, and go to bed, but now I guess we'll have to stay up for the eleven o'clock news to find out what happens at Wounded Knee after the ultimatum time passes. Even with the two hour time difference, they might know something by eleven. If things blow up out there, we may face some type of murder charge."

We switched television channels to see what another network was saying. The announcer was just finishing, "Lawyers of the duo testified they are reputable citizens, and Magistrate Karr released them on their own promise to appear March 16 at preliminary hearing."

"Did they say anything about my arrest in the paper?" Bill asked the girls.

Beth sighed. "We've been too busy to even think about it." She trotted out to the mailbox and returned with our local evening paper.

The headlines read "Wounded Knee Showdown Due," and beneath the headlines was a large picture of Bill that the newspaper had dredged from its files. In the photograph he was wearing his black high-crowned hat which we call his "Billy Jack hat," and beneath his photo was the sub-headline "Two Area Men Face Charges."

We bunched our heads together trying to read what the article said. "Oh, my gosh," I groaned, "they tell about the F.B.I. getting stuck on our road."

Bill laughed. "Good enough! Maybe they'll fix up our road now. If even the F.B.I. can't get through to get their man . . . I wonder who told the paper about the F.B.I. getting stuck?"

In a small voice I confessed, "I think I did. I've been so upset about these roads!"

The phone continued to ring constantly. Many of the callers were people from the news media, but others were strangers wishing Bill their blessings, or friends voicing concern. Bill disappeared into the bathroom for his long-awaited shower.

As I answered the phone another time, a welcome voice said, "Mom! How's Dad? Is he okay?"

It was Bruce, and obviously he'd heard some news about Bill's arrest.

"Dad's just fine," I assured him. "He's taking a shower right now."

"What happened?" Bruce insisted. "Was he really arrested?"

"Yes, he really was, but he's home now. Where are you, Bruce?"

He was just an hour's drive from home.

"I hate to talk too much on the phone, Bruce," I explained. "Everyone says our phone line may be tapped. Why don't we tell you all about it when you get here?"

An hour later Bruce came in the door, tanned and healthy-looking from his college-boy spring trip to Florida. Over his back he carried the obligatory gift from Florida—a mesh bag full of oranges. Poor Bruce. On any other day he would have entertained us with tales of his adventures in Florida. Instead, he brushed aside all talk of Florida. "I'll tell you about it another time. I just want to know all about Dad and Wounded Knee and what happened."

As Bill described the events of the past three days Bruce hung avidly on every word. Since he was an experienced flier holding a commercial pilot's license, he devoured the tales of the airplane episodes, and especially the precarious landing and take-off at Wounded Knee.

The eleven o'clock news carried no reports of whether there had been a settlement or a clash following the six P.M. deadline for evacuation of Wounded Knee. Our lawyers had indicated that the seriousness of the charges against Bill would be influenced greatly by whatever happened at Wounded Knee. If there were a peaceful settlement, Bill's crime of furnishing food might be considered a minor crime, but if people were hurt or killed out there, he might be charged as an accomplice to murder.

Exhausted as we were, it was difficult to sleep, knowing Bill's future might be decided within the next few hours. During the night persistent reporters continued to telephone and awaken us. Bill dared not leave the phone off the hook for fear a surgical patient might need him. He didn't wish to offend the people of the news media, but it was a struggle for him to keep the irritation out of his voice each time he was awakened.

In the morning we listened to the radio and learned there had been sporadic gunfire during the evening just before an agreed-upon cease fire went into effect. Negotiations were to continue between American Indian Movement leaders and the government again. An Indian had been wounded in the exchange of gunfire, and an ambulance had been allowed to enter Wounded Knee to collect the wounded man.

Little Joe, our tame yearling buffalo, climbed onto the back porch and bunted the door with his head, asking for his morning baby bottles of warm milk.

"Poor Joe," Bill sighed. "I've really neglected him this week. Guess I'd better get out there and give him some milk and attention." Bill put on his tattered red snowmobile suit and prepared three quarts of warm milk from the powdered calf-starter.

While Bill fed Joe, I busied myself clearing up the breakfast dishes and answering the telephone. One call was from the Chippewa Indian Tribal Council, the group we had given buffalo calves. They were outraged over Bill's arrest and wondered what they could do to help. Another call was from a local minister who, although he did not know us, volunteered to gather together at least a dozen local clergymen who would "pack the courtroom" at the hearing March 16. "We wouldn't say anything," he said. "Just don our clerical collars and sit there in a supportive manner."

I thanked him for his spontaneous gesture.

The back door slammed shut, and Bill bellowed, "Pinkie! Come here quick!"

I raced to the back door.

"I don't have enough problems what with being arrested by the F.B.I.!" he cried. "Now this tragedy has to strike our family!"

My heart flopped. Then I noticed the amusement twinkling in his brown eyes. "What happened?" I smiled.

He assumed a funereal expression. "Little Joe has gone gay!"

"Gay?" I didn't understand.

Exasperated, Bill shrugged. "You know, queer, fairy, homosexual. Gay. While I've been away, Joe has gone gay! I dropped a baby bottle. When I bent over to pick it up, Joe jumped on me. He tried to mount me!"

Little Joe's big eyes peered in the back window at us. Bill hugged me in mock fear. "He's after me, Pinkie! Don't let him get me!"

He collapsed laughing, and I shook my head in confusion. It wasn't easy having an ordinary buffalo in your backyard—but a sexually aggressive buffalo!

Smiling, Bill comforted me. "Little Joe's been raised to love people. He hasn't actually gone gay. Jumping on

151

me is his way of showing his affection for me. In his eyes, I'm his mother, and he's so glad to see me back!''

Bill gazed thoughtfully out the window. "I'll sure have to do something to channel his love in another direction. Little Joe is small now, but who wants to be hugged by a two-thousand pound grown-up buffalo?''

"You can expect a change in residence."
—Chinese fortune cookie

Back
on the
Reservation

14 That day following Bill's arrest was a blur of phone calls and the incessant noise from the radio, which we kept turned on, hoping for favorable news from Wounded Knee.

Bill's office nurse called to report that all of his scheduled surgery had been cancelled and transferred to other surgeons. Bill felt let down. Though some doctors who referred surgery to him remained loyal, many were quick to decide that Bill's professional career was ended. They believed it was unseemly for a doctor to get involved in rebellious events. Then, too, word had spread concerning the penalty Bill would suffer if convicted of this felony of aiding the Indians—five years in federal prison, and/or a ten thousand dollar fine. Aside from this severe punishment, Bill would suffer an additional heartbreak. If a doctor is convicted of a felony, he automatically loses his license to practice medicine, permanently. Many of the local doctors already had written him off as an ex-physician.

"Oh, well," Bill sighed, "I can't really take on any heavy surgical cases right now, since I don't know what will happen with the extradition hearing next week. Maybe at its conclusion, agents will handcuff me and take me off to South Dakota."

We would have to live in limbo for awhile.

Late in the afternoon the doorbell rang, and one of our neighbors stood on our porch, laughing, and waving the afternoon paper. "Did you see the paper, Doc? They're going to pave our road right up to your house. They must figure if the F.B.I. wants to come back in and get you, they don't want to get stuck again."

The newspaper showed a large picture of a very muddy road. The caption beneath explained that this was the section of Brooks Road where the vehicle of the F.B.I. agents got stuck on their way to arrest Dr. Cummings.

Bill chuckled. "Well, I've done my bit for our muddy road cause. Next time our road goes out, it's your turn."

"Have you seen all the heavy equipment working up the road?" the neighbor asked.

Since we hadn't left the house all day, we weren't aware of the massive effort one-half mile up the road in that notorious spot "where the F.B.I. got stuck." Out in our front yard we could hear the distant roar of earth-movers, bulldozers, and roadgraders. Huge dumptrucks were disgorging loads of gravel onto low spots. The road commission suddenly had become motivated to fix up our road and open it to traffic.

"It's ironic, isn't it?" Bill smiled grimly. "Remember my half-hour phone conversation with the road commissioner, pleading with him to just bring in a couple loads of gravel? He said nothing would help until the frost went out of the ground." That conversation had occurred just last Monday evening, the same evening the Indians called asking Bill to get food to Wounded Knee.

Soon a constant stream of cars bearing the curious battled their way through the ruts and mire. The sightseers must have been very curious to risk losing their mufflers and getting stuck just to see the infamous road, or see the home where "that buffalo doctor lives." We closed our draperies and huddled in the house wretchedly.

As twilight approached, Bill stepped out into the

backyard to give Little Joe his bedtime bottles of warm milk. Again, Joe leaped upon Bill in his ridiculous buffalo hug.

When the feeding and fondling was over, Bill came back in the house. "I wonder," he said thoughtfully. "Maybe we're going to have to castrate Joe. I think I'll call Don Hight to find out when he castrated his Buffalo Bill."

Don, the rancher in South Dakota whom Bill called the night before he flew to Wounded Knee, had a trained eighteen-year-old buffalo named "Bill." Don led his Buffalo Bill around on a little chain and took him to gala events such as supermarket grand openings and conventions.

After placing the long distance call to South Dakota, Bill glanced at me uneasily. "Don may be pretty mad at me for going out to Wounded Knee."

However, Don greeted Bill cheerily. "Hiya, Doc. How you doin'? We've been reading' about you here in the papers, and watchin' you on TV."

"I was afraid of that," Bill laughed. "Right now I need some advice about how to deal with an amorous buffalo. My tame yearling bull, Little Joe, is so glad to see me back that he keeps trying to mount me."

Don hooted. "No wonder! You've still got that squaw scent on ya," he laughed.

"Seriously," Bill stifled a laugh, "I wonder if I should make a steer out of him. When did you castrate old Bill?"

"When he was about one-hour old. Right when I took him away from his mother."

"Boy, I'm about a year late, then, aren't I?" Bill thought this over. He'd put off castrating Little Joe, partly because he preferred seeing an animal remain in its natural state, and partly because he wanted Joe's horns to grow into well-shaped bull's horns. If castrated before maturity, a buffalo bull develops horns which look like a buffalo cow's.

"Say, Doc," Don spoke up. "They're spelling your name right in our newspapers, and on television they're calling you The Buffalo Doctor. But there's something I think you ought to know. Right after the news reports telling about The Buffalo Doctor, they keep coming on with a report of how short we are of doctors out here in our federal penitentiary."

Bill burst out laughing. "Thanks a lot, Don. You sleep well tonight, too."

"Here's some advice for you, Doc," Don went on. "When you come out to Deadwood for your trial, don't waste your money buyin' a round trip ticket. You know Deadwood's been a hangin' town for a hundred years. People out here are riled up enough about our own Indians, to say nothing about you troublemakers from outside comin' in and stirrin' things up worse."

Tired as we were, Bill and I couldn't sleep. We discovered that being arrested by the F.B.I. is a very stressful upheaval. Half the night we sat up talking, debating future possibilities, and trying to assimilate our new situation. Toward dawn we dozed for a couple hours of restless, dream-filled sleep.

The next day sightseeing cars continued to struggle down our treacherous road. Some called Indian war whoops, and hollered, "Hey, Chief!" Some of the bolder curiosity-seekers leaned from their car windows and pointed, "That's where he lives! Where are the buffalo? See the windsock? That's for the airplane he used!"

Behind our barn fluttered an eight-foot long flaming orange windsock bearing the huge letters, "SHELL." But the gaudy windsock meant "landing field" to the onlookers, and they assumed our pasture was the takeoff point for the Wounded Knee airlift. Of course, the windsock had nothing to do with Bill. It was set up by Bruce for his guidance in landing his tail-wheel Champ.

When a car pulled into our driveway, I groaned, believing it to be a sightseer bolder than those who merely drove by or parked in front of our home. With relief I saw that it was friends of ours from central Michigan, Russell and Annette Kirk. On their car radio they had heard of Bill's arrest, and they came to offer their support and ad-

156

vice. Russell Kirk is a man of letters, a political historian, lecturer, and nationally-syndicated columnist, a brilliant man. We welcomed any advice he might give.

Bill related to him the events of the past few days, then added, "Say, Russell, would you like to meet Paul, the pilot? Let's go out to dinner together."

We picked up Paul at his hangar and went to a nearby Chinese restaurant. As we were being shown to our large table I had the distinct sensation that the whole dining room was staring at us. Of course, there are eight of us, I told myself, and I suppose a large group is bound to be conspicuous. In a few minutes, however, the waitress delivered a note to Bill. The note said, "Buffalo Doctor. Can I have your autograph? Thanks. The cook."

As we dined on Chinese food, our conversation centered on Indian affairs and problems. We discussed ways in which Indians are kept economically disadvantaged.

On the Pine Ridge Reservation, where Wounded Knee is located, a white farmer will lease land from an Indian for one year for about five dollars an acre. Then the white farmer puts this land into the federally-subsidized soil bank and receives fifteen dollars per acre from the government. The Indians can't put their land in the soil bank because the government says it doesn't pay subsidies on trust land. In 1972 seventeen farmers made eighteen thousand dollars or more just from subsidies of these lands. This soil bank program is a government program to keep certain lands idle, out of production, so all the rancher has to do is give the Indians a check for five dollars an acre for his lease, and the government will give the rancher a check for fifteen dollars an acre for not doing anything with the land. The rancher makes ten dollars an acre on the Indians' land without doing any work.

On this same reservation the Holy Rosary Church owns eighteen square miles of land, which is more than any Indian landowner has. Nine thousand people on the reservation own no land at all.

We talked about the high infant mortality rate among Indians, which is thirty percent higher than the national rate. On some reservations infant mortality is one hundred out of every one thousand births, almost twice the mortality rate of our worst ghettoes and four times that of white babies.

"We all know bureaucracy can be terribly wasteful," I added, "but I just read a report that was a real eye-opener. In 1970 federal funds allocated to Indians on reservations totalled four hundred sixty million dollars. This money came mostly from the Bureau of Indian Affairs, the Office of Economic Opportunity, and Health, Education and Welfare. If this money were given directly to the Indians, each family would receive five thousand six hundred dollars annually. However, the actual yearly income of a reservation family is one thousand five hundred dollars, and this includes money they make from land leases, jobs, and pensions. By the time that four hundred sixty million dollars filters down through the bureaucratic structures, there isn't much left for the Indian."

"The Indians just don't have any political clout," Bill explained. "There aren't enough Indians to make a significant voting bloc. Other minorities can retaliate against political indifference by trooping in numbers to the voting booth, but the Indian people are too scattered and too few to be fearsome to politicians. It's just very easy to take advantage of Indians.

"The Crow Indians losing their buffalo is an example of this," Bill continued. "I didn't hear about this until three years after it happened, and, of course, when I heard about it, I was furious. But the dirty deed by the government bureaucrats already had been accomplished, and there was nothing I could do about it. For twenty-eight years the Crow Indians in Montana had owned their own buffalo herd, which grazed in a four thousand acre pasture in the Big Horn Mountains of the reservation. The Crows were very proud of their buffalo, which represented the old ways of their people. Then one day the Crows were notified by the federal government that their buffalo herd was contaminated with brucellosis. The ranchers surrounding the Crow Reservation had registered complaints to the Department of Agriculture. The Department of Agriculture determined that the herd of sixty buffalo had to be destroyed. The Bureau of Indian Affairs was quick to cooperate with the Department of Agriculture, since the B.I.A. always has been insensitive to the suffering it causes the people it rules. There was no consideration of the magnitude of the problems of brucellosis. The herd simply was destroyed. The ranchers paid the B.I.A. one dollar sixty cents an acre for the buffalo grazing land, and the Crows despondently sank deeper into poverty.

"At the same time that the Crows' herd was destroyed, there were herds on private ranches throughout the West and in our parks which also were thought to be contaminated herds. The ranchers and the parks wouldn't permit the Department of Agriculture to go in and test and destroy the herds. Instead, with political pull and influence, the ranchers kept the Department of Agriculture away, while the ranchers privately tested and vaccinated their herds. After several years the ranchers were able to show evidence that their herds either were vaccinated or brucellosis-free. The ridiculousness of this brucellosis problem as related to buffalo is demonstrated by the fact that the deer, the elk, and the rabbits carry brucellosis. Unless the Department of Agriculture is going to go out and vaccinate every rabbit, every deer, and every elk, they aren't going to be able to wipe out brucellosis in the West."

From across the table, dark-haired Annette spoke up. "It just seems incredible that the government would go in and kill all those buffalo! Does this sort of thing happen often?"

Bill picked at his food. "There was a lot of it in Dakota when I was a kid. I remember when my family had three cows. Then one day the government men came and looked over our cows. They said they were diseased and would have to be shot. When the government men shot the three cows, they were careful not to let my dad bleed the animals. If animals aren't bled, the meat is no good. They dug a deep pit, shoved the cows in, and covered them with dirt. The ten of us kids stood there and watched in bewilderment, all the time our empty stomachs growling with hunger.''

"Were those three cows all the animals you had?" Annette asked.

"We had three pigs and four goats left," Bill answered. "We were what you would call 'poor.' In fact, we figured we were too poor to get on relief. In those days you had to be either richer than we were or have political pull to get on government relief rolls. That's why, as a kid, I had to be a slop collector. We had to have food for our pigs and goats. Some of the farmers near Rosholt let us go through their fields to gather the ears of corn they'd missed while picking corn, and we used that to feed the livestock, but it wasn't enough. My dad gave me the chore of calling daily at five or six places in Rosholt to collect slop for the pigs. I had a little slop wagon which I pulled. How I detested having people see me pulling my slop wagon around the village! But the pigs had to have food. My dog, Sport, always accompanied me on my daily rounds. I remember one bleak winter we acquired a new prize customer on our slop collection route—the North Star Hotel. The hotel had the best slop in town. Then, too, Mrs. Rose at the hotel was always very kind to me. She often treated me to a freshly-baked, warm cookie. The slop from the hotel usually contained many partially-eaten pork chops and steaks, which I'd dig out and give to Sport. I told my mother about these delicious-looking, discarded pieces of meat. Over and over again she warned me not to eat any food from the slop pails. She threatened a whipping if I did.

"I remember one bitterly cold day when I saw two pork chops perched on top of the hotel's five gallon slop can. The pork chops weren't covered with coffee grounds. I didn't see why Sport should get all that good stuff for himself. That day, Sport and I hid behind the outdoor three-hole privy and dined together.''

We all laughed over Bill's confession of his boyhood relapse to temptation; still, it was sad to think a young boy could be so hungry for meat that he'd eat meat scraps from garbage.

Bill continued his reminiscing. "You know, I learned many things on my slop collection route. One of the homes on my route always produced a five gallon can completely full because they used it for their toilet and for their soapy dishwater. I complained to Dad that their slop was no good to feed the pigs, and I didn't want to pick it up. My Dad told me I had to collect it anyway because the woman was a widow and her two fat daughters were too lazy to help her. Dad said for me to keep this unclean slop in a separate can and dump it alongside the road before I got home to the barn.

"Of course, using a pail for a toilet wasn't unusual during our Dakota winters. I know my family did when it was too cold to go out to the privy. We had a five gallon pail that the tar for our roof came in, and this was our toilet when the blizzards roared and the temperature plunged. Sometimes when I walked around town on my slop route a few days after a heavy snow, I noticed that in many backyards there was no path made out to the privy. I knew those people had the same sort of indoor toilet as my family did. These makeshift indoor toilets were usually emptied at night on the family garden, carefully dumped in the area which would grow peas and beans, never where they would plant carrots, radishes, or potatoes.

"One day I got a new customer, some real fancy people who had just moved to town. The husband worked in the farm implement store, and the wife referred to slop as "garbage." I told the lady that she didn't have to give me any garbage. All I wanted was slop for my pigs. She explained to me that garbage was the same thing as slop, and that my pigs would enjoy garbage just as much. My terrible humiliation over being a slop collector was eased. I was really coming up in the world. Now I collected garbage. I didn't have to haul that darn old slop anymore."

"Didn't you ever get any government assistance?" Annette asked.

Bill made a wry face. "One year towards spring my

161

Dad went to Sisseton and made friends with the people there. As a result, we got on relief, and we were eligible to get all that government food that relief people got. My mother always sent me to the general store to pick up the relief food because she didn't want to go. Usually, each week, we got one grapefruit apiece. But it was so disappointing. Many times the grapefruit had been frozen. They were dark, rotten, and inedible. Even as a little boy I always thought it was funny that the grapefruit which were sold in the same store weren't spoiled, and all the grapefruit came in on the same truck. I asked the store owner if he had any trouble keeping the government grapefruit and the "for sale" grapefruit separate. He told me, 'when you get something free, you can't expect it to be as good as if you pay for it.'

"Another kind of relief food we got was powdered milk, which I hated since I'd always had fresh whole milk from our cow. This powdered milk came in a bag. Frequently it had gotten wet, and by the time we got it, the powder was hard as stone and smelled sour. Most of the powdered milk was fed to our pigs or to Sport.

"One time when I was picking up relief food at the general store, I remembered I'd heard that the store owner's son had been accepted in the F.B.I. I told the owner that he must be very proud to have a son working for the F.B.I., and that I'd like to do something like that someday. He patted me on the head, and said, 'It's very hard to get to work for the F.B.I. You have to be a special type of person. But if you're a good Christian, work hard, don't steal, and are honest, someday your parents will be proud of you, too.'"

When we had finished eating, the little chinese waitress passed a tray of fortune cookies. All the fortunes were bland and innocuous until Bill opened his. The tiny scrap of paper predicted ominously, "You can expect a change in residence." We all laughed heartily. The thought of Bill residing in a federal penitentiary was so unthinkable that it seemed ridiculously funny.

162

*"You whites assumed we were savages.
You didn't understand our prayers. You didn't
try to understand. When we sang our praises
to the sun or moon or wind, you said we were
worshipping idols. Without understanding, you
condemned us as lost souls just because our form
of worship was different from yours."*
—Walking Buffalo, 1858

•

When the Choke- cherries Ripen

15 The Sunday morning papers brought us heartening news. The headlines read "Siege Ends at Wounded Knee," "U.S. Ends Wounded Knee Blockade."

The three hundred federal marshals and F.B.I. agents who had been encircling the village for nearly two weeks had been withdrawn. The chief U.S. marshal said, "The situation is back to normal for all practical purposes."

Our spirits soared. The confrontation had ended without anyone being killed or seriously injured. Much of our uneasiness evaporated and with light hearts we went about our tasks that Sunday, blissfully unaware that the short-lived peace had ended.

That evening a friend called, reporting the bad news. "Haven't you heard?" he said. "The Indians and F.B.I. agents exchanged gunfire, and an F.B.I. agent was shot."

Gloom dropped upon our home. We turned on radio and television, trying to learn details. Newsmen reported that about five miles west of Wounded Knee, F.B.I. agents had spotted the mud-daubed van, called a "tank" by the Indians, returning to Wounded Knee. The agents pursued the van, and there was an exchange of gunfire. Each side claimed the other fired first. One of the agents was

163

wounded in the right arm. A newscaster reported there were six bullet holes in the windshield of the F.B.I. car, apparently made by an agent firing through his own windshield. The fleeing Indians made it safely to the village, where they displayed their bullet-riddled "tank" to newsmen. A bullet hole punctured the passenger side of the windshield, and the rear panel windows had been shattered.

The following day news reports announced that road-blocks were being restored after the forty-eight hour moratorium. The Justice Department complained that the Indians had used their free access to Wounded Knee to replenish ammunition and weapons. The chief of the U.S. marshals told newsmen, "I'm sure as hell planning on changing their lifestyle, if that means starving, if it means being cold, not being able to read the evening paper, not being able to watch television, it means not being able to make telephone calls, it means not being able to get soap to wash your clothes."

The Indians tittered over this pronouncement. The Justice Department might think it was imposing a new life style, but the Indians accepted these inconveniences as the ordinary way of life on a reservation. On an Indian reservation, being cold and hungry in the wintertime is expected.

The Justice Department wanted to end the whole thing. They were uneasy over bringing about another Wounded Knee massacre, yet rumors spread among the reporters that the paratroopers of the 82nd Airborne were on the alert for action. Always, armed intervention was an awesome possibility.

Late Monday morning a lady named Pauline phoned. She explained that we didn't know her, and she didn't know us, but that she felt a tremendous calling to do something to help the doctor. "He performed a humanitarian act, and I think it's just terrible how he's being treated! I plan to organize a petition drive," she went on, "to request the government to drop charges against Dr. Cummings and Mr. Davids. I have an appointment with a lawyer this afternoon, and he's offered to donate his time and advice. I hesitated to go ahead without your permission. May I go ahead? Since your removal hearing is just four days off, I have to hurry on this," she said.

Gratefully, we mumbled our permission and our thanks.

Bill checked with our lawyer to make sure he wouldn't get in hotter water if citizens conducted a petition drive. Neal advised that petitions wouldn't do any harm, but unless they gathered at least three thousand names, petitions neither would draw attention nor be of any influence.

With the removal hearing for Bill and Paul scheduled in federal district court on Friday, we grew more nervous and uneasy as the time approached. At the close of the hearing, would they take Bill off to South Dakota in handcuffs? Would they put him in jail? Our life beyond Friday seemed a dark chasm.

Tuesday afternoon our lawyer called. His usually businesslike voice seemed tinged with humor. "I received a phone call from Chicago a few minutes ago. It seems they didn't wish to call your house because they suspected your line was tapped. At any rate, they left their number, and I'm supposed to return their call after talking with you. They would like The Buffalo Doctor to fly another load of food to Wounded Knee."

There was a long silence. I couldn't believe what he'd said. "You've got to be kidding!"

"No," Neal chuckled. "I think they're quite serious."

I felt a hot wave of irritation. Bill was in trouble over his eyeballs and they wanted him to repeat that dangerous trip with heaven knows what criminal consequences. "Well, of course it's unthinkable," I snapped.

"Absolutely, it isn't to be considered," Neal answered calmly. "But I do think we owe them the courtesy of a reply. Would you like me to take care of it? I'll thank them for their interest but explain that it's legally impossible."

"Yes, why don't you handle it," I agreed. I knew that

I wouldn't be gracious about their wanting to place Bill in double jeopardy.

Each phone call seemed to present a new problem, and my brain grew numb from trying to make instant decisions. One sweet old lady with an aged, shaky voice called to say that she had knit a whole boxful of mittens. She wondered if Bill would fly them out to the Indians. "I'd bring the mittens over to your house," she said, "but I saw in the paper that your road is impassable, and I doubt if I can get through to your house."

I explained that Bill wouldn't be able to fly to Wounded Knee again, that he had to appear in federal court on Friday.

Pauline called to say that she had gotten petitions printed and had obtained thirty-four volunteers to distribute the petitions to area businesses. Her peppery voice bubbled with enthusiasm. "Just everyone wants to sign these petitions. You'd be proud to know how many friends you have and how much sympathy there is for the Indian cause."

Wednesday evening, news commentators said that a continuing violent blizzard at Wounded Knee had quieted aggressions there. Everyone was busy just surviving. It was reported that the federal grand jury meeting in Sioux Falls, South Dakota, had announced indictments of thirty-one persons in connection with Wounded Knee.

Bill and I exchanged glances, wondering if he and Paul were among those thirty-one. Within an hour Neal telephoned. He'd just talked with the South Dakota authorities. The grand jury had indicted Bill and Paul.

Neither Bill nor I knew exactly what being "indicted by the grand jury" meant, but it sounded frighteningly serious, something that was done to big spies and gangsters.

Late Thursday evening Pauline called to tell us about the progress of the petition drive. Breathlessly, she began, "Mrs. Cummings, I just have to tell you about this marvelous experience we just had. We thought it might help you and the doctor get through the night, knowing that The Lord definitely is on your side."

She spoke to one of the voices murmuring in the background, and then continued. "Forgive me for the interruption, but we're so busy down here. I think we'll be up most of the night counting signatures. I think we have about five thousand signatures already, and in just three days' time! Isn't that nearly a miracle?"

I was amazed that so many people had signed the petition asking that charges be dropped. "I just don't know how you did it, Pauline," I said.

"Well, The Lord made it possible. But I have to share our experience with you. Do you have a minute so I can tell you what happened this evening?"

Of course, I wanted to know.

Pauline explained that they were gathered in a home near the center of the city, thinking it would be a convenient, central place for people to pick up and deliver petitions. Out on the white picket fence in front of the home they had placed a crudely-lettered sign saying "Petition Headquarters, Cummings-Davids Cause," to direct people to the proper place.

"Well," she said, "this afternoon we ran out of petitions, and people were coming to the house wanting additional blank petitions for signatures. I drove over to the printer's to get another one hundred copies. It took all the money I had so I didn't have a penny to put in the parking meter. When I came out of the printer's, I'd gotten a parking ticket.

"By this evening those one hundred petitions were gone, and people were arriving to get more. We didn't want to turn them away empty-handed. We all scraped around in our purses and pockets to see if we could collect five dollars and thirty cents, the price for another one hundred petitions. No one had any money. We were standing there in the kitchen, and I said to one of my friends, 'I think we'd better pray.' Now, I'm not a complicated woman, and I pray very simply. I just talk to The Lord, and he always seems to let me know what I should do. So I just told The Lord about our problem. I said, 'Lord, you know our predicament. We need some money in a hurry to get some more petitions. We need five dollars and thirty cents, and oh, yes, a penny for the parking meter. Amen.'

"No sooner had I said 'Amen' than there was a knocking at the door. We groaned because we figured it was another person wanting a blank petition, which we didn't have. Instead, it was a very old, crippled lady, all bent over, holding her arm in a twisted position. She explained that she was too old and too crippled to climb stairways and circulate petitions, but that she wanted to do something. 'Maybe you can find a use for this,' she said, thrusting her gnarled fist toward me. Into my hand she pressed two crumpled dollar bills and a pile of sweaty change. I tried to give her back the money, protesting, 'Oh, we don't want to take your last bit of money.' Very indignantly, this little old lady said, 'I'm not poor. I've got money in the bank. This is just all I could find around the house. God bless you.' And with that, she limped off.

"I took the money into the kitchen, and the other ladies crowded around. I dumped the two crumpled bills and the handful of moist change on the kitchen table, and we began to count the coins. Would you believe what it came to? Exactly five dollars and thirty-one cents! My prayer had been answered!"

As Pauline finished relating this experience, goose bumps rose on my arms. It was very strange. How could one explain it? It was either a very unlikely coincidence, or a prayer had been answered.

"It just makes me shiver," I said, my voice nearly a whisper.

"Yes, it does, doesn't it?" Pauline agreed. She said that while one of the women poured coffee for those waiting for petitions, she hurried to the printer's with the five dollars and thirty-one cents and returned in fifteen minutes with one hundred more blank petitions. "When I returned, many of the workers there were marvelling even yet over the unforgettable demonstration of the power of prayer."

168

As I related this experience to Bill, we both felt very humble. So many people were devoting their time, energy, and money to work for what they believed in, namely that an innocent act was being punished unjustly.

Nowadays, religious organizations and individuals seem to be especially sympathetic to Indians and their problems, but this wasn't always so. Until very recently the Christian world looked with disfavor upon the Indians' religious beliefs and social customs.

Missionaries who first came into contact with the Indian religious leader, the medicine man, were appalled and horrified. They looked upon the medicine man's feats as works of the devil, and they set out to obliterate all signs of Indian religion, and convert the tribes to Christianity. The early missionaries worked hard to teach the Ten Commandments, the various Creeds, and nineteenth century hymns. When the Indians had memorized these outward signs of religion, the churchworkers were relieved. They believed they had saved the Indians from barbaric paganism and brought them to true spirituality. They cajoled converted Indian men into cutting off their long black hair by persuading them that to be a good Christian, they must have short hair. How confused those barbered Indians must have become when they saw pictures of Christ and His Disciples with their long, flowing locks! Missionaries never had much success in trying to teach the Indians the meaning of "giving," which, of course, meant "giving to the church." An integral part of Indian religion had always been sharing. Among Indians it is a deeply ingrained tradition to share what you have with others. The churches wanted the Indian to put his donation into the collection plate and let the church decide who was in need of aid, but this was not the Indian way. Much of the Indian religion is based upon inter-personal relationships. Each member of Indian society has a unique, respected position, and sharing goods and caring for others who need care are basic tenets of Indian life. The Indians had developed a society in which they needed no locks on doors, no jails or poorhouse, and no orphanages. These were a people who watched out for each other. They *were* their brother's keeper.

Bill explained The Great Spirit as the Divine Power that can influence all things. The Great Spirit is made up of all spirits of all things. This places a personal obligation on each individual to develop good in his spirit, for if the majority of spirits that go into The Great Spirit are bad spirits, The Great Spirit will exert a bad influence.

The Sacred Hoop of the Sioux is the belief that when one dies, his spirit returns to Mother Earth as a part of the Great Spirit. The body nourishes the earth and makes the grass grow. The Sun brings spirit out of the earth through grass and the various plants. The buffalo take in spirit by eating the vegetation. The Sioux receives the same spirit from the buffalo when he eats the buffalo. Since the buffalo carries spirit from the ancestors, the Indian prays to the buffalo for forgiveness when he kills him. The Indian is reverent toward Mother Earth, the plants, and the buffalo, for they contain the spirits of his ancestors. When death comes, he will lie down on the earth, and the grass will cover him over like a warm blanket. His spirit will join his ancestors.

In their eagerness to convert Indians to Christianity, the early missionaries attacked with zeal all reminders of Indian civilization. They wanted to change the Indian into a dark-skinned white person. In this determination they were joined by the United States government.

Historically, white civilization has attacked the Indian in two ways. First, white invaders fought the Indian physically until they either had annihilated him or driven him, powerless, to specified reservations. For the final death blow, the government set out to destroy the surviving Indians' sense of being Indian. The Department of the Interior and the Department of the Army were issued orders to destroy every symbol of the Indian religion. Religious relics, medicine bundles, and sacred pipes were demolished, and the practice of any sort of Indian religion was prohibited. Medicine men, who were the religious leaders, were watched closely, and jailed if they practiced old ceremonies.

Until very recent years the Indian people actually have been denied freedom of religion, although this is a right guaranteed to them by our United States Constitution. The law which prohibited Indians from practicing their traditional religion was called the Indian Offenses Act and was sponsored and enforced by the Bureau of Indian Affairs. The Act disregarded our constitutional right of freedom to practice religion. Even so, the B.I.A. enforced it. Besides forbidding the old traditional Sioux religion, this Indian Offenses Act also prohibited the rites of the Native American Church, which is a combination of Indian and Christian beliefs. The penalty for practicing either religion was up to six months in jail or a fine of three hundred sixty dollars.

The Indian Offenses Act is no longer enforced, and the Indians may practice the religion of their choice. The Native American Church has become very popular. One Indian in four is a member of the Native American Church, and it is the largest single denomination on many reservations.

The ancient, traditional religion also has experienced a strong revival. If the Indian people had been a very literate people, depending upon books and writings to disseminate their religious beliefs, their traditional religion might have been squelched and completely forgotten. However, because their teachings always have been handed down by word of mouth, medicine men secretly continued to pass on knowledge and customs during that half-century when it was forbidden.

One ceremony which was forbidden, but now is being practiced openly is the Sun Dance, one of the oldest and most significant rituals of the Sioux. During the years when it was outlawed by white authorities, some traditional Indians continued to hold small secret ceremonies, risking jail in doing so. The Sun Dance was a symbol of union to the Sioux Nations. Many bands assembled joyously for this annual ritual. White authorities always feared having large groups of Indians assemble, and perhaps for this reason, the Sun Dance especially was suppressed.

As the Sioux practice the Sun Dance, it is a great feast, a prayer, and a sacrifice. Non-Indians misunderstand its meaning, believing it to be an initiation into manhood, which is not so. It is a personal ordeal in which the participant hopes to gain insight by vision, and by his sacrifice, help his people.

Bill became spiritually involved from afar in a Sun Dance procedure when a personal friend about his own age decided to do his first Sun Dance. With solemn honor old medicine men bear the scars of many Sun Dances. However, a medicine man's first Sun Dance is a powerful test of his spiritual strength. He must know his spirit well, for if his spirit weakens, he will die. Bill knew these ancient spiritual precepts, as did his medicine man friend, Selo Black Crow. Even though these ancient precepts never are verbalized, Indian children learn them before they can remember. To survive the Sun Dance ceremony, Black Crow's spiritual strength must be based on the Old Ways.

When Bill learned of Black Crow's decision to do the Sun Dance, Bill's first reaction was to stock his van with intravenous fluids and medical supplies and travel west to the ceremonial site. If Bill were parked there when his friend's time came, he could save Black Crow's life. However, he knew this could not be.

At the time of his vision, Black Crow would go into a coma caused by dehydration and physical suffering. If Bill were to administer intravenous fluids and drugs to bring Black Crow out of his coma, the medicine man would not get his vision. His spirit would be broken, and he would die in spite of any medications Bill used.

The Indian understands that his physical strength, his endurance, his entire state of health, are dependent directly upon his spiritual strength. Because he knows the importance of a strong spirit, the Indian's religion is a daily way of life. There is no room for hypocrisy.

The foundation of the Indians' spiritual strength is integrity, crucial above all else. The ancient precepts are:

INTEGRITY creates SPIRIT
HUMILITY creates STRENGTH
KINDNESS creates HONOR
HONESTY creates ACCURACY
EXERCISE creates HEALTH

Those familiar with the Old Ways know that the final precept which would determine whether Black Crow lived or died was: INTEGRITY CREATES SPIRIT. Black Crow would have to depend solely on his spirit to bring him out of the coma, which surely must come.

In the months before the time when the chokecherries ripen Black Crow prepared himself by testing his spirit daily. Alone, he would go to an isolated spot to meditate and pray to the Great Spirit. Again and again he went over in his mind the demanding conditions of the Sun Dance.

First, another medicine man would take Black Crow to the Sacred Place high in the Paha Sapa, The Black Hills, where Black Crow would be left in the vision pit, naked except for his blanket. There he would remain for four days and four nights with nothing to eat or drink. At the end of this time the medicine man would come for Black Crow and take him to the ceremonial place. The skin over Black Crow's heart would be pierced with eagles' claws, or incisions made with tree branches inserted through the skin.

Then would come Black Crow's time of prayer and struggle. He must pull against his tether to tear the flesh on his chest and free himself from the bondage. Even though dehydrated, weak, and stiff from four days in the vision pit, Black Crow must conquer the piercing and free himself from the tether without responding to the pain. This would take hours, sometimes days. When free, Black Crow would be given only bitter-sweet chokecherry juice to regain his strength.

The Sun Dance is a very "Indian" ceremony and difficult for outsiders to understand. Once, when an Indian was explaining the Sun Dance to me, I shuddered and commented that it sounded like a gruesome, barbaric ceremony.

The Indian smiled and shrugged. "Christians pray to Jesus, who was nailed to a cross for the sake of his people," he said. "We don't call you Christians 'uncivilized' for believing this. We Indians believe in the redeeming qualities of suffering, just as you Christians do, but there is one big difference. Christians believe in the suffering of someone else who lived long ago and far away. We believe that each of us must suffer ourselves. You talk much of the crucifixion; we have our Sun Dance."

In the old days before it was forbidden, the Sun Dance was a grand gathering of Plains Indians. Held at the time when the chokecherries ripen, the earth was fruitful, and hearts were glad. This occasion was a happy reunion of old friends and relatives. It was a marvelous opportunity for boys and girls to meet, and many a long marriage had its beginning at this ceremonial gathering.

During the years when the practice of Indian religion was forbidden, only a handful of faithful traditionalists continued the Sun Dance in secret. Since Wounded Knee 1973 the Indians practice the religion more openly in spite of the Indian Offenses Act. Indians flock to the annual Sun Dance ceremonies, eager to learn about their lost heritage.

After years of being ashamed of being Indian, present-day Indians are asserting a sense of pride over being Indian. They wear buttons and T-shirts proclaiming, "Indian and Proud," and "Red is Beautiful." They delight in reviving their old traditional ways. They are defying the churches and missionaries who said, "Our way is the only right way. You must learn our ways." Typical is a sign erected over one Indian mission school by zealous church people. The sign warned: "Tradition is the enemy of progress."

174

"So many people want to be Indian," a tribal chairman commented to us once. "At least people from the East and those who really don't know many Indians." He shook his head and sighed. "For instance, two years ago a nice young man came here from New York City to be a teacher in our high school. He's an Italian fellow, with a very Italian surname. After he'd been here a year he began calling himself Tony White Feather, never using his Italian name. We just grinned and figured if it made him happy to have an Indian name, it didn't hurt us any. But last week he became ill and had to enter the Public Health Service hospital here. He signed himself in as one-quarter Indian blood, which allows him to receive free medical care. Now this scares me, and I'm going to have to go to the hospital and talk to Tony. I'm sure he doesn't realize it, but he's defrauding the United States government by representing himself as one-quarter Indian, and he could get into legal difficulty."

So many people claim to be part Indian. One gets the idea that everyone loves Indians. Conservatives usually have accepted Indians because they are docile and don't move into all-white neighborhoods. Liberals like the Indian because he is the most oppressed of all people. Revolutionaries looked toward the Indian people to furnish them with fellow angry militants. Ecologists love the Indian as part of the ecosystem.

People living far from large concentrations of Indian population can't imagine that there is prejudice and hatred of Indian people. Anti-Indian feeling grows steadily as one nears an Indian reservation or an inner-city Indian ghetto. In our society it seems that antagonism toward a minority group grows in relation to the number and power of that minority group.

I was first introduced to the hostility of white people toward Indians several years ago on the Sisseton Indian Reservation in South Dakota, where Bill was raised. It was in the late 1950's when Bill took me and the children back to see his birthplace. Toward evening we grew hungry and

175

sought out a restaurant. It was a very ordinary, truck-stop sort of cafe. We seated ourselves at the oilcloth-covered table. When the middle-aged waitress approached our table, Bill greeted her. "Good evening. Is this a pretty good place to eat?" he smiled.

"Oh, yes, sir," she replied. "It's a very good place. We use separate dishes for Indians and whites."

I couldn't believe what I'd heard. Quickly, I ordered sandwiches for the children and myself. With tight lips Bill placed his order, and as the waitress turned to go, Bill added quietly, "Be sure to use the Indian plates for my food. I'm part Indian."

Later we were able to laugh about it, such a ridiculous, foolish situation. But it is a memory we can't forget, and there's that nagging suspicion that even now there may be restaurants who boast of using separate dishes for Indians and whites.

Most of us have read or heard those often-quoted, infamous words of General Sheridan: "The only good Indians I ever saw were dead." But few white people imagine that Indians have a counterpart saying which goes: "A good white man has yet to be born."

Until recent times and the coming of television, reservation Indians had little contact with white civilization. They met white people only as dealers in pawn shops, used cars, and whiskey. These contacts did nothing to improve the white man's image in the minds of reservation Indians. Their other meeting with the white world was with Christian missionaries and teachers. The Indians listened politely to the Christian teachings, but it was the acts of Christians which appalled them. Christians believed in and practiced the beating of children. Indians never spanked or whipped their children. They enticed them with trust and patience to learn what they had to know. Indians could not understand a religion which preached peace, love, and kindness, and yet condoned beating children. When Indian children entered the mission schools, they were bewildered when their hands were beaten with rubber hoses by their Christian teachers.

For generations the Indian people have suffered stoically and silently. Now the spark of defiance and pride has been kindled. The Indian people say, "We have been listening to you white people for three hundred years. Now it's your turn to listen to us."

*"Man's capacity for justice
makes democracy possible, but man's inclination
to injustice makes democracy necessary."*
    —Reinhold Niebuhr, 1944

A Day in Court

16 On the morning of the court hearing Bill went to the hospital to see his patients. When he returned home he wore in his lapel a fresh white carnation, a gift from a patient, "For luck."

None of us had any appetite for lunch. We drove to Grand Haven where we were to pick up Tom and Neal, our lawyers. When Tom climbed into our station wagon he explained that Neal already had gone to the federal building. An hour before, Neal had received a telephone call requesting his presence at a pre-hearing conference there.

We parked in the underground parking ramp beside the federal building. I gave hasty instructions to the girls. "Stick together with Dad and me. Follow us close, as there may be a crowd, and don't get separated."

In front of the federal building stood dozens of Indian people, some carrying placards. As we approached, none of them acknowledged our presence. They acted as if they didn't know us because they didn't wish to complicate our court case or intimidate us. This is the Indian way. We were concerned that the Indians might be cited for contempt of court for demonstrating on the grounds of a federal building. One Indian youth wearing a black "Billy

Jack" hat adorned with many colorful feathers, carried a delightful large sign. It said, "LET THE BUFFALO DOCTOR ROAM."

On the sidewalk two teen-age girls sat crosslegged, their black braids shining in the spring sunshine. They waved their signs toward passing autos. One placard said, "CUSTER WAS A REDNECK." The other said "CUSTER WORE AN ARROW SHIRT."

On the steps leading into the federal building stood a pretty young girl wearing a beaded headband. She shyly gripped a sign which said, "THE BUFFALO DOCTOR IS LOVE." Her placard was decorated with red hearts. Farther up the steps an erect, defiant young man offered the straight arm, clenched fist, power salute. He, too, wore a headband, and his eyes were hidden behind mirror-lens sunglasses. His placard protested, "ISN'T IT AGAINST THE LAW TO STARVE PEOPLE IN THE U.S.A.?"

Although we didn't know it until later when we read the newspaper accounts, Grand Rapids police were stationed on a hillside and highway overpass overlooking the federal building, where they scanned everyone with binoculars and took pictures with long-range cameras. This was said to be usual procedure at public demonstrations.

As we entered the lobby we encountered over one hundred more supporters, most of them Indian. Everything was peaceful. The supporters merely stood about, waiting quietly. Among them we spotted a few close friends who had come to lend their moral support. A uniformed security officer tended the door, where he warned everyone that no protest signs would be allowed inside the building. Uneasily, I noticed he carried a billy club. Uniformed police weren't in evidence, but an unaccountably large number of maintenance men moved around the building, carrying ladders or mops.

When we stepped onto a crowded elevator to take us to the sixth floor Bill and I recognized one of our fellow-passengers as an F.B.I. agent. Instead of the usual dark business suit, he was decked out in coveralls. The place was crawling with F.B.I. agents in disguise!

As we stepped off the elevator Neal rushed up, saying he wanted to talk with us. He asked a uniformed security guard if we could use a small conference room for a few minutes. We were ushered into a room containing a long table surrounded by dark oak armchairs.

"Okay," Neal said, "here's the deal. I've been talking with the federal prosecuting attorney and the magistrate. We need time to study the indictment handed down by the grand jury, and they've agreed that they will allow my request for a ninety-day postponement. So all we're going to do is go in there, listen to them read the charges, and then I'll ask for a postponement."

Neal leaned his stocky body against the wall. "Now what do we do with all these Indians? As you can see, there's room for very few people in that courtroom. Let me see if I can get them to give us a large room to have everyone wait in during the proceedings. Then afterwards, you can make your statement for the press there."

Neal stepped into the hallway and made these arrangements with an official. As he strode back in he asked sharply, "Now, how are you going to select who gets into that small courtroom? Paul's wife and five kids will take up one row, and your family will take another. That leaves room for about twenty-five people. How do you want to choose them?"

"Let Chief Shalifoe choose those who come in," Bill answered.

"Okay," Neal agreed. "Where's the Chief? Is he downstairs in the lobby?"

We didn't know.

Bill stood up. "I'll go find him."

"Oh, no!" Neal cried. "I don't want you roaming around out there with all those reporters." He turned to me. "Do you know the Chief?"

As soon as I nodded "yes" I wondered if I'd really

recognize Chief Shalifoe again. I had seen him only the one time when he presented Bill with the Indian headdress.

As Neal and I stood waiting for the elevator to take us down to the lobby, a stout Indian woman with an incredibly sweet face approached me. She slipped a printed card into my fingers, squeezed my hand, and said, "We're behind The Buffalo Doctor all the way."

In the elevator I glanced at the card and saw that she was the secretary of the Michigan Commission on Indian Affairs, an arm of the Governor's office. Her warm manner and her official position were comforting.

Just off the lobby was a large room into which all the supporters had been herded. Newsmen and television cameramen also had been shuttled into this room, and the television men were getting their lights set up.

"Okay, where's the Chief?" Neal prodded me, impatient to get going.

Never had I seen so many Indians in one place at one time. There must have been over one hundred fifty Indians in that room. I searched the crowd of faces for that of the Chief. At last I caught sight of Stella, who I knew was the daughter of Chief Shalifoe.

I gripped her arm, and whispered, "Where's your father?"

Stella pointed him out to me, and Neal and I explained to him that we would appreciate his choosing a delegation to be seated in the courtroom.

Again, on the elevator ride back upstairs we were accompanied by another maintenance man. Was he guarding me, I wondered, or guarding our nation *against* me?

In the small courtroom Beth, Brenda and I seated ourselves in the front row on the left side. Between us and the judge's bench was a long table for the defendants and their lawyers. Bill and our two lawyers seated themselves at the left side of the table, and Paul strode to the right side. Though I'd never met them, I knew this must be Paul's wife and five children. As other people began crowding into the seats behind us, I caught Mrs. Davids's eye, and we exchanged trembling smiles of understanding sympathy. At the rear of the courtroom several F.B.I. agents, their arms folded, leaned against the wall.

From a door behind the bench the black-robed magistrate entered the room, and the clerk called out, "All rise." It was just like in the movies. The U. S. District Attorney rose and read the charges, beginning "The United States of America vs. Paul Davids and Dwain Cummings."

His voice droned on, reading that the two accused men "did willfully obstruct, impede and interfere with federal law enforcement officials engaged in the lawful performance of their official duties incident to and during the commission of a civil disorder at Wounded Knee, South Dakota."

My mind wandered, and I didn't realize the prosecuting attorney had proceeded to the reading of the grand jury indictment.

Suddenly a phrase broke through my consciousness— "armed riflemen." The indictment had accused Bill and Paul of flying in supplies and "armed riflemen." I jerked my head up, bewildered, and saw one of Paul's attorneys half-rise from his seat, only to be restrained by the other lawyer.

I looked at Bill for his reaction, but could see only the back of his dark head. As the reading went on, my thoughts were confused. Had I heard correctly? Were they actually accusing Bill and Paul of hauling riflemen in that tiny plane along with that huge load of supplies? No mention had been made of that earlier accusation that they delivered a bazooka and armor-piercing shells. How had the bazooka become transformed into armed riflemen? Or maybe it was the toilet paper and Kotex which changed themselves into riflemen. It was so ridiculous that I decided to disregard it. However, when I noticed the grim scowl on the face of Paul's attorney, I felt uneasy.

The moment the District Attorney finished reading his papers, Neal rose quickly, and addressed the bench, beginning, "Your honor." He explained that more time was needed to study the grand jury indictment and to prepare our case. He requested a postponement of the proceedings.

As previously agreed upon, the magistrate granted a postponement of ninety days and ordered that the defendants appear again in this same courtroom on June 15 at two in the afternoon. At the time, ninety days seemed a long time, a welcome reprieve. Summer would be upon us before the next court appearance when we'd have to face extradition to South Dakota.

As we left the courtroom and stepped onto an elevator, Neal whispered to Bill, "Now we'll go downstairs, and you can read your statement to the press. Just read what you and I agreed upon, say nothing else, and we'll get out of there."

Bill nodded. I saw an unkempt, long-haired young man standing directly behind him reach out and pat Bill affectionately on the back. "Nice going, Doc. You're doing okay." I assumed the fellow was there as a protester, but later Bill told me that the stringy-haired man was an F.B.I. agent, a narcotics undercover man. He'd seen him in the F.B.I. offices on the day of his arrest. Bill felt a special warmth toward this agent because of his thankless, dangerous job and because the agent trusted Bill.

When our elevator arrived at the first floor and the doors opened, we were blinded by the glare of floodlights. Cameramen with portable television cameras resting on their shoulders pointed their lenses at Bill, and as he strode across the lobby, the cameramen walked backwards, keeping their cameras homed in on Bill. The girls and I trooped behind, following Bill and our lawyers into the large room filled with people and reporters. As we entered the room the supporters broke into pleased applause. Several microphones had been set up at the front of the room, and Bill and our two lawyers stepped up to them. The girls and I stood directly behind Bill.

In the crowd of faces I noticed a few old friends. All eyes were on Bill. He looked so handsome and dignified I felt a lump begin swelling in my throat. He stood tall and slender in his black western-cut suit, pointed western boots, and string-tie, which was a beaded black-and-white thunderbird motif. From his inside jacket pocket Bill removed the typewritten statement he would read.

"For the last week I have been requested to make a public statement concerning the Federal charge placed against me arising out of the 'Wounded Knee' incident. Upon the advice of my attorneys I have declined to make any comment until this time. Now that the situation is somewhat clearer, I have the following statement.

"As a child, I was raised upon an Indian reservation. The rigors of a South Dakota winter coupled with the scarcity of good food are not unfamiliar to me."

Bill was reading slowly and clearly, but I was aware that his voice was unusually deep and emotional.

"It was believed unreasonable to expect men to negotiate their difficulties with clarity of mind and purpose when at the same time they lacked food and medical supplies. Apparently, others have recognized this situation as it is now reported through the news media that various parties have been allowed to bring food and medical supplies to the Indians at Wounded Knee."

At this point, Bill's voice cracked, and he paused to regain his composure. Uneasily, I reached out to touch his elbow in a gesture of warmth, then thought better of it. Always cool-nerved in any crisis, now Bill struggled to overcome strong emotions.

He continued. "The incident at Wounded Knee is symptomatic of the ills that our country is experiencing. Whether it be Watts, California; Kent, Ohio; or Olean, New York; all of these incidents are reminders that there are certain internal problems presently sapping the strength of this great country."

Bill's voice wavered and broke. Tears streamed down his cheeks. Television cameramen zeroed in close, and flashbulbs popped. I knew the anguish and humiliation that Bill was enduring by having the news people record his breakdown. As I glanced past Bill's head toward the audience, I saw tears streaming down many faces. Bill

185

tried to hand his typed statement to Neal, but the lawyer only gripped Bill's wrist firmly and refused to take the paper.

Bill took a deep breath, regained his composure, and went on, his voice strong and sure once again.

"Through no fault of our own, we have been made citizens of the world with the awesome responsibility of trying to remedy the various problems of other nations. Some of the basic human needs of our fellow Americans have gone too long unanswered. 'Out of sight, out of mind' can no longer be the rule.

"The present problems of our country are manmade; and, therefore, they can be solved by men. It is my hope that with all the resources available to us at this point in history the problems manifested at Wounded Knee may be brought to resolution without further unrest.

"I thank you all," he finished softly.

From the rear of the room a man's voice called out, "Amen!" and voices in the crowd echoed, "Amen."

Neal grasped Bill's arm and with a quick gesture, motioned us all toward the door. A few photographers followed us all the way to our car in the parking ramp, but the television people stayed behind. Later, at home we were able to watch the television coverage of what occurred after our hasty exit.

As we drove the forty miles to Grand Haven to return Tom to his law office, Bill groaned, "I really blew it, didn't I? I don't know why I got so emotional reading that statement. I haven't cried since I was a kid."

"It was a beautiful statement," I assured Bill, "and you did just fine. No one will think less of you for having strong feelings."

Tom agreed. "Don't give it another thought. You did very well. Everyone there felt emotional about the situation. There was hardly a dry eye in the crowd."

Speeding west along the four-lane divided highway, we were more than half-way home when we noticed two cars stopped on the shoulder of the east bound lanes. Casually curious, we glanced toward the cars. As we rolled past I cried out, "I think someone's lying on the trunk of that car!"

Bill slammed on the brakes and pulled onto the shoulder. Without a word he jumped from the car and raced across our lanes of the highway and out onto the wide, grassy median dividing the west and east-bound lanes. Tom followed Bill, not far behind.

We had travelled quite a distance beyond the two parked cars, and it was hard to see what was going on. It was obviously some sort of emergency. I could make out the figure of a man desperately waving his arms at cars speeding past. I assumed that someone had suffered a heart attack.

For ten minutes the children and I watched the distant figures. Then an ambulance screamed up, and Bill and Tom returned to our station wagon.

"What was it?" we all wanted to know.

It seems a young father had been driving along with his two sons in the backseat. The little boys grew quiet, and the father thought they had fallen asleep. When he turned to check on them, he noticed the face of the younger child had turned a peculiar color, and he realized the boys were asphyxiated from exhaust fumes. Frantically, he stopped the car and dragged the three-year-old from the back seat. The child appeared dead. The anguished father began waving, trying to flag down passing cars. At last a car stopped, and the driver went to work on the boy, giving him mouth-to-mouth resuscitation. It was at this point that we came along, and Bill and Tom dashed across to give assistance. When Bill raced up, the older child was conscious and breathing, but the younger boy lay unmoving. His skin had the telltale flushed, reddish-pink color of carbon monoxide poisoning. Bill administered resuscitation, and the child began to respond. When the ambulance arrived, Bill turned the children over to the emergency personnel who had oxygen available.

"They'll be all right," Bill assured us.

Tom wiped his forehead with his handkerchief. Medical emergencies weren't supposed to be a part of a lawyer's day. Tom shook his head. "I felt so sorry for that poor father. He was just hysterical, not knowing what to do."

We dropped Tom off at his law office and went home, where we gratefully put on comfortable jeans and sweatshirts. By this time we were hungry, having eaten nothing since breakfast. I groaned, wondering if I had the energy to prepare supper.

"I'll fix supper," Beth volunteered. "But it's a surprise, and you have to promise to eat it."

Supper turned out to be French crepes, a sort of sophisticated pancake. Beth was about to embark for France with her high school French class, and they had been collecting and testing French recipes to accustom their palates to foreign food.

Settling ourselves on the living room floor to watch the evening news on television, we nibbled crepes smothered in various fattening sauces.

Bill's court hearing was the first item of news. Upon our television screen appeared the federal building with scores of Indians standing on the steps, holding placards.

The announcer described the scene: "A popular West Michigan doctor, Dwain Cummings, and pilot Paul Davids, who were arrested last week on charges of taking food to the Indians at Wounded Knee, were in court in Grand Rapids today fighting the removal of their preliminary hearing to South Dakota. Supporters went with them. While Grand Rapids police stood on a hillside across the street scanning the federal building with binoculars, two hundred supporters of the two men gathered inside and picketed outside, awaiting word of the pair's hearing. Lawyers for osteopath Dwain Cummings and pilot Paul Davids were asking federal magistrate Stephen Karr to postpone the hearing for ninety days. The men were arrested last week on a complaint filed by federal authorities in South Dakota. Since that time a federal grand jury has indicted the men for interfering with federal officers by flying food to Wounded Knee. Davids's attorney argues that the preliminary hearing on the original complaint to determine if the men should stand trial, should be held in Michigan. Attorneys said they needed time to review the indictment and the demand that Cummings and Davids be removed to South Dakota to answer the charges. When Cummings left the courtroom his supporters learned that Magistrate Karr has postponed for ninety days the pair's hearing on removal to South Dakota.''

The television screen showed Bill and Neal leaving the elevator, the girls and me tagging behind, crossing the federal building lobby. Then switching to the large room the cameras panned across the faces of the Indian supporters. The newsman described the scene: ''The smiling defendants left the courtroom with their families and went to a room on the main floor of the federal building to meet with several hundred waiting supporters. Those supporters, mainly Indians from across Western Michigan, were orderly and patient, which made the heavy security precautions seem unnecessary. Cummings, called by many, 'The Buffalo Doctor' because of the herd of buffalo he owns in Stanwood, read a short statement approved in advance by his attorney and containing no reference to the alleged flight to Wounded Knee.''

The camera turned to a close-up of Bill reading his statement. I glanced across the living room at Bill. His face was tense, and he chewed nervously on the side of his index finger. He was braced, waiting for the cameras to reveal his cracking voice and wet cheeks.

Instead, the television camera turned toward the crowd, zeroing in on weeping faces and wringing hands. The newsman's voice condensed the remaining part of the statement: ''Cummings said that the incident at Wounded Knee is symptomatic of the ills that are sapping the strength of this great country.''

Bill and I exchanged happy grins. ''They were kind to me!'' Bill whispered. ''That was real good of them!'' The television people hadn't exposed Bill's tremendous struggle.

It was at this point that Neal had rushed us all out of

the room. Now, on television, we got a peek at what ensued. As the cameras panned across the weeping crowd, a young Indian man stepped forward and asked everyone to join hands in prayer and as a symbol of unity. The camera zeroed in on a white woman wrapped in an elegant fur coat. Her very white hand was gripping firmly the brown hand of the blue-jean clad Indian girl beside her. The camera dwelled lovingly on that clasping of hands for several seconds, while the Indian man prayed, "that other Americans may open their hearts to the agonizing cries of the first Americans. We are all wholeheartedly behind Mr. Davids and Dr. Cummings."

The newscaster continued, "Cummings's backers joined hands and prayed that justice might begin here, and that the charges against Cummings and Davids be dismissed. Backers of the two men say that seven thousand people have signed petitions on their behalf. The petitions call upon federal authorities to avoid compounding the embarrassment already caused Cummings and Davids, and describes their alleged flight of food to the Indians as 'humanitarian' and calls for dismissal of federal charges."

The newsman picked up a piece of paper just placed before him and read, "On his way home from court Dr. Cummings rescued two youngsters who were overcome by exhaust fumes in an old car. The children, three and six years old, passed out. Their father started to flag down cars on Interstate ninety-six near Grand Haven and one of the first cars was that containing Dr. Cummings and his family. Cummings gave the children mouth-to-mouth resuscitation, got them breathing, then drove off as police took the children to a hospital."

The news continued, covering other area events.

Bill and I smiled at each other happily. The news media, so powerful in what they choose to tell and to show, had been kind to Bill. They had described the Indian supporters as orderly and patient and hinted that the government had over-reacted in supplying such heavy security precautions. We changed channels and ate more crepes, licking the blueberry jam and powdered sugar from our fingers. The other stations covered the hearing in the same sympathetic manner.

The national news reported that the National Council of Churches was apparently going to increase food shipments to Indians occupying Wounded Knee. "According to Indian leaders in Wounded Knee, there is no fuel, and they have been living on a subsistence diet," the commentator said. "Talks between the Indians and federal officials, stalled for three days by a blizzard, are scheduled to be resumed tomorrow."

That night we slept soundly, our first good night's sleep in twelve days. Completely exhausted from worry and dealing with frequent new experiences, we now could relax. Ninety days must pass before Bill could be extradited to South Dakota to face the hostile authorities there. We vowed to enjoy the reprieve and freedom of the ensuing ninety days.

The next day we instituted a family work party with the purpose of cleaning up the backyard. A winter's collection of manure and hay was unsightly. Each of us armed himself with a rake or shovel. Our large wheelbarrow was filled dozens of times, and each load was wheeled to our vegetable garden area and dumped. When plowed into the soil, these buffalo chips would provide good fertilizer for our garden. Slowly, our backyard began to look less like a dirty barnyard and more like a normal, grassy lawn.

During our clean-up operations Little Joe followed us about curiously. Once, when Bill was stooping to shovel up a dried buffalo chip, Little Joe jumped on his back.

Bill chuckled and rubbed Joe's neck affectionately. "I'm afraid we're going to have to castrate you, Joe," he warned. "We sure can't have you jumping on me when you weigh a ton."

Later, when my back was turned, I received the same loving hug from Joe, and it frightened me. The large hoof of his forefoot skidded past my right ear and grazed my jaw before I leaped out of his reach. His hoof and much of his weight came down on my instep. Three-quarters mad and one-quarter hurting, I blinked back tears and glared angrily at Bill. "Look what he did!" I sputtered, rubbing my throbbing instep.

"Well, at least we know Joe isn't only homosexual!" Bill laughed.

This only made me madder, and I limped around for awhile. No one had time to give me a sympathetic glance, so eventually I forgot to limp.

Since Joe's amorous hugs seemed to be increasing in frequency, Bill decided that it was time to operate on Joe. He would have to become a steer, if he were going to remain a manageable backyard pet.

Four farmer-neighbors who were experienced in castrating calves came to help perform the operation. We tied Little Joe to a white clump birch tree in our front yard. Joe didn't like being restrained, so I held a dark-colored blindfold over his eyes, and this quieted him. Deftly and quickly, the men cut away Little Joe's testicles, inflicting only a minimum of pain. As soon as we were certain there would be no excessive bleeding, we returned Little Joe to the pasture.

Sisseton Sioux, who always felt motherly to Joe, immediately galloped up to him and began sniffing and licking his wounds. Though Sisseton Sioux hadn't yet been a mother, she felt strong maternal instincts toward Joe. Joe was pretty touchy about his new wounds, but Sisseton Sioux was persistent and continued to apply the healing benefits of her sandpaper tongue.

When Barely Kicking von Holstein came running up to check out the commotion, Sisseton Sioux swung her horns, warning Barely to keep her distance.

Joe healed quickly with no complications, and we hoped his surgery would put an end to his clumsy buffalo hugs.

"A hungry people listens not to reason,
nor cares for justice,
nor is bent by any prayers."
  —Seneca

•

Deadwood
Beckons

17 Following that first March 16 extradition
hearing we basked in the sunshine of relief.
For two weeks tension had kept our nerves
quivering. With the ninety-day reprieve from traveling to
South Dakota and becoming enmeshed in the web of the
federal court system there, we began to unwind.

The annual meeting of the National Buffalo Association was to be held in Denver, Colorado, at the end of the
week. These meetings were delightful occasions, a chance
to get together with old friends in the buffalo business,
and an opportunity to exchange information in the world
of buffalo husbandry.

As a member of the Board of Directors and chairman
of the Research Committee, Bill's attendance at these
meetings was important. This year, especially, he wanted
to be there to gain the support and encouragement of the
association in changing government policy concerning the
disposal of surplus buffalo from the federal parks. In
August, 1970, the National Buffalo Association members
drafted a resolution requesting the United States Department of the Interior and the Department of Agriculture to
give their surplus buffalo from parks, refuges, and ranges
to Indians on reservations throughout the United States.

The resolution declared that the one thousand buffalo declared surplus annually by the parks should, by rights, be given to American Indians on the reservations, as previously agreed by Memorandum N1427 signed December 10, 1965, by the Bureau of Indian Affairs and the National Parks. Reservation Indians suffer from an inadequate and low-protein diet. High in protein, buffalo meat would help battle this malnutrition. It was hoped that this resolution, coming from a national association, would have some influence. But now three years had gone by, and there was no change in policy of disposing of surplus buffalo from the federal parks.

Annually, federal parks must cull out extra animals to keep the herd numbers down so there will be enough grass to feed them. These surplus buffalo are auctioned off to the highest bidders, or shot by "great white hunters" who want to brag that they've shot a buffalo.

Shooting a buffalo is no more sport than walking into a barnyard and shooting a riding horse or a milk cow. The buffalo is not a sporty hunting animal like a deer. A deer will dash off into the woods and lead his pursuer a challenging chase. Strictly a herd animal, the buffalo stays with his herd for preservation. If one of the herd is shot, the others mill around their fallen comrade. This trait of remaining with the wounded made it possible for the buffalo hide hunters of the last century to kill whole herds of buffalo, stopping only when their buffalo guns overheated.

Everyone who raises buffalo knows that it's no great sport to hunt a buffalo. Because of its thick hide, heavy skull, and dense coat, the animal must be shot at a certain point the size of a silver dollar just below the ear, in order to penetrate and kill. Other than taking careful aim, no great skill or bravery is needed. One need only drive up to within shooting range of the buffalo. Curious creatures, the buffalo victim most likely will stand very still and stare at the intrepid hunter, giving plenty of time for precise aim.

Though the buffalo isn't a challenging animal to hunt,

it is an excellent source of high-protein meat. Buffalo breeders who get to know and appreciate the animal, get almost a mystic feeling about its purpose. We come to believe that the buffalo was meant to be the beef of North America. In so many ways it is superior to the cows which white civilization imported to replace our native beef, the buffalo. Indians revere buffalo. Wild meat—buffalo, deer, rabbit—are part of their heritage. Many of their religious ceremonies call for a feast of wild meat. Surplus buffalo from the United States government would be most welcome. Because of its great size, one buffalo provides a large amount of nourishing meat.

We hoped that the National Buffalo Association could be a force in persuading the powers-that-be to direct surplus buffalo to Indians. Though the passage of the Resolution three years before had produced no results, Bill hoped that further insistence by the Association might jar the established bureaucracy into changing its policy.

Bill wanted very much to attend the Denver meeting, but he didn't know if the F.B.I. would allow him to leave the state. He called Neal and explained to the lawyer why he felt his presence at the Denver meeting was necessary. Neal composed a letter to the F.B.I. detailing Bill's efforts at peaceable help to Indians through National Buffalo Association auspices, and F.B.I. permission was granted for Bill to travel to Denver.

We would be gone only four days, but I eagerly anticipated escaping the pressures of the telephone for even so short a time.

We were wary over what sort of reception we'd receive from the buffalo association members. Many of our best friends in the association were western ranchers, a group who holds no great love or admiration for the American Indian. If an Indian adapts himself to the white man's way of life, the ranchers will accept him and respect him. But of the reservation Indian who holds to the old ways and lives in poverty, the ranchers speak with contempt.

Whenever two different cultures exist close together perhaps it is inevitable there be misunderstanding and even clashes. But there was a monetary consideration, too. Ranchers hungrily eye the reservation land. The vast stretches of unused grasslands on the western reservations beckon the rancher. Here would be grass for his cattle, room for expansion for his ranchlands. The Indians see the ranchers as invaders, conquerors who slew their buffalo and herded the Indian people onto reservations, usually the least desirable land in the area. Indians say, "Our land is so poor, we have to fertilize it to make bricks out of it."

Our rancher friends had little respect for modern day Indians and an active hatred for malcontent Indians who tried to change the status quo. A militant Indian was intolerable, and in the rancher's view, Indian sympathizers were either fools or communists. How would the ranchers receive Bill's involvement in Wounded Knee, we wondered.

In the hotel dining room in Denver we met our first rancher, an energetic, attractive widow who ran cattle, sheep, and buffalo on her large Wyoming ranch. "Well, Doc," she greeted Bill, "you really put your foot into it, didn't you? You're not all bad, but you'll do 'til bad comes along!" At least she was smiling.

"Hi, Toots," we greeted her. Bill rubbed his chin and grinned. "You gonna come to my trial, Toots?"

"I wouldn't miss it," the petite woman laughed. "We haven't had a hangin' for five years, and we figure your trial might be the closest thing to a hangin' we'll have for awhile," she drawled.

Other members arrived, and soon buffalo breeders filled a large portion of the dining room. The ranchers took a charitable view of Bill's involvement in Indian protest. Their attitude seemed to be that Doc wouldn't intentionally do anything bad. He was just a naughty boy who got his hand caught in the cookie jar. They had a lot of fun teasing him.

"We're going to hold our next annual meeting at Leavenworth," one of the members announced. "That way Doc can attend." Apparently Bill was forgiven.

A Denver television crew came to the Buffalo meeting to interview some of the buffalo breeders, including Bill, as chairman of the Research Committee. Bill explained to the young interviewer that under no circumstances could he discuss the situation at Wounded Knee or his involvement in it. "My attorney strictly forbids me to discuss those aspects," he said. The interviewer promised not to ask any questions which might jeopardize Bill's legal standing.

Bill began, "What we're really trying to do is convert a bureaucratic shuffle to a meaningful, productive buffalo dance." He went on to discuss with the interviewer the many excellent characteristics of buffalo meat—the fact that it is non-allergenic, its low cholesterol content, its richness in essential amino acids, the fact that pound for pound, it is higher in protein than beef. Very carefully he discussed the severe nutrition problem on Indian reservations and described how surplus buffalo from the federal parks could be used to great advantage by the Indians. The interviewer seemed interested, and a lot of footage was taken.

When the interview was completed, I congratulated Bill. "You really did a good job. I think you got the message across that the reservation Indians need and will make good use of buffalo."

Two weeks later we found out I was wrong.

Housewives were promoting a national meat boycott, protesting the high price of beef. Network television had picked up the interview with Bill, and, cutting all references to Indians, they ran a portion of the interview on the national news in conjunction with the meat boycott. It came across that buffalo meat might be a good substitute for beef. That was the only part of Bill's interview that was used. Once again we were disillusioned. Despairing, we wondered why the message never came through straight. Getting buffalo back to the Indians wasn't an easy undertaking.

On May 7 a letter from the United States Attorney in South Dakota arrived, ordering Bill to appear for arraignment in the federal courtroom in Deadwood, South Dakota, on May 21.

We were dumbfounded. How could they do this? We'd thought we were free from worries of extradition to South Dakota until after the June 15 hearing. And Deadwood!—the hanging town!

Bill called Neal. The lawyer said he had dictated a letter to the United States Attorney protesting that this order to appear in Deadwood was contrary to court rule.

We worried. Should we make arrangements to leave? Plane reservations? How much bail would be needed in South Dakota? So many unknowns.

While we uneasily awaited word, the seige and confrontation at Wounded Knee ended. For seventy days the Indians and the government authorities had locked horns. Now an agreement had been reached, and the armed conflict was over. For the Indian participants and for others involved, like Bill and Paul, many troubles lay ahead, but it was a real relief to know that guns were no longer being pointed at Americans by Americans.

At last we received a letter from Neal telling us that he had heard from the South Dakota authorities. They said they had made a mistake in ordering Bill to appear for arraignment on May 21. They would await the outcome of the decision of federal court in Grand Rapids on June 15.

As Bill's June 15 court appearance drew closer, friends tried to cheer us. "Oh, don't worry," they said. "You'll get off. They wouldn't convict anyone for giving food to Indians."

We weren't encouraged by these supportive words, however. The surprise notice to appear in Deadwood had given us an inkling that the gears of government were grinding on, and Bill was enmeshed. In the juggernaut of the federal court system, Bill was just another accused felon.

Bill grew increasingly grateful to the D.O.s at Stanwood. They expressed their loyalty by continuing to have Bill perform their surgery. Thursday became the one day of the week that Bill practiced his profession of surgery.

He enjoyed those Thursdays. He could focus all his attention on patient care and block out the worries of legal defense, at least for that day.

But even that day of sanctuary was to be invaded by the F.B.I. one Thursday morning in late May. Bill was dictating a surgical report between cases when the head nurse came into the doctors' lounge at the Stanwood hospital.

"Excuse me, Dr. Cummings, you're to return a long distance call. I've written the number down." She handed him a slip of paper.

Bill took the note. "Thanks, Mrs. Sedine."

The nurse moved to leave, then hesitated, and cleared her throat. "He said you're to ask for John Tinker of the Iowa Bureau of Investigation."

Bill raised his eyebrows and reached for the phone. "Maybe he has information that'll get me out of this F.B.I. mess. I'll use any help I can get."

When John Tinker came on the line, he got right to the point. "Doctor, I'm investigating a triple baby murder. I'd like to ask you some questions."

Bill caught his breath. A triple baby murder! This had nothing to do with Wounded Knee!

The investigator went on. "Do you keep any personal records of the work that you did here in Des Moines?"

"No," Bill answered. "I was a resident in surgery, and all the medical records were kept by the hospital."

"Perhaps you kept a calendar or appointment book in your personal things," the agent suggested.

"I don't think so, but I can look. They'd be stored at my home in Muskegon. What is it you want me to look for?"

"You arranged for the adoption of a newborn illegitimate baby March 20, 1958. Do you remember about that?"

"Well, that's a long time ago." Bill searched his memory. "I didn't deliver the baby, but I do remember arranging for the adoption of a baby. The family doctor wanted some uninvolved physician to turn the baby over to the adoption attorney so there would be no way for the

199

natural mother to trace the baby in later years. But that was fifteen years ago!"

"I know it was a long time ago. But I thought you might have an old appointment book or some kind of record."

"I suppose the fire at the hospital ten or twelve years ago destroyed the records?"

"That's right, doctor. When the old part of the hospital burned, all the records went with it. Was the baby a boy or a girl?"

"I have no idea. But I know I turned that baby over to the adoption attorney. I think the child is in a good home. You won't be doing it any good by tying it in with something like this. Why don't you talk to the family physician? I wasn't even in practice at that time. All my records were kept by the hospital."

"We will contact the family physician. A girl friend of the baby's mother said you arranged the adoption, so we are contacting you. The public and the news media are very upset that three dead babies are found, and no one knows anything about it."

"How does my arranging for the adoption of a baby relate to a triple baby murder?" Bill asked. "I don't understand how information about my arranging for an adoption is going to help you solve the triple baby murder."

"We're trying to filter out all the facts," the F.B.I. agent said. "We found three mummified babies in a trunk near Ames. One of the babies was wrapped in a newspaper dated 1955. A second baby was wrapped in a newspaper dated 1956, and we assume that these are the dates the newborn babies were placed in the trunk. The third baby was in a grocery bag, so there is no date. We're trying to establish whether this third baby was the baby that you were supposed to have adopted out, or whether the mother did, in fact, have four babies in all, and the baby you were involved with continues to live."

"My God, what a ghastly thing! Three mummified babies in a trunk!" Bill thought a moment. "It's quite a coincidence that you should be questioning me about this at this particular time."

"What do you mean?" the agent asked.

"I'm the Buffalo Doctor. I'm under indictment by the F.B.I. out here in Michigan for flying food into Wounded Knee."

"I don't know anything about Wounded Knee," the agent replied. "I was instructed to find out from you any information relative to your arranging for an adoption of an illegitimate baby born March 20, 1958. Will you look in your records from that time and see if you have anything about the adoption?"

"I don't know of any records that I would have, but I'll look through my old stored things," Bill sighed. "Possibly you can get some information from the attorney who legalized the adoption."

"We'll continue the investigation," the agent said. "See if you can find anything on the adoption, and I'll call you back in a couple days. Good-bye, doctor."

Bill hung up the phone.

"What on earth was that all about?" Mrs. Sedine asked. "Three mummified babies in a trunk?"

"I don't know," Bill said, "but I sure have the feeling the F.B.I. is trying to intimidate me—involving me in a triple baby murder."

"It gives me the willies," Mrs. Sedine shuddered.

"It gives me gastritis," Bill said. "I'm going to see if they have any dill pickle juice down in the kitchen."

The next day Bill searched through our old storage trunks, but could find no diary and no record of the adoption. Several days went by, and there was no call from agent Tinker. On June 5 Bill called the Iowa bureau to talk to the agent and had to leave a message for agent Tinker to return the call. The agent didn't return the call. We never heard from the Iowa bureau again. The specter of being involved in the investigation of a triple baby murder was added tension to cope with.

At the June 15 hearing our lawyer was planning to ask for another ninety day postponement, and he hoped it would be granted. Neal wanted to keep Bill in Michigan as long as possible in order to let tempers in South Dakota cool.

Many people had warned us that a trial held in South Dakota meant instant conviction of any Indian or Indian sympathizer. As one of our Dakota rancher friends said to Bill, "Out here everyone gets a fair trial before he's hung."

The June 15 court hearing was pretty much a re-run of the March 16 appearance, though not so chaotic or emotional. The magistrate granted Neal's request for postponement, and September 14 was set as the next court appearance date.

The day following the hearing the children and I left for southern Colorado. Beth and two of her girl friends had gotten summer jobs at a dude ranch, and I had promised to drive them west.

After unloading their belongings and saying good-bye to the three girls in Colorado, Bruce, Brenda and I decided to return to Michigan via a more northerly route, one that would take us through Wounded Knee. That village had profoundly affected our lives, and we were curious.

It was late in the afternoon when we neared the historical hamlet, and we were rewarded with the sight of the little white Catholic church far across the valley on a distant hill. As we drove into the village desolate silence surrounded us. Wounded Knee was deserted. There wasn't a human being in sight, not a sound to be heard. At first, this frightened me. I'd feared we'd driven into some sort of ambush, or into a forbidden area. Then I decided that the government hadn't allowed the residents to return as yet. The trading post was a pile of ashes, covered by its huge crumpled roof, intact, but lying flush with the ground. Across the street and scattered about the village were several house trailers and small homes. All were apparently abandoned, at least for the time being.

At the end of the main street a gently sloping hill curved upward, and Sacred Heart Church stood on its crown, commanding a view of the countryside. At the base of the hill we stopped to read a large yellow sign which began "The Battle of Wounded Knee." It described the terrible slaughter of Big Foot's starving and freezing band on this exact site eighty-three years before. There was no village and no Catholic Church here then, only a small stream known as Chankpe Opi Wakpala to the Sioux, called Wounded Knee Creek by the army.

As I stood on the spot where so many were slain, I recalled what I'd read about that awful December day in 1890 when Big Foot's fearful people were being disarmed by their old enemy, the Seventh Cavalry. A shot had rung out, and the alarmed soldiers began shooting. On the top of the hill where the white church now stands were Hotchkiss guns, capable of hurling explosives two miles. These guns began pumping death at the fleeing, screaming people, composed mainly of women, children, and old men. Several soldiers were killed from their own crossfire. At the end of the shooting spree, one hundred fifty-three Indian bodies were accounted for, but it was thought that an equal number of Big Foot's band were mortally wounded and crawled off into the creek beds and died.

A few days later a burial detail gathered the one hundred fifty-three frozen bodies and placed them in a huge common grave on the crown of the hill. Eventually the little white church was built beside the graveyard.

Nowadays, most of us think of this tragic 1890 encounter as a horrid mistake, but contemporary newspaper reports of the incident dwelt upon the treachery of the Indians and were written in the tone of "the only good Indian is a dead Indian." On the day of the encounter, the New York Times reported, "The Hotchkiss gun was also run up . . . and a withering fire was poured upon the reds . . . It is doubted if by night either buck or squaw out of all Big Foot's Band is left to tell the tale of this day's treachery. The members of the Seventh Calvary have once more shown themselves to be heroes of deeds of daring."

Just beyond the billboard describing the awful Wounded Knee "battle," was the pasture slough which we believed must be the place where Bill and Paul had landed their Cessna.

We drove up the hill and parked beside the church, which was locked, its windows boarded shut. The white siding was pock-marked with bullet holes, and a sign tacked to the front door reported that all furniture and accessories from the church had been removed.

Behind the church was a small archway, topped by a cross, opening into the cemetery. In some ways it was a typical small cemetery located beside countless rural churches throughout our country. But one thing stood out and made it very different from other cemeteries, and that was the huge mass grave containing the bodies of Big Foot's slaughtered band. About six feet wide, and dozens of feet long, the grave was marked by a cement curbing outlining the grisly shape. Pots of artificial flowers surrounded the burial pit. Off to one side lay a fresh grave, completely smothered with bouquets of artificial flowers and bearing two small American flags. I assumed this to be the grave of one of the Indian men killed during the most recent confrontation, the 1973 battle at Wounded Knee. Many small monuments throughout the cemetery told the sad story of high infant mortality on Indian reservations. There were several markers commemorating children of less than three years old. I noticed a couple monuments bearing American flags and veterans' insignias, and from the dates on the stones, it seemed they had been soldiers killed in action. None of the stone monuments were pretentious, and many graves were marked only by small wooden crosses. The whole cemetery spoke of poverty and tragedy. With new insights in Indian suffering, we left Wounded Knee and headed for home.

With Beth away in Colorado for her summer job, our family population was decreased, and then it was to dwindle more. Little Joe was the next to leave.

A friend of Bill's who owned and managed the Bucking E Rodeo asked if he could borrow Little Joe for the summer. He wanted Little Joe to travel with his rodeo throughout the Midwest to serve as an attention-getter for the rodeo to increase attendance.

Bill agreed, and this surprised me. I couldn't imagine Bill parting with his beloved Little Joe, even for a few months.

"The discipline will be good for Joe," Bill explained. "He's been getting pretty stubborn, and he doesn't lead well. We don't work with him enough. Those cowhands will make him mind. I'll sure miss Joe, but I think the rodeo will be good for him."

During the next few months Bill and I kept busy writing to congressmen and speaking before groups, trying to make people aware that the surplus buffalo from the parks should go to the Indians on the reservations.

When nearly six months had passed since Bill's arrest, we were confronted with a money crisis. Our income had dropped to the point where we barely could meet office overhead. There was the burden of heavy legal fees and ranch expenses. We needed several thousand dollars. It was a hard decision, but there was only one way to get that much money. We had to sell the Texas longhorns and this year's crop of buffalo calves. It took us nearly two weeks working with a rodeo crew to round up and ship the wild longhorns and to separate the buffalo calves from their protective mothers.

Selling all those animals was a real set-back to our future progress in crossbreeding. Even so, our primary concern for now had to be keeping Bill out of federal prison and getting him free of the felony charge.

Throughout the winter the court continued to grant sixty day postponements. Due to the press of heavy court schedule in South Dakota, authorities there were in no hurry to begin prosecuting Bill. It was hard to have this somber threat of jail hanging over Bill's head for so long.

Well-meaning friends said, "Wouldn't you just like to get it over with? It's mean for them to keep dragging it out like this."

We were in no hurry to be prosecuted. We didn't feel that giving food to hungry Indians was a crime. But how

205

would a South Dakota jury view it? Then there was the added worry of the heavy expenses we would incur when Bill went to trial. The legal fees would be tremendous, but added to these would be the expenses of transportation to South Dakota for us, lawyers, witnesses, and food and lodging there. No, we weren't in any hurry to go to trial. We welcomed the extra time to save money for those future trial expenses.

Early in 1974 the first Wounded Knee trial got underway in St. Paul, Minnesota. This was the so-called "leadership" trial of Dennis Banks and Russell Means. They were co-defendants on trial for their leadership roles in the Wounded Knee confrontation. Federal Judge Fred Nichol of South Dakota had moved his court to St. Paul after he agreed with defense attorneys that it would be impossible to get an impartial jury for the two men in South Dakota.

Bill and I were anxious to follow the proceedings, since the fate of the lesser defendants like Bill and Paul might hinge upon the outcome of this leadership trial. News reports on the trial were minimal. Only South Dakota and Minnesota papers seemed to carry this news. At last, friends and relatives in those states began sending us newspaper clippings about the trial, and we were able to follow its progress.

It promised to be a long and complicated trial, perhaps lasting a whole year. One event which caused a four-week delay in the trial was intriguing to us. The defense brought in evidence concerning an alleged illegal wire-tap in which the F.B.I. monitored phone calls coming from the Wounded Knee Trading Post by listening to an extension phone located at a roadblock. In mid-March a telephone company employee came forward with the story that he had installed an extension phone from the line going into Wounded Knee, the extra phone conveniently located at a federal roadblock. Judge Nichol expressed horror at this revelation, excused the jury, and began the month-long hearings on this illegal surveillance question, concerning government misconduct. Defense attorneys were irate over the fact that the F.B.I. agents had listened in on phone conversations because they had been assured by both the Bureau of Indian Affairs Superintendent and the U.S. Chief Negotiator at Wounded Knee that the line was clean, and the client-attorney relationship would be safe. At first, the government maintained that they had installed the extension phone to facilitate negotiations with the Indians. However, as witness after witness took the stand, it became clear that no one could testify that the phone had been used, even once, for negotiations. In fact, no one knew how to ring up the trading post phone, since a complicated dialing code is needed to call a phone on the same party line. At last, the prosecution admitted that the phone was "essentially useless for any purpose other than overhearing."

At the very beginning of the wiretap hearing, Judge Nichol asked Joseph Trimbach, divisional head of the F.B.I. in the Minnesota-Dakota area, if there were any wiretaps in Wounded Knee during the occupation. Mr. Trimbach assured the judge that there were none. During the hearing itself Mr. Trimbach testified that he never saw an application for a court-approved wiretap, and he said that he didn't remember assuring Judge Nichol that there had been no wiretapping.

This put the judge in the peculiar position of having to decide whether he should step down from the bench and become a witness in his own court to testify concerning what the F.B.I. director had told him.

After Mr. Trimbach's testimony that he had never participated in the making of an affidavit seeking a wiretap, two exhibits were entered which showed otherwise. Defense attorneys submitted an affidavit dated March 7, 1973, signed by Trimbach himself, referring to the phone inside Wounded Knee. "The telephone which is sought to be tapped has been used extensively by the leaderhsip of the American Indian Movement," the affidavit said. Defense attorneys promptly accused Trimbach of perjury, and filed a motion asking that a copy of his testimony be forwarded to the U.S. Attorney's office for possible prosecution.

Also, during this hearing there was considerable testimony revealing that the government had not turned over to the defense attorneys all the required pieces of evidence. The judge grew impatient with the F.B.I., charging them with negligent conduct in complying with rules of federal trial evidence. At the conclusion of the hearings the judge said that the negligent and dilatory conduct by the F.B.I. had "brought this court to the brink of dismissing this case." However, he decided that the misconduct was not "gross enough" to warrant dismissing the criminal charges against Means and Banks.

Judge Nichol observed that "although the F.B.I. has had the well-deserved reputation of being the world's most effective crime-fighting organization, it must be remembered if our system of freedom is to be preserved, that the F.B.I. must be servile to our system of justice. The F.B.I. in this case failed as a 'servant of the law.'"

The trial resumed, and Means and Banks were permitted to become co-counsels with their own lawyers. This new tack permitted them to cross-examine witnesses.

There were times when the trial threatened to become a Keystone Kops comedy. An F.B.I. agent had admitted on the witness stand that he had broken the law and could be arrested and prosecuted. As the agent concluded his testimony, Means and Banks attempted to make a citizens' arrest. The judge informed them that they could not arrest anyone in his courtroom, or in the court building. Immediately, several sympathetic Indian spectators left the courtroom and stationed themselves encircling the federal building, intending to arrest the agent as he emerged. But the F.B.I. is known for its *esprit de corps,* and fellow agents grouped themselves around the threatened brother, hustled him out of the courtroom, and helped him escape through a skylight across roof tops, using a next door bank as his exit route. The image of the F.B.I. couldn't survive Means and Banks arresting an agent and sending him off to jail.

Later, the defense submitted documents and requested that a trial transcript be furnished the U. S. Attorney. With this action they sought a grand jury indictment of two F.B.I. agents for breaking the federal wire-tap laws and perjury.

Some of the news coming out of the trial was heart-breaking, some frightening, and some amusing. It appeared that the outcome of the trial very definitely would affect Bill and Paul, and all the other Wounded Knee defendants. The government indicated that it was in no hurry to prosecute the lesser defendants until this leadership trial was concluded.

All we could do was wait and worry. In the meantime our life had to go on. Bill had to perform surgery, and the animals had to be cared for. The long shadow of a federal prison term for Bill hung there, but we were learning to live under this threat.

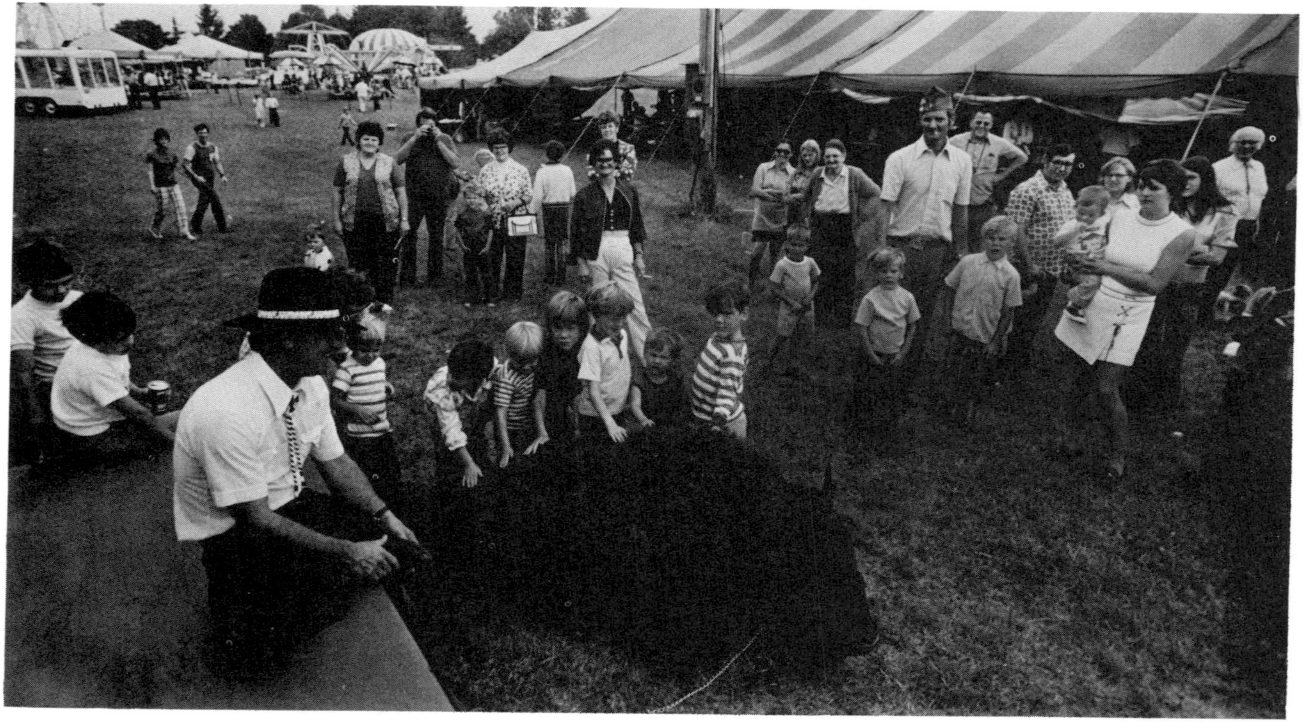

Photo Courtesy of Rudy

*"Strong and content
I travel the open road."*
   —Walt Whitman

•

Following
That
Yellow
Line

18 While waiting at the airport in New York
City following a seminar on cancer and im-
munology Bill met some interesting people.
As they chatted, Bill mentioned buffalo and Indians, and
soon his two new friends were absorbed and fascinated
with the problem of how modern day Indians could be
helped. They were especially interested in helping Bill pro-
mote his campaign to get the government to give their
surplus buffalo from the parks to reservation Indians. As
they talked, Bill discovered that the man named Allen was
from Detroit.

When they parted at the end of the flight, Allen
assured Bill, "You'll be hearing from me. I'm concerned
about Indians, and I want to help. I have some friends
who are active in radio and television. We can launch a
publicity campaign to inform the public about the surplus
buffalo that are available. I think people would agree that
the Indians should have first choice on buffalo being
disposed of. If I can set up some radio and television appearances, will you come to Detroit to present your
ideas?"

Bill agreed enthusiastically. "I'll bring Little Joe to
Detroit to help. Joe gets people's attention real fast."

Over the next two months Allen telephoned several times, reporting his progress in setting up press interviews and television and radio appearances. "Of course, you'll be my guests while you're in Detroit," Allen offered, "but I'm still looking for suitable people to play host to Little Joe." He chuckled. "I certainly never dreamed I'd be looking for a buffalo babysitter."

Over the Christmas holidays while Bruce was home to help, we took Barely Kicking von Holstein and her mother, Bertha, back over to the ranch. Barely was now approaching two years of age, old enough to become pregnant. Bertha, too, should be earning her keep by bearing us another cattalo calf. At the ranch they had their choice of Kahtanka or The Black Bull for companionship. Their conjugal visit to the main ranch at Stanwood would be only temporary. As soon as either of them showed positive signs of pregnancy, we intended to return them to our backyard where we could supervise their pregnancies with a watchful eye. In the meantime I would thoroughly enjoy being rid of the bellowing, belligerent Barely.

In January Bill was granted another sixty-day postponement, until March 14. Nearly a whole year had passed since Bill's arrest. We were beginning to expect these postponements as almost a matter of course. There was always that hidden worry, however, that we might be living in a fool's paradise, that one of these times, they would not grant a postponement, but ship Bill to South Dakota.

In mid-February we left for Detroit to take part in the interviews and appearances Allen had arranged. Little Joe climbed eagerly into the homemade, two-wheel trailer we'd built for him.

Bill laughed. "After all Joe's traveling with the rodeo last summer, he's had a pretty stay-at-home life with us. I think he's glad to hit the road and get a change of scenery."

When we arrived at Allen's apartment building, we learned that Allen had managed to find a family eager to babysit with Little Joe. "They have a fenced backyard," he said, "and they'll be happy to bed him down for tonight."

Allen climbed into the van with us and directed us to the Mondello's, where Joe would be staying. Al Mondello, an interior decorator, greeted us warmly, and motioned us to back Joe's trailer into their backyard. There, Bill unloaded Joe, and with a long rope tied him to a tree. This area was used for a small vegetable garden. The remainder of the yard was like a Japanese garden. We spread a bale of hay to make a bed for Joe and laid out several piles of hay and grain for his supper. Joe gazed at his new surroundings calmly, as if saying to himself, "So this is the big city!"

Mondello's next-door neighbor started down his back steps, then stopped in surprise as his gaze fell on Joe. "My gosh, that's the biggest dog I ever saw!" he blurted. Then, leaning forward, the neighbor squinted and his mouth gaped. Slowly he shook his head. "That isn't a dog!" he accused.

We all laughed and invited him to come over and meet Joe. Word spread fast. Soon people from up and down the street arrived, having heard the crazy rumor that someone had a buffalo in his backyard.

With Joe cozily bedded down in the suburban backyard, Bill and I went to Allen's apartment where we spent the night. I was fascinated with Allen's huge city apartment, beautifully decorated with priceless Oriental antiques and paintings.

We had to get up at four o'clock the next morning in order to pick up Little Joe and get to the television station by six-thirty. Allen served us breakfast of coffee and bagels. He was amazed that neither Bill nor I had ever tasted a bagel.

In the dark we loaded Joe into his trailer and drove to the television station. At the parking lot, Bill brushed Joe's coat clean from any hay or dust and gently polished his horns and hoofs. When Bill led Little Joe into the building, stagehands, cameramen, and script girls clustered around him.

"Is it a real buffalo?" they asked. "Where'd you get him? Aren't they extinct?"

As Joe moseyed about casually, peering in doorways and down hallways, Bill answered their questions. The program manager of the early morning show, a young woman, approached Bill. Indignantly, she said, "He's much too large. I thought he was a baby buffalo."

"He's a young buffalo," Bill answered. "Only two years old. He has a lot of growing to do yet."

The woman was terrified of the buffalo, and she refused to allow Joe to appear on the show with Bill. "Each of those four television cameras cost eighty thousand dollars," she said. "If that creature goes wild on the set, the bill would be astronomical! There's no way that I'll permit that bull on my Morning Show set!"

Bill tried to calm her. "Little Joe is a gentleman. He won't misbehave if you'll just stay calm and leave him alone."

The woman's nervous tizzy was upsetting to Joe, but she seemed to enjoy the attention she was getting from her fuss. She raved on.

Bill put an end to the scene by insisting that he talk to the director. With only three minutes to go before his scheduled appearance, Bill assured the director that Joe would be no problem. "We've brought Little Joe all the way to Detroit specifically for this show," Bill said. "If Joe isn't on the show, I won't be on the show."

The director decided that Joe would be on the show. The manager gave in reluctantly, but by this time she'd upset the show's host, who was to interview Bill. Everyone on the set was on edge.

Bill stood in front of the podium, holding a very docile and placid Joe by a dog chain leash. The host huddled behind the podium, eyeing the beast warily. Quietly, Bill explained his purpose in bringing Joe to Detroit, that of publicizing the fact that surplus buffalo from our parks and ranges should be given to Indians on reservations. "If people agree with me that this is just," Bill said, "I'd like them to write to me, expressing their approval. I'll forward their letters to the appropriate members of Congress to demonstrate the wishes of the public.''

The cameras panned in close, and Bill continued, ''People can write to me at a very simple address. Write to 'The Buffalo Doctor, Stanwood, Michigan.' ''

At this point Joe began to rub his neck on the interviewer's podium, trying to relieve an itchy spot. His eyes half-closed, the buffalo rubbed gently, but it rattled the host. The poor man was closer to a buffalo than he wanted to be. As Joe swung his head, he brushed the script with all the buffalo questions to the floor. Quickly, the host terminated the interview, but the cameramen followed Joe's exit through the studio as the buffalo casually avoided the expensive television cameras.

We returned Little Joe to Mondello's Japanese garden backyard and hurried downtown to a radio station where Bill was scheduled for a noon interview. The radio interviewer was excellent and enthusiastic. With ease, he asked the right questions, helping Bill explain to the listening audience what some of the needs of American Indians are.

''For five years,'' Bill explained, ''I've been writing letters, trying to get our federal parks to live up to their 1965 agreement and give their surplus buffalo to the Indians. The parks produce about one thousand surplus buffalo each year. These surplus animals they auction off to the highest bidder, or have a buffalo hunt. I believe that the Indians can use them very well, as a food supply, or in research projects such as crossbreeding buffalo and beef to get a rugged hybrid animal.''

''Are reservation Indians actually short on food?'' the interviewer asked.

''Last summer,'' Bill answered, ''on the Rosebud and Pine Ridge reservations in South Dakota, during the month of July, people were supplied with two pounds of canned chopped meat, per person. In August each person received only one-half pound of canned meat, and in September there was no meat. Many people think that one hundred years ago the white man mistreated the Indian. What most people don't know is that this same treatment of starvation is going on today on our Indian reservations.''

"Doctor, has there been marked resistence from the government agencies toward this proposal of giving the surplus buffalo to the Indians?"

"I wouldn't call it 'resistence,' Bill answered. "It's more of an ignoring of the problem. This is why I feel that if we can arouse public interest in these projects, and public awareness of the starving situation on the reservations, we can conquer two problems at the same time. Buffalo would provide both work and food for the Indian people. At one time the western tribes lived on buffalo. Buffalo are still a part of their religious ceremonies and the spiritual basis of the Indian people."

After the radio interview we gathered up Little Joe and his trailer and drove to two different newspaper offices, where Bill and Joe were photographed and interviewed.

It had been a long day. At dusk we bid good-bye to our new Detroit friends and headed west for Muskegon on the other side of the state. A cold drizzle followed us all the way home. In the dark we unloaded Joe from his trailer. Beth's horse whinnied his delight to greet the shaggy traveler's return, but Joe plodded into the pasture reluctantly.

Bill laughed. "How're we gonna keep him down on the farm now that he's seen Detroit and a Japanese garden?"

I tossed together a quick sandwich and soup supper, and we sat down to eat. Outside in the front yard Bruno began barking. The barking continued, and we tried to ignore it. Probably a wandering tomcat, we figured.

Suddenly, squealing tires drowned out the barking. I opened the front door and peered into the darkness. In the middle of the road intersection, silhouetted in the headlights of a stopped car, were the shapes of two buffalo.

"The buffalo are out!" I cried.

Like firemen at the sound of the alarm, we all moved quickly. No one needed to be told what to do. Pulling on coat and boots, we each grabbed a protective whip and collected cans of enticing grain. As we stepped into the side yard, we could make out the dim shape of Little Joe, standing serenely beside his trailer, chewing his cud.

"That big ham, Joe!" Bill laughed. "All he wants to do is go, go, go. Just follow that yellow line!"

The pasture gate gaped open. It was easy to see what had happened. Restless and bored after an hour's confinement in the pasture, Joe had pushed down the gate to get to that symbol of excitement, his trailer. But Joe wasn't the problem. Sisseton Sioux and Good Cow also had escaped through the open gate, and they weren't standing around docilely. They seemed to be heading north. Bill fastened a lead rope around Joe's neck and led him in pursuit of the fleeing buffalo cows. Using Joe as a decoy, Bill hoped to get the escapees to follow Joe back into the pasture. He called over his shoulder as he disappeared into the blackness, "If you see them coming back, get the big gate open quick!"

The cold rain had stopped, but thick clouds shut out any moonlight. In the murky darkness, every bush and pine tree looked like a charging buffalo. The squeak of rubbing tree branches sounded like approaching buffalo hoofs. "Cowards die many times," I lectured myself. "Brave men taste of death but once. Stop being a coward!"

I strained, listening. Where were the two escaped cows, and where was Bill? Then distantly I heard pounding hoofs. Quickly, the thudding sound grew louder. I fumbled with the padlock and threw open the drive-in gate. Just as I leaped aside, a dark buffalo shape thundered past, rushing through the opening and into the pasture. I hesitated. Should I swing the gate shut, or was the other buffalo coming, too? From behind me, very close, came a low grunt. Startled, I whirled toward the sound and saw that it was Good Cow, my old adversary. Silently, she'd slipped up and was staring at me.

From far off, Bill's voice shouted, "Get away from the gate, Pinkie! She won't go in while you're standing there! Get around behind her!"

Timidly I backed away.

Good Cow inched closer to the open gate, then changed her mind and sauntered toward me. Like a frightened child covering his head with blankets, I slid behind a blue spruce tree. Immediately I was sorry, since I couldn't see what was coming at me.

I gasped with relief when Bill called, "She's heading toward the gate again. Get behind her now, Pinkie, and wave your arms! Don't let her think you're afraid of her!"

But I *was* afraid of her, and I was positive Good Cow knew this. With a resigned sigh, I ran toward the fearsome buffalo, waving my arms and yelling like a banshee. Good Cow stood her ground for a few unnerving moments as I rushed toward her. Then with a disgusted grunt, she turned and sauntered casually into the pasture.

I closed the gate and leaned against it weakly. Soon Bill came across the road, leading Joe, chatting amiably all the way.

"I know you like to travel, Joe," Bill said, unhooking the lead rope, "but we can't just go, go, go all the time." Bill opened the gate and Joe plodded into the pasture.

"That's a good boy, Joe," Bill chuckled, patting the shaggy brown flank. "I'll tell you what. If you're good, maybe I'll take you with me to Florida, fishing."

As we walked toward the house, I threw Bill a sharp glance. "Take Joe on a fishing trip to Florida?" I said each word clearly and distinctly.

"Why not?" Bill grinned. "In Florida Joe could stir up public interest toward getting the government's surplus buffalo to the Indians. Besides, Joe has never seen the ocean."

And so it happened that early in April Bill and his fishing friends departed for Florida, towing behind them a two-horse trailer carrying Little Joe the Buffalo.

Somehow I found it embarrassing. Neighbors and friends missed seeing Joe in the pasture, and asked where he was. The answer always caught in my throat. The truth: "He's down in Florida with my husband, fishing," brought blank stares. No one believed it for a moment.

218

Joe had a grand time during his holiday in Florida. He gazed with interest at the strange-looking palm trees. He loved to roll and dust himself in the white sand on the beach. But most of all, he was impressed with the Gulf of Mexico. Ankle deep in salt water, Joe loved to watch the endless, rhythmic surf pound in.

Joe experienced another "first" in Florida. He made his first appearance on a radio show.

"Radio!" I exclaimed, when Bill told me about it. "What on earth could Little Joe do on radio?"

"He was just great," Bill chuckled. "He was a real gentleman. Right away he lay down on the carpeting in the studio. We were on the air for a whole hour, and Joe behaved beautifully. The interviewer was tremendous. She did a good job getting across the whole Surplus Buffalo to Indians concept. Whenever she had to stop to read a commercial, she always tied the commercial in to Little Joe, and Buffalo-to-the-Indians. When she advertised stationery, she said, 'You can use this stationery to write to The Buffalo Doctor, Stanwood, Michigan to give your support.' About half way through the program, Joe started chewing his cud, and she got right down on the floor beside him and held the microphone close to his mouth so the listeners could hear the sounds of a buffalo chewing his cud. Later on, Joe began to snore, and she made sure she picked that up on the mike."

Back home from his trip to Florida, Joe grazed contentedly in the pasture. Apparently, the long trip had satisfied his travel urge for the time being. He was beginning to shed his winter fur, and Bill brushed and curried him daily, since the loosening fur made Joe itch. One day as Bill was brushing Joe vigorously, I commented, "Joe really liked the Gulf of Mexico, huh?" Then, wistfully, "I've never seen the Gulf of Mexico."

Bill waved the brush at me. "Well, if you're good like Joe, maybe I'll take you some day."

219

Photo Courtesy of Rudy

*"There is no such thing as justice—
in or out of court."*
    —Clarence Darrow, 1936

•

Get Us Some Buffalo!

19 Late in July at the Means-Banks trial in St. Paul, the United States government prosecutors completed their case, and Judge Nichol gave the jury a two-week vacation before the defense lawyers began their presentation.

During the trial recess we learned that the fall Board of Directors meeting of the National Buffalo Association was to be held in Custer State Park in the Black Hills of South Dakota. Bill was expected to attend.

"Let's make a vacation out of it, Pinkie," Bill proposed. "If we drive the van, we can sleep in it and save motel costs. On the way to the Black Hills we can stop in St. Paul and spend some time at the Wounded Knee trial, then visit Indian reservations as we cross South Dakota. I want to see first hand how the Indian hospitals are doing."

A two week vacation sounded great, even though it would be a working vacation, centering on Indian problems and ways of getting surplus buffalo to the Indians. Since Bruce and Beth wouldn't be going back to college until the middle of September, they could stay home and care for the animals and be stand-in father and mother to Brenda.

Another federal court hearing was scheduled for September 16. This meant we would have to hurry home after the Black Hills Board of Directors meeting. On this trip Bill hoped to establish some understandings between the ranchers and the Indians, and he hoped to spend time on the reservations to get some agreements activated. Having to rush back for the scheduled hearing would cut short some of the accomplishments Bill hoped to achieve. For seventeen months we had been dominated by these periodic hearings. Over and over again, the hearings were scheduled, then postponed for sixty days. Though grateful for the postponements, we wished we could know a week in advance that our appearance in court wasn't necessary. We were never informed of the postponement until the day before, or sometimes the very morning of the scheduled hearing. Several times Bill had talked to and written Neal, our attorney, asking if this couldn't be corrected. Each time one of these hearings was scheduled, Bill dared not schedule any surgery for two or three days before the hearing date. There was always the possibility that the hearing would be held and Bill transferred to the court in South Dakota. If the surgical patient developed problems, Bill would be far off in South Dakota, and unable to care for his patient.

Also, surgical patients must be scheduled and prepared several days ahead of the day of their operation. The scheduled and then postponed hearings made for much uncertainty here. The Stanwood hospital was greatly inconvenienced by the hearings. For several years the patients and hospital staff had depended upon Bill being there to do surgery on Thursdays.

Bill explained this to our attorney, telling him, "Every time a hearing is scheduled, it causes delays and prolonged hospital stays which could be avoided if you and the Justice Department attorney would reach an agreement three or four days earlier as to whether the hearing will be held or postponed once again." Still, the last minute postponements continued.

As we began to lay plans for our western trip, Bill grew

exasperated that another hearing was going to cut short his projected visits to Indian reservations. This time he wrote a long letter to our lawyer describing the scheduling problems with his patients and asking for another postponement, this time well in advance of the hearing date. Bill sent a carbon copy of the letter to the presiding judge of the federal court holding jurisdiction over his case.

Neal phoned Bill. "Doc," he advised. "You mustn't consider going back to the South Dakota reservations where there's so much tension. You might get caught in the conflict between the Bureau of Indian Affairs Indians and American Indian Movement Indians, or in the conflict between the Indians and the white ranchers."

"I'm really the only one working on this project of Buffalo to the Indians," Bill argued, "and the related research projects. I'm close friends with many of the Indians and the white ranchers involved in the conflicts. The buffalo research projects are badly needed by the ranchers, and the Indians are desperate for meaningful work. Possibly these buffalo projects can establish lines of communication and cooperation between the Indians and the white ranchers."

"I won't be responsible in any way," Neal said, "if you persist in going to South Dakota. If you're arrested out there, I won't be able to defend you. Doc, out there you'll be strictly on your own, and I don't like the smell of this whole deal. There's a way out of this that I've been working on. I got a call from the assistant prosecuting attorney in Deadwood. The Justice Department is offering to let you plead guilty to three counts of illegal operation of aircraft, five hundred dollars fine on each count for a total of fifteen hundred dollars fine if it's all settled out of court. Possibly we can negotiate this a little more and get it down to one thousand dollars. But they keep reading about you out there, Doc. They know your wife is a writer, and they figure you're getting rich off this thing."

Bill snorted. "Neal, you know I don't get a dime from those articles. In fact, publicity can be a real pain in the neck. Publicity attracts the attention of promoters and emotionally unstable individuals who figure they have an excuse to come to my home, even when I've never seen them before."

"We have to consider this plea bargaining offer they've submitted," Neal continued. "The thing I like about it is that it takes us off the hook on the felony charge and gets us out of criminal court and into only a civil charge, which is a lot easier to handle. Remember, Doc, as long as you're under a federal felony charge, your license to practice surgery and medicine anywhere in this country is in jeopardy. You know you made the flight. Why don't you let them rap your knuckles and take your punishment like a good boy? This way neither side wins, but neither side gets hurt too badly. It's a good compromise, and I think you should take it, especially before you go back out to Dakota where you run the risk of having further charges piled on you. You might get in deeper than you already are."

Bill shook his head. "You know, Neal, it's very difficult to compromise on principles without damaging one's spirit and losing one's principles. If I should plead guilty to these aircraft charges, where does this leave Paul and his pilot's license, as well as the other defendants in the Wounded Knee trials?"

"Paul will be all right," Neal answered. "I asked the government attorneys about that."

"The Indians must be able to trust me if they're going to make these buffalo projects work. If I buy my way out of this thing when they can't, they won't respect me, man to man."

"You don't have to make a decision right this minute," Neal said. "But I urge you to take this chance to get out of the felony charge."

"I want to do a little digging on this and try to find out what's going on. I'll get in touch with you later," Bill answered.

Bill made some phone calls, and between the information he got, and Dakota newspaper articles, we pieced together a more realistic picture of what was taking place in the trials, so far.

We learned that on August 10, 1974, in St. Paul, Minnesota, Judge Nichol had dismissed charges of obstruction of justice against Russell Means and Dennis Banks. The charges were dismissed because a Brigadier general and his staff from the 82nd Airborne had been at Wounded Knee with the F.B.I. and federal marshals, along with army equipment which was used during the confrontation. It is unconstitutional for the army to become involved in a civil disturbance without a presidential order, and no presidential order had been given. The makers of our Constitution showed great wisdom in making this restriction on use of the army. The instability of many Latin American governments is increased because their armies interfere, moving in on a civil disturbance, ousting the president, and taking over the government.

On August 14, the very day the assistant prosecuting attorney phoned Neal with the plea bargaining offer, Judge Urbom in Lincoln, Nebraska, dismissed obstruction of justice charges against two Wounded Knee defendants because the government had not proved it was at Wounded Knee legally. The judge emphasized that his ruling did not mean the government was there illegally; it meant the government had not proved it was there legally.

After we had digested all this new information, I asked Bill what he thought.

Bill laid aside the clippings. "It looks to me as if the Justice Department has lost their charge of obstruction of justice. I think they're trying to snag me into pleading guilty to as heavy a charge as they can, without having to go to court to prove it. I'll plead guilty to disorderly conduct and frequenting a disorderly place." Bill picked up the phone. "I'm going to tell Neal about the dismissal of these obstruction of justice charges."

The lawyer appreciated the information, but reminded Bill that this didn't necessarily mean that the Justice Department would drop charges of obstruction of justice. Neal said the government could have more evidence that they hadn't gotten admitted to the other trials. They might wish to get this additional evidence admitted into court, and might want to take Bill and Paul to trial to do so.

"I'm going out to Dakota," Bill told Neal. "Maybe while I'm gone, you and the prosecuting attorney can do some straight talking and see if we can't get a better understanding."

Bill and I spent several days loading the van with cooking utensils, food, sleeping bags, jeans, and formal dress for the diversified trip ahead of us. When we waved goodbye to the children and backed out of our driveway, Little Joe was standing beside the pasture fence watching the van. As we passed Joe, he gave a loud snort, kicked up a swirl of dust, and pounded along the fence line, chasing our van.

"Joe wants to go along," Bill chuckled. "He knows it's going to be an interesting trip, and he wants to go."

It was very early in the morning when Bill and I arrived in St. Paul and presented ourselves at the law offices of the American Indian Movement defense attorneys to request passes, which were necessary to gain admittance to the Means-Banks trial.

A copy machine was flipping out copies of legal documents. Third-year law students and young Indian girls, all volunteers, were busy gathering papers, filing, and typing. Obviously, the office was geared for quick response to every new twist in the trial procedures.

When Bill introduced himself, an Indian girl's black eyes flashed recognition. "Oh, you're the Buffalo Doctor!" she said. "The one who flew the food to Wounded Knee." She handed us mugs of welcome coffee.

Soon the defense attorneys began arriving. We were introduced to William Kunstler, Mark Lane, and Kenneth Tilsen, who questioned Bill about the way his defense was going. The three attorneys offered helpful advice, explaining that they would be happy to cooperate with our lawyer in any way. I was impressed with their sincere concern for the defense of the people charged with the Wounded Knee effort. These attorneys with their amateur and inexperienced help, much of it volunteer, were opposing the mighty resources of the federal government with all its expertise, and making a good accounting of themselves.

Only thirty people a day were admitted as spectators to the trial. American Indian Movement security was in charge of selecting those thirty people. When we arrived at the federal building, we found it under tight security. Just inside the front entrance were uniformed guards, and everyone entering the building for any reason had to have a specific admittance pass and walk through a metal detecting device.

After passing through the metal detector, we were ushered onto an elevator going only to the seventh floor, the location of Judge Nichol's courtroom. The elevator operator was a United States marshal. As we stepped out onto the seventh floor, we faced another search for metallic articles and dangerous weapons. Male spectators were directed to one line where they were searched by a marshal, and women were checked out by a female deputy. A metal detector was passed over our bodies, front and back, and purses and briefcases were searched.

Just ahead of me in line was a grandmotherly-type lady with bluish hair. The female deputy searching this woman's purse frowned and held up a plastic rat-tail comb. "I'll have to keep this," she said, dropping the dangerous comb into a Manila envelope. My purse also contained a forbidden weapon—my fingernail file, which was confiscated and placed in a brown envelope. Now I was really nervous. With such tight security and fear of combs and nailfiles, was a riot expected? My stomach churned. Perhaps we shouldn't be here, I worried.

Inside the courtroom there were six rows of benches which served as the spectator section. A half dozen reporters occupied the first row. The rest of the audience was mostly Indian people. Behind the judge's bench the wall was decorated with strips of bronze metal running floor to ceiling, overlaid with a bronze plaque of an eagle and shield. Along the left wall of the courtroom were sixteen seats for the jurors, including the usual twelve, plus four alternate jurors. The defense attorneys, whom we'd met earlier, filed in and took their places at their table along the right wall, and the prosecuting attorneys seated themselves at the table in the center of the courtroom.

Several men in dark business suits placed themselves in different seats about the courtroom. Each of these men wore a small square lapel pin, one-half of which was green, the other half, gold. As one of these dark-suited figures slid in beside Bill, we realized these men were United States marshals.

The two defendants, Means and Banks, strolled toward the defense table. Both wore blue jeans, and Russell Means wore a flowered shirt. His hair flowed long and wavy down his back. Dennis Banks wore a levi denim jacket sewn with streamers of the five American Indian Movement colors. His shiny black hair was drawn tight into two long braids, each wrapped in bright blue ribbon. A big man, tall and ruggedly handsome, Means casually pushed his chair back against the wall, folded his arms, and appeared to drowse. Banks began leafing through legal documents. Though scarcely forty years old, Banks resembled a wise old patriarch. The perpetual scowl on his face hinted that he carried the burdens of all the Indian people.

When black-robed Judge Nichol entered his courtroom, most of us stood. In the audience a few Indians remained seated, and Means and Banks did not rise. The judge ignored this gesture and rapped his gavel. I knew the purpose of those who remained seated. It was a gesture of independence, and perhaps, defiance. Earlier in the summer at an Indian trial in Sioux Falls, some Indian spectators refused to rise when Federal Judge Bottum entered his courtroom. Infuriated, the judge ordered the marshals to clear the courtroom, and an angry riot ensued. Many people were injured, and the courthouse was damaged. A little research turned up the fact that there is no law requiring people to stand when the judge makes his entrance. It is merely a custom. In protest to the harassment of Indians, many supporters had decided not to follow the old custom of rising for the judge. Judge Nichol had decided to ignore those who did not stand.

I studied the jury, made up of nine women and three men. Of the four alternate jurors, three were women. It was a young jury. Only one looked elderly, and many appeared to be in their twenties. A youthful jury, I thought, should be favorable to the Indian cause. The jurors had been sitting there for eight months, listening to testimony and legal maneuverings. I wondered how they felt. They seemed to be listening carefully, but their faces showed no emotion.

In his opening remarks Judge Nichol explained that he hoped today and tomorrow would finish the testimony. Closing arguments would be presented next week, followed by his instructions. The jury then would be sequestered at a downtown hotel where they would decide upon a verdict.

We were getting in on the last two days of the trial, which should prove interesting and perhaps very important.

The first witness was sworn in, and the defense attorneys began questioning him. It took Bill and me awhile to figure out what was going on. All the testimony referred to a young Indian man, Louis Moves Camp, a star witness for the government, who had testified two weeks earlier. At that time, Moves Camp, a defector from the American Indian Movement, had claimed to have been at Wounded Knee during most of the seventy-one day occupation. He substantiated charges against Means and Banks. As he made his accusations from the witness stand, his mother jumped from her seat in the audience and rushed ed toward him down the aisle, screaming, "You're lying, you're lying! Why are you lying?"

When defense attorney William Kunstler began cross-examining Moves Camp, the Indian testified that he had seen Means and Banks confer with representatives of China, East Germany, West Germany, and Russia.

Kunstler jeered, "Do you know that if what you say is true, this is the first time that East and West Germany have agreed on something?'' Spectators laughed and jeered, and the judge ordered them to leave the courtroom. In the ensuing confusion a United States marshal used Mace and fists generously. The angry judge put Kunstler and Mark Lane into jail for the night.

Now, two weeks following this outburst, the courtroom scene was quiet, but defense attorneys were busy attempting to discredit the prior testimony of Louis Moves Camp, who had been under the protective custody of the F.B.I. while awaiting his turn in court. The defense learned that Moves Camp, while in the care of the F.B.I., had been kept at a resort motel in Wisconsin, and that he had been accused of rape of a high school girl in a small Wisconsin town. The rape charges had been dropped, and the defense attorneys charged that the F.B.I. had suppressed the charge to preserve Moves Camp's credibility as a witness.

I wondered how the jury felt. As I listened to the testimony, I grew convinced that a rape had been committed, and that the F.B.I. had pressured the local authorities, the raped girl and her mother, not to prosecute this star witness.

During a mid-morning recess of the trial we moved into the lobby outside the courtroom. Russell Means approached Bill and introduced himself. We chatted for a few moments, then Means invited us into the defense rooms.

The defense rooms consisted of a conference room where defense lawyers could confer with their clients during recesses, and another larger room filled with many chairs. This seemed to be a lounge room for Indian sympathizers and witnesses waiting to be called to the stand. A gnarled, toothless Indian man hunched in one of the chairs, looking miserable in a wrinkled suit and pink shirt many sizes too large. Bill offered him a cigarette, which the old man took with a grunt.

A younger man lounging on the radiator leaned forward. "This is George Gap. He's going to be a witness, and I'm his interpreter." I'd forgotten that English is not the native language of this land. George Gap had been called as a witness to confess that he requested the American Indian Movement Indians to seize Wounded Knee. As an elder and a chief, George claimed to be the real leader, and the one whom the government should prosecute.

During the afternoon court session Bill opened his small address book, then reached into his coat pocket for his reading glasses, or I should say, his spectacles, which describes them better. They are very old, wire-framed spectacles. Bill keeps them in their original case, a metal envelope.

When Bill pulled the wire glasses from the metal case, the United States marshal sitting in front of him whirled around, alarmed, half-rising from his seat. A marshal from the back of the courtroom immediately dashed to our aisle. Apparently, the sliding metallic sound resembled the screech of a knife being removed from its scabbard. This incident was a reminder of the tension that invaded the courtroom, and in fact, most Indian-white encounters. Suspicion and distrust were everywhere. The marshal sitting beside Bill had seen the glasses, and he assured the others that everything was all right.

After observing court proceedings for two days we grew more and more disillusioned. Our faith in the honesty and integrity of the Justice Department was growing dim.

As we walked from the federal building for the last time and stood waiting for a red light to change, a dilapidated pickup truck rattled up to the curb. Russell Means leaned out the window and waved, "Keep up the good work, Doc! Get us some buffalo!"

*"Lo, the poor Indian! who's untutor'd mind
Sees God in clouds, or hears him in the wind."*
  —Alexander Pope

The Sacred Pipe

20 From St. Paul we headed northwest, toward Indian Country. Our first destination was the village of Rosholt on the Sisseton Reservation, Bill's birthplace, and his home until he was fifteen years old. One of Bill's eight sisters still lived at Rosholt, and we planned to visit her family for a few days before moving on to the more western Sioux reservations.

On the Sisseton Reservation we found Indian-white tensions running high. Daily, there were minor confrontations, and some erupted into real violence. Though she didn't agree with Bill's sympathy and help toward Indian causes, Bill's sister offered to guide us around the area. Bill had been gone for thirty years.

"It sure looks a lot more prosperous than when I was a kid," he mused. "I'd like to see Sieche Hollow," he proposed. Sieche Hollow had been an Indian powwow grounds when Bill was a boy. To make money, Bill's family had sold pop at these powwows, and Bill had fond memories of participating in some Indian dancing, much to his mother's disapproval. Now a state park, Sieche Hollow remains a beautiful spot, preserved naturally, made up of steep hills and cozy hollows. Little springs gush from hillsides and trickle into the hollow to form a bubbling brook.

Bill's sister, Geneva, Bill and I hiked along narrow paths, picking and eating rosehips, high in vitamin C, Bill said.

He led us to a large, grassy plain. "I want you women to be silent for once," he said. "Listen to the grass. Be still now. Don't move or talk until you hear my whistle."

He moved off, out of sight. I knew Bill's reason for wanting to return to Sieche Hollow. He wanted to listen to the grass.

We had no idea how long Bill would stay here, but it was pleasant sitting in the tall grass, warmed by the sun and sheltered from the incessant wind. The stiff breeze made varied waves in the feathery grass tops. The whistle of the wind changed in pitch and volume from moment to moment, just as my thoughts were changing. I sat quietly going over details of our problems. My thoughts wandered like the wind in the grass tops above me. At times the wind grew strong and blew from one direction for a few moments. The random facets of our problems came together into focus. If Bill should go to court, and lose, the specter of the penitentiary and the loss of his license to practice was there. We didn't have the money to fight the government in court. It appeared Bill would have to abandon principle and accept plea bargaining.

The wind died down to a gentle breeze again. The air grew chilly as the sun slipped behind a western hill. As darkness closed upon us it grew very silent, except for the quiet sounds of insects in the grass.

The stillness was broken by a sudden gust of breeze, which grew into a strong wind from a new direction. Bill's distinct short whistle announced his return and broke our solitude. He motioned us to follow him down the dim moonlit path. Though he remained silent, he moved with new determination.

As I stepped carefully down the steep path, I asked Geneva if the wind always blew like this in Dakota.

"It seems a little strange," she said. "The last few days

the wind can't seem to make up its mind which way to blow. You know, pioneer women found the Dakota winds blowing through the grass very threatening. It drove some of them mad. They heard all sorts of things from the grass."

As he drove us back to Geneva's farm, Bill remained quiet and thoughtful.

I asked Geneva what was happening with the Indian people on the Sisseton Reservation.

She pursed her lips. "A few days ago we had a riot and burning episode just down the road from us." A restaurant owner, she said, had received several worthless checks written by Indians. When he took the checks to the sheriff for help in collecting them, the sheriff told him that the Indian check-writers had no property, no money, and no wages to garnishee. There was no way to recover the money. Angrily, the restaurant owner tacked up a sign, "No Indian checks." Outraged over this insulting sign, the Indian people retaliated by not only boycotting the establishment, but forming a cordon around it to prevent anyone from entering.

"It's a bad situation," Geneva said.

"It seems to me the restaurant owner went out of his way to insult the Indian people," I observed. "He could have put up a sign saying 'checks cashed at owner's discretion,' and then chosen which checks he wished to accept. What if he'd gotten a bad check from a farmer, and put up a 'no farmer checks' sign? The farmers wouldn't like that."

The next day we went to Sisseton, the county seat. Bill drove to the Indian hospital, which he wanted to visit. Though Sisseton is only a small country town, it struggles to maintain two separate hospitals, one Indian, administered by the Bureau of Indian Affairs, and the other, white, administered by the county. Each hospital maintained thirty beds, but had only fifty percent occupancy. When Bill talked with the two public health service doctors staffing the Indian hospital, he learned that theirs was a constant struggle with lack of funds, equipment, and facilities. Laboratory tests which should be done on-the-spot for immediate reading and accurate results, had to be mailed all the way to Creighton University, a distance of nearly three hundred miles.

From the Sisseton Reservation we set out for the Rosebud Reservation, west of the Missouri River, in southern South Dakota. Bill had heard that the Indians on the Rosebud had received some surplus buffalo, and he hoped to talk with the tribal chairman and find out how their buffalo-raising project was progressing.

Most towns on Indian reservations look seedy. If there is a nice residential section, it is a white neighborhood. The Indian section consists of a depressing collection of unpainted shacks and rusting automobiles. The town of Mission, where we spent the night, was typical. It was late when we pulled into town, and we were hungry. We drove the length of main street twice, looking for a restaurant, but saw only dingy saloons. Finally we stopped at a motel to ask about a place to eat.

"Oh, you'll want to go out to the country club to eat," the lady proprietor said. "That's the place to eat here. I'll have to give you pass cards to get in, and I'll call out there and let them know you're coming." She clucked her tongue and tucked a wisp of gray hair behind her ear. "You see, we had a little trouble out there a few weeks ago, and now they have very tight security arrangements."

We accepted the pass cards and drove toward the country club, following her directions. We knew what the "little trouble" had been. A few weeks before, some Indians, including Russell Means, had entered this country club and asked to be served. They were told it was a private club, and were asked to leave. A fight broke out, and Indians were arrested, including Russell Means. It was a private club as far as Indians were concerned, but an open eating place to us, strangers and transients, because we appeared to be white people.

As we stepped up to the door of the country club, we saw that it was locked, and a sign said, "Ring Bell." The bartender came to the door and peered at us through a small window. Bill held up the two pass cards, and the door was quickly opened.

It was a small dining room and bar, not elaborate, typical of small town country clubs around the country. A handful of people sat at the bar. Bill and I were the only guests eating. We devoured our steaks with amusement. Because we looked non-Indian, we were receiving friendly, gracious service. Wouldn't the waitress and bartender be horrified if they knew Bill was an accused felon, indicted for involvement at Wounded Knee?

Early the next morning when we drove into the little town of Rosebud, we saw that this was no ordinary Indian town. Set in gorgeous, rolling country with copper-colored cliffs and green hills dotted with dark pine groves, the town of Rosebud was immaculate, almost manicured, and prosperous looking. There were many B.I.A. offices, government cars, and a good-sized hospital. All the official houses, buildings, and vehicles were painted the same color of "government green." We remained in Rosebud several hours, and every inhabitant we saw was Indian.

At the police station Bill asked where he could find Bob Burnette, the tribal chairman. An obliging B.I.A. policeman hopped into a squad car and led us directly to Burnette's home, an attractive, modern ranch-style house, surrounded by homes of the same caliber.

Bill knocked on the door, identified himself, and disappeared inside. Soon he beckoned me to join him. Though we were complete strangers to the Burnettes, we were greeted warmly, and given breakfast.

As I spread a slice of toast with homemade chokecherry jam, I told Mr. Burnette, "I enjoyed your book, *The Road to Wounded Knee*, very much. I wish I'd thought to bring it along so I could have you autograph it."

"No problem," he said, rising from the table and returning with a new copy of the book, which he autographed to Bill and me. I autographed a copy of my book to him, and our exchange was complete.

Bill chuckled. "Bob, I want to thank you for devoting two pages in your book to my flight to Wounded Knee."

Burnette blinked, and then his face lit up. "Oh, you're the doctor who flew the food to Wounded Knee! Now I know who you are!"

Quietly, Mrs. Burnette added, "We had a son at Wounded Knee."

"Have they dropped the charges against you?" Burnette asked.

"No, I'm still under indictment for obstruction of justice."

Burnette shook his head sympathetically. Then he began describing some of his ambitious plans for improving life on the Rosebud Reservation. He explained about the improvement in medical care which soon would be brought about by a computer program which would exchange medical information quickly. A beautiful, expensive home was being built with the hope of attracting and keeping a permanent doctor at Rosebud. For many years the doctors staffing the hospital had been mostly young men just out of medical school who chose to serve two years with the Indian Health Service in lieu of serving time in Viet Nam. With the end of the draft, the influx of young doctors had disappeared. Now the reservation had to do something quickly to insure itself of adequate medical care.

As tribal chairman, Burnette had been working hard to regain Indian lands previously sold to non-Indians. In recent months the tribal council had purchased thousands of acres of land. This was land within the reservation boundaries which, over the years, had passed out of Indian or tribal ownership.

"Let me show you our proposed wildlife refuge," he said. "This is where we hope to put our buffalo—when we get them. I'd like you to tell me if it looks like suitable buffalo land."

Bill and I climbed into Burnette's big four-wheel drive pickup truck and were given a tour of the Rosebud area. We passed through a powwow grounds, recognizable by the circular enclosure of wooden posts, covered with pine boughs, now dry and brown. Bill climbed out and opened a gate, through which we drove into a large pasture area. The persistent wind blew his hat off. Bill ran across the rocky terrain to retrieve it.

"All this land is now tribal land." Burnette waved his arm in a sweeping motion. "Twenty-seven thousand acres, all enclosed by fence, and there's some cross-fencing in it. As far as you can see in any direction, this is Rosebud land now."

We bounced up a steady rise and stopped at the peak. A green valley many miles wide spread out before us. Pink cliffs bordered a small river snaking through the valley. Clusters of white pine trees grew thick and green throughout. Much of the land of the Rosebud and Pine Ridge Reservations is bleak and desert-like. This vast expanse of acreage was different. It was both lush and spectacularly beautiful.

"Buffalo will love it," Bill breathed. "They love variety in the landscape, and this is perfect."

Bill's main suggestion concerned fences. The outside fences were too low. He recommended that another strand of barbed wire be tacked on top of the posts, bringing the height up to what might be adequate. "If buffalo have enough room and variety, they probably won't bother the outside fences," Bill said. "And with this beautiful twenty-seven thousand acres, they ought to be happy buffalo."

When we returned to Burnette's home, several people were waiting to see him about various problems. We left him to his duties. Being tribal chairman is much more demanding than being mayor of a town. Burnette has the same duties as a mayor, but in addition, he is expected to be a marriage counselor, lawyer, and father-image for his people. Along with the complicated executive duties to be performed, the modern tribal chairman, like the chiefs of olden times, must fulfill the positon of adjudicator in personal crises arising among the people. Each day he must be responsive to the needs of his people.

Visiting the Pine Ridge Reservation was touchy. I was apprehensive about Bill's returning there while still under indictment. Though we were visiting friends there, it still amounted to the "criminal returning to the scene of the crime." Bill was eager to visit Wounded Knee and see what it looked like from the ground. Bill and Paul had been on the ground only eight minutes unloading the food, and Bill's memory of the layout was dim.

We found our reservation friends upset over continuing injustices occurring on the Pine Ridge. They were especially irate over the distribution of a recent donation of a large supply of lumber and building materials. Some East Coast churches had donated these supplies to be used for the rebuilding of Wounded Knee and for improving inadequate housing on the reservation. When the supplies arrived, they were stockpiled in Pine Ridge. Immediately, our friends said, surrounding white ranchers and well-to-do Indians began arriving in pickup trucks pulling trailers, into which they loaded quantities of lumber, roofing, and plywood. Several ranchers had built whole houses and barns with this donated lumber. They said one rancher used dozens of sheets of heavy plywood to make feed troughs for his cattle.

"The poor people, those for whom the lumber was intended, lost out, for the most part," our friends grieved. "They had no trailers to haul the lumber in. They had to scrounge to borrow a truck in running condition from friends. They told of their neighbor, an elderly widow, who made two trips to the lumber stockpile. Each time she was told nothing was available at the moment, that she should come back another time. All this poor woman wanted was enough lumber and roofing to put a cover on her basement-home so she could live in it, come winter.

"It just makes me burn," one of our young friends said, "to think of all the well-off ranchers who carted away most of that donated lumber. It wasn't meant for them, and they knew it! Those eastern churches meant well and did a fine thing. It was the corrupt distribution methods here that were wrong."

"We get so aggravated," one of the young men added, "over continuing injustices here on the reservation. Back in 1942 the War Department and the Bureau of Indian Affairs confiscated five hundred square miles of this reservation land to use as a practice bombing range. The Indian-owners were given less than a month to evacuate their homes. They were told that it was patriotic to give up their land, and they were assured that the land would be returned to them when the war ended."

He told us that the land had not been returned. "The war ended, and years passed by," he said. "In 1965 the War Department declared the land "surplus" and gave it to the General Services Administration."

A blue-eyed, bearded teacher spoke up. "And now more than thirty years have gone by, and the Indians still want their land back. But do you know what the government has done with this supposedly "borrowed" land? Because of heavy lobbying by conservationists, the Sierra Club, and ranchers, Congress has passed a law making this a sanctuary for the black-footed ferret."

"What's a black-footed ferret?" I asked.

"It's a sort of weasel," he said. "It goes down into the burrows of animals such as rabbits and prairie dogs and sucks their blood." His lips curled with disgust. "And you know, the ferret isn't even an animal native to North America. It originates in Africa. Here, again, you have to say that the Indian lands are being used to serve the white ranchers who are always eager to get rid of the prairie dogs and other wildlife that burrows holes. Ranchers' cattle and horses may step in a burrow and break a leg. With the black-footed ferret working for them, they don't have to poison these animals."

When it came time to leave our friends, we told them of our plans to pass through Wounded Knee.

"You know, don't you, that the church at Wounded Knee was burned down?" the teacher asked.

"Yes, we'd heard that," Bill said. "But who did it?"

The young man shrugged. "That's a big question here on the reservation. The B.I.A. people say that American

241

Indian Movement members burned it down in defiance of Christianity. The A.I.M. people say that the government had it burned to destroy the evidence of all the bullet holes. The B.I.A. police didn't seem to make any serious effort to find out who burned the church, and the A.I.M. people can't find out anything about it."

A young woman spoke up. "All the A.I.M. people I know wanted the church to stand. It had just as many bullet holes as the Alamo, except those bullet holes were put there by the United States government."

As Bill and I approached Wounded Knee, our van cruised over a slope, and we looked out over the wide valley in which the village huddles. It was hard to get our bearings, since the little white Sacred Heart Church on the hill was gone.

We drove slowly into the hamlet, parking beside the hilltop cemetery. Where the church had stood, there was only a scar, a gaping hole of concrete basement filled with refuse.

His back to the burned-out church, Bill faced south and pointed out the field where he and Paul had landed. "We came in over those trees," he said softly. For a long time he gazed at the autumn-dry pasture, and I knew he was reliving those dangerous moments when they'd brought the little Cessna down onto the frozen slough that cold March day. He stood facing into the brisk wind. The wind now was strong and blowing persistently in one direction, perhaps part of a mammoth storm system. I shivered. Was everything all right at home?

Not a living soul was in sight. The wind whistled through the dry weeds, and we turned to walk through the cemetery. The long mass grave outlined by cement was bare sand, not even a blade of grass grew on it. A year before, when the children and I stopped there, the whole grave had been covered by a carpet of artificial flowers. Now it was barren. The cemetery was in disreputable shape. Beer and pop cans were strewn about, and on one child's grave a soiled disposable diaper had been dropped.

Near dusk we left Wounded Knee and drove west toward the Black Hills, the legendary Paha Sapa of the Sioux, the place where the Great Spirit dwells. We drove warily along the reservation road. On an Indian reservation Saturday night is a dangerous night to be traveling. On most reservations liquor is not sold. Therefore, Indians drive to border towns to drink, and return to their homes under the influence. Terrible Saturday night auto accidents are the single major cause of Indian deaths on reservations.

In the beautiful pine-covered Black Hills we stayed at the rustic Custer Park Game Lodge, and were lodged in the President Coolidge Suite. In 1927 the Game Lodge had been the Summer White House, and our room, along with a little sun porch, had been President and Mrs. Coolidge's bedroom. The furniture was exactly as it was when the President stayed there, the twin beds, even the President's desk with a quaint little triangular, three-legged stool. Next to our room was the Eisenhower room, where President Eisenhower had stayed one night during the 1950's. Another buffalo-raising couple was lodged there. We were delighted to be staying in these historic rooms, but there was one disadvantage. Everyone wanted to see the Coolidge and Eisenhower rooms, and we found ourselves giving frequent guided tours. I had to keep the room tidy all the time.

Bill had written letters to the tribal chairmen of several Indian reservations, inviting them to send representatives to our National Buffalo Association meeting, so they could learn some of the technicalities of handling buffalo. Several Indians from different tribes attended.

One group of Sioux Indians, especially appreciative of Bill's efforts at getting surplus buffalo from the government to the Indians, wished to hold a pipe-smoking ceremony with Bill as a sign of friendship and honor. Bill's friend, Selo Black Crow, conducted the ceremony, which was entirely in the Sioux language. Beforehand, he very thoughtfully explained in English what he would be doing, and the meaning of the symbolism.

"The power of the Almighty," he said, "you call it

God, we call it WakanTanka, the Great Spirit, is represented by six directions. I will hold this sacred pipe and
point it first to Father Sun, then down to Mother Earth.
Then I will pray to each of the four directions, thanking
them for their blessings to us. I will pray to the North
which puts the earth to sleep each winter, to the East
where the sun is born every day, to the South, from which
summer and production comes every year, and to the
West, the land of spirit power. Each of these directions is
represented by one of our sacred colors, which are four:
white, red, yellow, and black. These colors also represent
the four races of mankind. We are all brothers.''

After this explanation in English, the medicine man
filled his sacred pipe, and began his ritual, praying in his
native language. The group standing around all bowed
their heads. The prayer grew long for me because I didn't
understand the Sioux language. I remembered that Christian prayers sometimes were long and more like a sermon
than a prayer.

The prayer concluded, Black Crow struck a match and
lit the tobacco pressed tightly into the red Catlinite
pipebowl. The long wooden pipestem made drawing on
the pipe very difficult, but at last the tobacco glowed. The
medicine man puffed, then handed the pipe to Bill.
Ceremoniously, Bill received the sacred pipe and took
long, slow puffs from it.

''Now say 'All my relatives, how!''' Selo quietly instructed. ''This means you are remembering all your
relatives, all of us, everyone upon this earth, even tiny insects and plants.''

Holding the pipe out toward Black Crow, Bill said,
''All my relatives, how.''

The medicine man, however, did not reach out for the
pipe, but said ''Hand it to your wife.''

I was stunned. I dared not look at Bill. Though I
respected the seriousness of the pipe-smoking ceremony, I
had no idea women were active participants. In the movies
and television I never once had seen an Indian woman

share the peacepipe ceremony. Perhaps Women's Liberation has hit the Indian reservations, I thought.

I raised my eyes just enough to see Bill's hands thrusting the pipe toward mine, and I grasped the wooden stem, worrying that I might be committing some awful breach of etiquette by grasping the pipe in an awkward manner. I took two mighty puffs, but the pipe went out. I looked up helplessly at Black Crow. "All my relatives, how," I mumbled and returned the cold pipe quickly.

Selo turned his back to the strong wind and re-lit the pipe. He passed it to the old Indian on his left. Apparently, I had committed no great sacrilege by allowing the pipe to go out.

Sighing in relief, I lowered my eyes to my shoes, and concentrated on thinking solemn thoughts. This is so nice of Selo to welcome Bill in this way, I told myself. And surely, it's no stranger a ceremony than our Christian, Hebrew, or Moslem customs.

Afterwards, when Bill and I had a moment alone together, we exchanged smiles. "That was a nice ceremony," Bill said, "and I feel very honored they wanted to smoke the pipe with us."

Selo's peacepipe ceremony for Bill was good-bye and time to head home.

Our two-week journey to the Wounded Knee trial, the Indian reservations, and the buffalo meeting had been enjoyable and informative, and we believed we had made progress in Bill's Buffalo to the Indians project.

When we arrived home we learned that the Wounded Knee trial in St. Paul had gone to the jury. The jury was sequestered, deliberating. Anxiously, we awaited the results, wondering about the verdict.

"Hear me in my sorrow,
for I may never call again.
O make my people live!"
   —Black Elk, 1931

•

The Hurricane

21 But there was to be no jury verdict. One of the jurors suffered a stroke, severe enough to prevent her from continuing to deliberate with the jury. Judge Nichol hoped that both the prosecution and defense would approve the continuance of jury deliberations with the eleven remaining jurors. In a federal court, both sides must approve of such a decision. The defense lawyers quickly gave their approval for an eleven-man jury, but the government prosecutors refused.

Angered, Judge Nichol announced that he was dismissing all charges against the defendants. Reminding the court that the F.B.I. had driven him to the brink of dismissal several times during the trial, he said, "It's only fair to say I am now over the brink."

The defendants would have preferred an acquittal from the jury rather than this dismissal given by the judge. When the jurors were interviewed after the dismissal ruling, it became obvious that the jury vote would have gone for acquittal. At any rate, the Indians were elated. They spoke of this decision being a "blow for freedom" and a vindication of the Wounded Knee occupation.

After the major television networks carried the outcome of the trial, many well-wishers called us to congratulate Bill on being "off the hook." Everyone assumed that the government would drop its charges against Bill and Paul.

"Wouldn't it be wonderful to be out from under that criminal indictment?" I sighed.

"It'd be a real relief," Bill agreed. "I'd like to concentrate on getting the government to give up its surplus buffalo to the Indians. If I have to go to trial and fight the whole United States Department of Justice, I won't have time or money to do anything else."

In our local paper an editorial discussed the outcome of the Means-Banks trial, and hinted that this should affect other defendants, such as The Buffalo Doctor. The editorial concluded with a notice of the upcoming federal hearing of Dr. Cummings and added, "hopefully, the months of anguish and recurring harassment will come to a quick end."

But Judge Nichol's dismissal of the charges against Means and Banks didn't lead the government to drop charges against the other defendants. Instead, the government filed an appeal of the dismissal. Our attorney continued with his plea bargaining communications with the federal prosecuting attorney in South Dakota.

Bill worried about pleading guilty to the illegal operation of aircraft charges proposed by the prosecuting attorney. Bill explained to Neal that he'd been doing some flying with Bruce, and that he was hoping to get his pilot's license someday. "Can't the prosecutor come up with a charge that's outside the area of flying?" he asked. "If I plead guilty to illegal operation of aircraft, the F.A.A. might prosecute me."

Neal promised to see what he could do.

Bill called Paul to report the new legal entanglements, but Paul wasn't too interested. His mind was on other things.

"Say, Doc," Paul interrupted, "the Muskegon Indians want you and Little Joe to be in a fund-raising parade for my trip to Honduras."

"What trip to Honduras?" Bill asked.

248

"Hurricane Fifi hit Honduras with one hundred seventy-five mile per hour winds and thirty-six inches of rain in twenty-four hours. It's a real mess down there, and the Indians here in Muskegon want me to take down some food and supplies," Paul explained.

"Your little plane isn't going to do much if they've got a big disaster going down there, Paul."

"On short wave radio I've been talking to a missionary's wife in Honduras. Her name is Ruth Paz, and she's a ham operator," Paul said. "Ruth says the Red Cross and Salvation Army have tons of supplies at Puerto Cortes and La Lima Airport, but the Honduran army is holding it. They can't or won't get it out to the small native villages where it's needed. I'm going to load up my Cessna with beans and penicillin and take it out to those isolated village people."

"Now, Paul," Bill said, "just once I wish you'd stick to the piloting and leave the doctoring to me. The first thing we'll have to do is get our tropical diseases shots, so we can recover from them before we leave."

"I hate shots," Paul grumbled.

Bill and Paul unconsciously had fallen into the ancient Indian custom of leadership in which the chief says, "I will go fight," without asking anyone to join him. Those who wish to help, follow him of their own free will.

Bill went on. "I have to talk to this Ruth Paz in Honduras so I can know what kind of food and medicine we're going to take in."

"Okay," Paul agreed. "Nils is the ham radio operator out here in North Muskegon. I'll call Nils and we'll set up a time for you to talk to Ruth. What about the Indian parade?"

"Little Joe and I will be happy to be there. Say, Paul," Bill added, "we've got to clear this with the F.B.I. They'll really be sticking their necks out if they give you and me permission to leave the country."

The next few days became a whirlwind of preparations. The F.B.I. granted permission for Bill and Paul to go.

At Nils's home over his powerful ham radio Bill talked with Ruth Paz. She confirmed that supplies were stuck at the seaport and airport. Ruth's voice crackled over the radio. "I don't know why the Honduran government can't move those supplies out to the people who need them. They have armed soldiers guarding the supplies in the warehouses."

"I get real worked up when the government oppresses its own people," Bill replied. "I sure feel a government exists to serve the people. And if it does, the people will be willing to serve their government."

"Doctor," Ruth's far-off voice continued, "we've got to have help from outside if we're going to survive. Weakened older people and young children are dying from dysentery and dehydration."

"They'll need lots of sulfa, intravenous Lactated Ringer's solution and concentrated baby formula," Bill noted.

"If you come, be sure and bring your own water," Ruth instructed. "Our only uncontaminated water is what rain we can catch running off the trees and roof tops. We have no telephone communications, and our roads and railroads are flooded out. The floods have brought the snakes out of their burrows. Our snakes here are the fer-de-lance. They're predatory and highly poisonous."

By the next day the necessary supplies had been collected. We gathered at Paul's hangar to weigh and itemize the dozens of huge cardboard cartons. There was far too much weight to get it all on the small plane. Bill suggested that more medication could be taken if it were removed from the heavy and cumbersone packaging, and dumped into plastic kitchen and trash bags. A group of us sat about Paul's office, pouring pills into plastic bags, getting rid of the hundreds of small but weighty glass bottles. Bill told us that the pharmacists and hospitals had given all the drugs and intravenous fluids that the plane could carry.

"The Indians have raised two hundred fifty dollars," Paul said, "and the local churches told me they will guarantee the rest of our expenses, which should come to about nine hundred dollars.''

One-half of Paul's office floor was covered with air maps for the trip. Paul was busy with his plotter and ruler, marking the route, and where they would land for gas. Paul looked up from his calculations. "Doc, this should be a breeze except for two areas that I want you to be aware of.''

Bill pulled off his cowboy boots, and in their stocking feet the two men walked over the air maps, fitted together like a giant jigsaw puzzle.

"Here,'' Paul pointed to one section of the maps, "south of Villahermosa, is two hundred miles of uncharted jungle of Yucatan and Guatemala.''

Bill snapped his fingers. "That reminds me. I've got to put in my machete.''

Paul went on. "There are no VORs down there, and ADF radio isn't so accurate. Anyway, I've used it before, and it's better than nothing.''

"Okay, Paul,'' Bill nodded, "so what else do we have?''

Paul's usually smiling face was serious. "With the tropical rains they're having down there, this Sula valley could be a bear to get into. We'll have to play it by ear, but that's where we meet our contact.''

At sunrise, October 1, 1974, Bill and Paul climbed into the Cessna and took off, heading south. The flight was uneventful until the heavily loaded plane reached the warm tropical air in Mexico. Then flying became more difficult. In Veracruz they removed the co-pilot seat and moved forward the heavy cases of baby milk to balance the plane's center of gravity. From that point on these unpadded cartons served as Bill's uncomfortable co-pilot's seat.

The first real danger occurred over the vast Yucatan peninsula. After the checkpoint of Minatitlan Paul flew at two thousand five hundred feet so they had visual contact with the ground. Suddenly the Cessna was surrounded by a storm pattern of dense jungle rain.

251

"I'm going to get up out of this," Paul said, pointing the nose up.

In the moist tropical air the plane gained altitude sluggishly. At five thousand feet they broke out of the clouds and continued to climb until they reached six thousand five hundred feet, but with the load and the hot, moist air, the plane couldn't gain higher altitude.

They continued on for an hour at this altitude, flying by radio navigation with the ADF radio tuned to Minatitlan and Villahermosa. Ahead of them appeared dense storm clouds, too high to fly over. The air became turbulent, and Paul struggled to steady his plane. At last he found a hole in the clouds and descended through it until once again they could see the ground. Startled, the two men saw that they were surrounded by mountains. According to their ADF signals, they should be far from mountains.

Bill's heart sank as he thought, we're lost over the jungle! Below there was nothing but a dense tangle of green and occasional mountain peaks. He scanned the ground for some significant land mark. They flew on for ten minutes, searching. Then Bill spotted a large river which formed an inverted "W" as it coiled its way out of the mountains.

That river must be on the airmap, Bill figured. But when he tried to study the airmap, his fatigued eyes wouldn't focus on the small print. Quickly he dug through the plane's glove compartment and found his wire spectacles. On the airmap he found the river forming the inverted "W" and pointed it out to Paul.

"But how can that be!" Paul protested. "That would make us at least thirty miles off course."

Bill's voice was tight. "And it also means that in that soup up ahead of us is a nine thousand foot mountain peak!"

Paul banked the plane and turned back north. The plane couldn't get enough altitude to fly over that high a mountain.

As they headed out of the mountain range and approached Villahermosa, the ADF radio corrected its error, and the men knew where they were.

"Keep those spectacles handy, Doc," Paul grinned. "I have a new respect for them. Just keep reading those air maps like you've been doing, and I won't call you Benjamin Franklin anymore."

Over the jungles of northern Guatemala treacherous weather again surrounded them. Thick steam rose from the jungle swamps, obliterating the ground. Intermittently, tropical downpours pelted the plane, but at the same time the rain settled the jungle steam so they could get a glimpse of the ground.

"You're not supposed to fly over this Guatemalan jungle," Paul said. "It's uncharted, and the Guatemalan government doesn't take kindly to stray aircraft violating their airspace."

Buffeted by increasingly turbulent storm clouds, the men picked up the ADF out of Flores and headed for it. Each time the plane dropped into an air pocket, it tried to go into a steep dive. As the plane was twisted around, Paul battled with the controls, all the time the stall buzzer blaring its warning. After a twenty minute search, they spotted the large lake that was the landmark which would lead them to Flores.

From the radio a noisy squawking requested information about a lone plane flying in the Flores area. Paul picked up the microphone and reported his plane's numbers, altitude and destination.

Immediately an excited voice screeched from the receiver, but the words in broken English with a heavy Spanish accent were so garbled that Paul had to ask for a repeat twice.

The accented voice finally turned to international code, yelling, "LIMA, EVIL, VICTOR, EVIL, LIMA!" Paul had begun to catch the message on the word "evil," and completely confused, he asked the radio operator to repeat.

Again, the voice shouted, "LIMA, EVIL, VICTOR, EVIL, LIMA!"

Paul repeated the code words to Bill, who wrote them down. The words spelled "level." The man wanted to know their level, their altitude.

Paul reported their altitude of four thousand feet and their destination, La Lima Airport, Honduras.

"No!" the radio voice screamed. "You no go La Lima! You die! You land Puerto Barrios! You land Puerto Barrios!"

The air map showed Puerto Barrios to be a Guatemalan military establishment on the coast not far from Honduras. Its five thousand foot runway was just off the beach of the Gulf of Mexico. The radio operator there spoke fluent English and guided their plane in. The moment the Cessna came to a stop it was surrounded by young soldiers.

A man rode up on a bicycle and explained that he was the radio operator who had guided them in. The weather in the Sula Valley was very bad, he said. Only a few hours earlier a small Cessna like Paul's had crashed, trying to get into the valley. The radio operator advised Bill and Paul to wait until morning when the weather would be improved.

The next morning the men took off early. As they entered the Sula Valley they could see the docks at Puerto Cortes which were stacked with supplies. Air traffic was busy at the La Lima Airport, with dozens of helicopters buzzing in and out. As Paul taxied the Cessna up to the terminal building, Bill noted the many huge military and civilian cargo planes from the United States, Great Britain, Cuba, and Mexico parked on the ramp. The aprons and parking ramps were overflowing with supplies. Huge drums of banana paste were stacked in rows outside the filled warehouses.

The airport aviation official approached their plane and introduced himself as "Joe." He made arrangements for their cargo to be cleared by customs agents, while Bill and Paul left to get hold of Ruth Paz, the Honduran ham radio operator. Within thirty minutes after landing at La

Lima Airport, they were transferring their cargo to a Land Rover sent by the mission.

As the missionary-driver steered the Land Rover out of the airport, he explained to Bill and Paul that they were delivering the supplies to the village of Progresso. Many roads were impassable, and their route took them through mud, deep water, and washouts. As he drove, the missionary described the Sula Valley, which had been intensely farmed before Hurricane Fifi.

"This whole valley floor," he said, "was covered with sugar cane fields and an extensive network of railroads." He pointed toward the mountain slopes. "Years ago the people cleared the jungle trees from those slopes and planted banana trees. They piled the old trees on the margins of their property as boundaries. When Hurricane Fifi hit and dumped thirty-six inches of rain, all those old trees, fences, and houses were washed down into the valley. The debris created dams and water piled up twenty feet deep. Many of the people not killed by the winds were drowned by the instant lake which covered the valley."

The missionary's voice deepened with sadness. "Chaloma, a city of nine thousand people, was completely wiped out. The survivors are trying to burn the dead. There are just too many to bury. Our heavy rainy season has started, and the rains keep putting out the fires and floating more bodies up out of the mud. The stench there is awful!"

At Progresso the hurricane survivors milled about in bewilderment and shock. The Land Rover pulled up before a Catholic mission converted into a first aid station. There a volunteer doctor from Costa Rica was calmly caring for the needs of distraught mothers and their babies.

As Bill and Paul unloaded the cartons of supplies, the Costa Rican doctor caught sight of the baby milk. He was delighted. This was the first baby milk in Progresso since the hurricane hit.

For the next few days Bill waded through water and mud, helping where he could. He made friends with some Cuban doctors who had set up hospital facilities down the road. Most of the medical problems were due to tropical infections and parasites, and there was little need for Bill's surgical skills. In this international setting Bill was embarrassed by his halting, bare-minimum fluency in Spanish. However, he became very proud of the services performed by the American helicopter pilots. These brave pilots literally chopped the tops out of the dense jungle trees to descend low enough to get ropes on flood victims. It took great courage and accuracy on the part of the pilots, for if their blades hit a branch too large, it could break their rotor, and they would crash.

The rainy season for Honduras had begun. Each day brought torrential rains and more flooding. The Sula Valley supply of aviation gasoline was exhausted, and La Lima airport was being flooded. The men were told that in a matter of hours the airport would be under water, and a new supply of gasoline wasn't expected for a week.

Since there wasn't much more they could do, Bill and Paul decided to try to get out. Most of the roads to La Lima Airport were flooded out. Again and again they had to backtrack and try another road. When they were a mile and a half from the airport and stopped again by a washed-out road, they decided to walk the rest of the way. They put their packs on their backs and waded into the waist-deep, swirling waters. Carefully avoiding the downside of the road which had ten-foot deep treacherous washouts, they felt their way through the rushing water. As they approached a bridge whose roadway was two feet under water, Bill spotted a large snake being swept past by the current. When the snake saw Bill and Paul, it immediately changed direction and began battling upstream, swimming against the current toward the men.

Holding onto the beam of the bridge, Bill reached down into the muddy water and grabbed a fistful of small stones. One at a time he threw the rocks at the approaching snake. The fourth rock caught the attacker's snout, and the snake slid beneath the surface.

On the far side of the bridge the men reached higher

ground, where they emptied the water from their boots and then ran for the airport.

Enough gasoline remained in the plane for them to get to Belize, but Joe, the aviation official, told them he was closing the airport. One-third of the runway already was under water. After some persuasion Joe agreed to let them take off. If they were sure they could get off the runway by the first turn-off, he would hold off closing down until after they left.

Paul filed his flight plan with Joe, checked out the weather, and started the engine. Now empty of cargo, the Cessna lifted off easily, well ahead of the flooded section of runway.

On the two-day flight back to Michigan the men were rewarded with much improved weather. Paul used the opportunity to give Bill many more hours of flight instruction, and by the time the Cessna taxied up to Paul's hangar, Bill felt comfortable flying this different type of aircraft.

The welcome home scene at Paul's hangar was reminiscent of that eighteen months earlier when Bill and Paul returned from their flight to Wounded Knee. The same group of Indian people gathered to greet the fliers and to thank them for delivering the supplies to the Honduran people.

Two weeks later Bill received a gracious letter from Phillipe Sanchez, the American ambassador to Honduras, expressing thanks for the much-needed aid. Bill was surprised to receive the letter, as he'd met the ambassador only briefly out on the flooded roads of Honduras.

"Laws are like cobwebs,
which may catch small flies,
but let wasps and hornets break through."
    —Jonathan Swift, 1707

•

Alias
The
Buffalo
Doctor

22 Our lawyer had continued his communications with the Justice Department, referred to as "plea bargaining." Soon after Bill returned from Honduras, federal attorneys in South Dakota made a definite offer to drop the criminal proceedings and felony charges against Bill if he would plead guilty to three counts of illegal operation of aircraft and pay a fine of five hundred dollars for each count, totaling fifteen hundred dollars.

One of the counts was "operating an aircraft within five hundred feet of a restricted area." Objecting to this count, Neal wrote to the prosecutor, informing him that no "Notams" (restrictions) regarding flight in the vicinity of Wounded Knee had been filed at the Muskegon County Airport at the time of the alleged flight. Neal also objected to Bill's pleading guilty to the count charging "reckless and careless" flying, but acquiesced on the third count, agreeing that Bill would plead guilty to operating an aircraft with a load in excess of legal limits and pay five hundred dollars in fine.

For several weeks the attorneys continued to dicker. The final offer coming from the Justice Department was that they would drop the one count of flying in a restricted area, but they insisted that Bill plead guilty to the remaining two counts and pay a total fine of one thousand dollars. This offer included another warning. The U. S. Attorney promised that if Bill pleaded guilty to these counts, the Federal Aviation Agency had agreed they would not use the guilty plea as a bar to Bill receiving a pilot's license in the future. However, the letter warned, if Bill did not plead guilty, the F.A.A. would begin proceedings of their own in addition to the charges of the Justice Department, "proceedings which would have an untoward effect on the issuance of a private pilot's license."

Bill was wedged. If he chose to go to trial and defend himself against the criminal felony charges, the F.A.A. would begin proceedings against him. He couldn't defend himself against both the Justice Department and the Federal Aviation Agency. We just didn't have the money. We were feeling the financial pinch of keeping two children in college. The burden of going to trial was beyond our means.

Regretfully, Bill accepted Neal's advice to plead guilty to the two counts.

"You're doing the right thing, Doc," Neal said. "These counts are just civil proceedings. You'll be out of the criminal charges, and your license to practice medicine won't be endangered. I'll contact the prosecutors right away about this. Your next federal court hearing is scheduled for March 17. Probably we can wrap everything up at that time, and be done with it."

Winter dragged on while we wondered what would happen.

On St. Patrick's Day morning, 1975, Neal telephoned. "Be at federal court in Grand Rapids at three this afternoon, and we'll finish things off. Bring a cashier's check or money order for one thousand dollars."

As Bill was preparing to leave for the hospital to see his patients, a reporter telephoned. Apparently he'd checked the court docket and learned that Bill's case was scheduled. Bill filled the reporter in on the details.

"Well, doctor," the reporter said, "it's cost you several thousand dollars and considerable concern. Is it all worth it?"

"There are some things in our government which need tending to," Bill answered. "I believe that any efforts we make toward achieving improvements in our government are very important and worthwhile right now. Our government will work if we go back to the original ideas of the founders of our Constitution, a government of the people, by the people, and for the people. If we can produce that kind of responsive government, it will be a government that our young people once again will be proud to serve and fight for."

At noon Bill telephoned me from the hospital. "I have an emergency here," he said. "It's our friend, Zelda, the rabbi's wife. She needs immediate surgery, and she insists that I do it. I'm just going into surgery now. If you'll come over to the hospital and pick me up, that'll save a few minutes. Maybe we can make it to court on time."

In spite of being held up by the emergency operation, we arrived at the federal building in Grand Rapids just fifteen minutes late. Bill hurried upstairs to the judge's chambers, where he was supposed to meet Neal. I waited in the empty, marble-walled lobby which seemed like a mausoleum. It had been two years and one day since this same lobby was packed with protesting Indians, television cameras, and noisy reporters, all intent in finding out what was going to happen to The Buffalo Doctor.

Now, two years later, the Day of Judgment had arrived, and Bill was upstairs, facing the outcome alone. No F.B.I. agents disguised as maintenance men prowled about. The lone security guard slumped at his post, dozing behind a newspaper. For two years we'd been agonizing over the outcome of Bill's Wounded Knee involvement. Now, in this cold tomb of a building, it was ending.

In the judge's chambers Bill watched quietly as Neal and the prosecuting attorney executed the necessary legal papers. They moved into the courtroom to have the guilty

261

plea read into the permanent court record, and the proceedings were concluded.

When Neal and Bill stepped off the elevator into the lobby, I searched their faces for a sign of the outcome. Bill looked grim, Neal was business-like.

"Is it done?" I asked.

Neal nodded. "All done. Doc pleaded guilty to flying an overloaded plane and to reckless flying, and he paid one thousand dollars in fine. Now the Justice Department will drop their charges of obstruction of justice."

"Then it's all over?" I wanted to know.

"It's all over," Neal answered.

But upstairs in the seventh floor F.B.I. headquarters, information was being fed into the giant computer web for permanent records, information saying, "Dwain W. Cummings, D.O., alias The Buffalo Doctor, accused felon . . . "

Epilogue

The 1965 agreement, if implemented with integrity, would provide one thousand buffalo a year to Indians on the reservations. They could be used to:

1) Bring much needed protein into the diet.

2) Conduct nutritional studies to teach us all the importance of diet management.

3) Produce a genuine buffalo-cattle crossbreed for our northern beef ranges.

4) Produce a serum to prevent organ rejection in transplant patients.

5) Produce an anti-cancer vaccine.

6) Provide buffalo leather, horns, etc. for Indian art work and crafts.

These projects on the reservations would provide industry that is meaningful and appealing to Indian people.

In the last fourteen years the bureaucrats of Yellowstone National Park have not given up any of their buffalo to the Indian people. Instead, each spring there are rotting buffalo carcasses from a winter of starvation. The grass and foliage in the park can support only so many animals. The surplus die. The surviving animals are weakened because of the short food supply. The research biologist of Yellowstone has informed us there are no surplus buffalo at Yellowstone and there will not be in the future. They are all used in the ecosystem of Yellowstone. The insectivorous birds feed on the larval insects which are abundant on carcasses.

From 1964 to 1974 the annual number of buffalo at Yellowstone varied from four hundred to eight hundred seventy-five. When the herd population reaches eight hundred there is massive starvation, damage to the entire herd, and hundreds of animals die. The entire herd is weakened for several years. The 1979 buffalo population at Yellowstone was fifteen hundred fifty-five. Soon the maggots will have the biggest buffalo feast of all time.

* * *

Memorandum N1427-ORW dated November 4, 1965 to Commissioner, Bureau of Indian Affairs
From: Director, National Park Service
Subject: Disposal and utilization of surplus wildlife, National Park Service

There are seven conditions of this agreement that the National Park Service agrees to:

1) Notify B.I.A. before June 15 each year of species, numbers, locations of surplus animals available for Bureau use.

2) Live trap surplus animals to extent possible

3) Transfer to Bureau all elk and bison for direct reduction at no cost or other expenses

4) Carry out and bear all expenses associated with field killing

5) Provide or arrange for vet services

6) Endeavor to maintain park roads utilized

7) Report all requests for bison and elk meat received from American Indian groups, individuals or others directly to the Bureau for evaluation and action.

The B.I.A. agrees to:

1) Accept full responsibility for the animal carcasses transferred to it as a result of this agreement.

2) Bear all costs directly and indirectly related to the commercial slaughter, packaging and storage of subject carcasses, including the transportation of live animals or carcasses from the point of pickup within the Park or Monument to designated slaughtering establishments.

3) Maintain a sufficient quantity of bison and elk meat in storage to meet legitimate Departmental and Indian requests for such meat in connection with ceremonials or special dinners.

4) Limit distribution and use of all other meat resulting from this agreement to approved, noncommercial Bureau functions and related programs.

This agreement entered into on November 4, 1965. Signed by A. C. Stratton, Acting Director, National Park Service. Accepted and signed by Philleo Nash, Commissioner, Bureau of Indian Affairs, and by Robert E. Vaughan, Deputy Assistant Secretary, Public Land Management on December 10, 1965.

* * *

Just what did the F.B.I. have stored in their files concerning Bill? In a brave moment, we decided to try to find out. Under the Freedom of Information Act we wrote to the F.B.I. in Washington, D.C. and requested their records on Bill. Very quickly we received a form letter saying they were processing our request.

Two months later and just as this book is about to go to print, we received a letter—not a form letter—cautioning us that the entire content of Bill's record would not be disclosed, and that "processing of these documents may result in charges of approximately six hundred and sixty dollars." The letter instructed us to send no money at this time, but that they would need written notification from Bill indicating his willingness to pay fees of approximately six hundred sixty dollars.

That certainly put a damper on our curiosity. Six hundred sixty dollars! And what would we get in return? Perhaps only a transcript of the hearings, or the grand jury indictment.

Apparently the Freedom of Information Act has some loopholes in it. The information isn't free, and the disclosure of the information isn't complete. The bureaucrats with their computers have a great ability to intimidate each of us. Possibly we can control the bureaucrats with computer information on them. But their records aren't worth six hundred sixty dollars to us.

*   *   *

Little Joe the Buffalo is now eight years old and weighs about a ton. He still loves to stand on our back porch. It seems he remembers his younger days of waiting there for his baby bottles of milk. And he loves to come into the house, though my squeals of protest have made his visits infrequent. He is so big that he fills the doorways and can turn around only in the living room.

But occasionally, when Bill sees Joe gazing wistfully at the house, Bill gets an impish twinkle in his eye, and says, "Joe wants to come in and visit."

Then we go into the ritual of my pleading, "Oh, no, don't bring him in, no."

As I sputter, Bill is already on his way to the back door. "Okay, Joe. You haven't seen our new carpeting, have you? You better come in before the bureaucrats pass a law against buffalo in the house."